EMBROIDERY

EMBROIDERY

consultant editor Pauline Brown

Villard Books New York 1987

Copyright © 1986 by Marshall Editions Limited

All rights reserved under International and Pan-American Copyright Conventions. Published in the United States by Villard Books, a division of Random House, Inc., New York, and simultaneously in Canada by Random House of Canada Limited, Toronto. First published in Great Britain by William Collins Sons & Co. Ltd.

Conceived, edited and designed by
Marshall Editions Ltd,
170 Piccadilly, London W1V 9DD

Consultant editor/
Author of Design Your Own
Pauline Brown

Managing editor	**Ruth Binney**
Editor	**Carole McGlynn**
Sub editor	**Hazel Harrison**
Editorial assistants	**Vivienne Quay**
	Pat Hunter
Advisory editor	**Maggi McCormick**
Art editor	**Daphne Mattingly**
Art assistant	**Richard McAndrew**
Picture coordinator	**Zilda Tandy**
Picture assistant	**Sarah Wergan**
Production	**Barry Baker**
Production assistant	**Rosanna Scott**
Production secretary	**Nikki Ingram**

Typeset by Filmtype Services Ltd, Scarborough, UK
Reproduced by Reprocolor Llovet SA,
Barcelona, Spain
Printed and bound in West Germany by
Mohndruck Graphische Betriebe GMBH

CONTENTS

HOW TO USE THIS BOOK

EMBROIDERY is designed for anyone, irrespective of their experience, who wants to explore the craft of embroidery in a creative, imaginative way. How you use this book will depend on your level of skill and on your goals as an embroiderer; but our hope is that through its use both your skill and your goals will develop enormously.

Three distinct, but interrelated parts make up the book; the Embroidery Design Collection of patterns and the two other sections of this book, "Design Your Own" and "Embroidery Basics". The 46 original patterns each give complete instructions for making an embroidered piece of work, be it a garment, a household item, a picture, panel or a wallhanging.

A moderately experienced embroiderer can use many of the patterns without referring to the rest of the book. For the beginner or the embroiderer whose experience does not extend to a particular technique, the book will provide invaluable guidance; cross-references to the relevant pages are given where these will prove most helpful.

Design Your Own is a comprehensive exploration of design as the "heart" of embroidery. It begins with an introduction to the equipment required for embroidery —design tools and materials as well as the needles, the amazing diversity of threads and the wealth of different fabrics that come into play in modern embroidery. The principles of good design as found in any art form are explained, and then applied to embroidery techniques in particular. The various design sources and the media through which to interpret them are explored in detail—from using photographs and drawings to creating patterned designs with cut paper shapes, collage and geometric forms. This helps to establish as broad a base as possible from which to embark on your own original embroideries.

Readers are encouraged to be innovative with backgrounds too—an often neglected aspect of embroidery—by using fabric dyes or paints creatively.

The rest of this part of the book is concerned with free, experimental interpretation of the various embroidery techniques. It is intended to be used hand in hand with the Embroidery Basics section, and to take you a stage further. Once you know how to work any of the surface stitches in a conventional way, you will be receptive to ideas for trying them out using an unusual bouclé thread, for example, to produce a rough texture, or imaginatively varying the spacing to create effects of color shading.

All of the "experimental" sections in Design Your Own cover an important element of embroidery design: color, texture, lines and shapes, fabrics, threads and stitches. Each one relates to a range of embroidery techniques and should be treated as broadly as possible. Creative smocking, for example, is discussed in the section entitled "Experiment with Fabrics", since it is a means of manipulating fabric, though it is also relevant to "Texture", since it is a way of creating textural effects, and to "Lines and Shapes" as it is also a basically linear exercise. The demarcations are not rigid—the intent is to extend the embroiderer's scope. Specially commissioned embroidered "samples" illustrate this experimental approach. It is hoped that these will stimulate the embroiderer and give inspiration for including similar creative ideas in a finished piece of work.

Whether or not you feel inclined to use any of these examples in a practical way, simply reading and studying them will help you to understand the process of embroidery design. When you do begin to design your own pieces of work, they will serve as inspiration and guides.

In Embroidery Basics (pp. 62–140) you will find detailed, illustrated instructions for all the essential embroidery techniques from surface stitchery and needlepoint to related crafts such as quilting and appliqué. This section of the book is especially valuable for its illustrated library of stitches (64 in Surface Stitchery and 50 in Needlepoint), many of which are used in other forms of embroidery too. Many of the needlepoint principles and stitches, for example, apply to other counted thread methods such as blackwork, drawn and pulled thread work, cross stitch and Assisi work.

Any unfamiliar terms or techniques on a Design Collection pattern can be clarified by referring to this section of the book. For the complete beginner, Embroidery Basics will, of course, be the starting point.

Embroidery is a pastime that should be enjoyable and satisfying; designing your own embroideries can also give wide scope for self-expression. We hope that EMBROIDERY will enhance your enjoyment of this diverse and stimulating craft.

THE EMBROIDERY DESIGN COLLECTION

Easy-to-follow instructions accompany every pattern.

A comprehensive list of materials is given, with details of the finished size where relevant.

"Options" gives ideas for adapting the instructions to make something simpler or slightly different, or for using alternative yarns and color combinations.

Full-color photograph of the finished article shows how the embroidery technique is used and its major design features.

6

DESIGN YOUR OWN

Embroidered "samples" illustrate the experimental possibilities within a particular category, in this case fabrics.

The potential of using sheer fabrics is illustrated here in cutwork, Italian and trapunto shadow quilting, shadow appliqué and machine embroidery.

All the relevant embroidery techniques are explored within each category of the Design Your Own section of the book.

EMBROIDERY BASICS

The photograph shows the stitches or technique explained on that page; each stitch is worked over a large enough area to show some of the textural and two-color effects that can be achieved.

A longer introduction is given for a "family" of stitches, or for a stitch that is particularly versatile and lends itself to a host of different effects.

Clear line drawings show how to work each stitch step by step, and indicate how the stitches are built up.

Useful tips and special features enable you to work a stitch or perform a certain technique in the most efficient way, and to achieve a professional-looking finish.

DESIGN YOUR OWN

All design begins with an idea, and the inspiration for an embroidery design can come from many sources. Ideas abound if you are sensitive enough to your surroundings to recognize the potential all around you. Being visually aware means seeing not only nature's most dramatic effects, such as a wonderful sunset or the spectacular colors of autumn, but looking closely at less obvious features, like the pattern of brickwork, the texture of lichen on a rock; the rusty colors in a heap of scrap metal; the shape and lines made by rooftops and chimneys – all of which could be translated into a design for embroidery.

Any research you can do will pay dividends in terms of widening the scope of your designs, so visit your local library or museum; go to exhibitions whenever you can, particularly craft fairs, and try to analyze the designer's source of inspiration; also note the use of shape, pattern, texture and color. Look at old embroideries in museums or ethnic or native work if you get the chance on vacation – ideas for techniques or subject matter may well evolve from these. Carry a notebook or sketchbook around with you and make notes and/or sketches to remind you of what you have seen.

There is no reason to feel daunted by the prospect of making your own designs. Even if you cannot draw well, there are many other ways to start. You can design from photographs – your own or one in a magazine – with paper shapes, even by ''accident'' using ink blots; or you can create more rigid geometric designs based on lines or shapes; all these subjects are covered in detail on pages 22–29.

The range of possible design sources for embroidery can be roughly categorized as follows. *Natural forms*, which include the elements – skies, water, landscapes – as well as all forms of plant life, and animals, insects, birds and fish. *Man-made forms*, which cover a wide range of possibilities such as your own home (from the whole exterior to a small corner of one room), or machinery of all kinds; a wheel, for example, could translate well into a design for a quilted circular pillow. *Geometric forms*, based on lines such as stripes or zigzags, or shapes such as squares, triangles or circles, any of which may be seen in a backyard fence, a window frame or even a printed fabric. *Lettering*, which has traditionally played its part in embroidery design, particularly in the form of samplers. Letters and numbers can also be adapted to form a design in their own right, as in interlocking monograms.

There is no format to designing your own embroideries. You may hit upon an idea for a design – say, a bowl of fruit – before choosing the embroidery technique; you might then decide between

The initial inspiration for an embroidery design often comes from a photograph. But the original source can be embellished or adapted in several ways before arriving at the final design; many other elements may well be included in the final composition.

It is well worth working small samples before embarking on the embroidery itself. They will help you to make decisions about the type and thickness of yarn, the best kind of stitch, and the most suitable background fabric (in this case the gauge of canvas) to use.

8

A border can finish off an embroidered picture perfectly. It may be continuous or made up of repeating motifs, as here. The chosen motifs might duplicate an element found in the main part of the design or can simply echo its subject or mood.

In a single stitch embroidery – like this needlepoint picture worked almost entirely in tent stitch – the choice of colors and threads is especially important. The strong, bright shades chosen here suggest the atmosphere of a hot summer's day.

surface stitchery, appliqué or even blackwork, and adapt your design accordingly. Equally, you could be keen to do some quilting, for example, and then look around for a suitable design motif – it might be based on shells, or more abstract swirling forms. Whatever the starting point, you will then have to compose your design, arranging the elements into a coherent whole; considerations of line, space and form all play a part in a successful composition. At the same time you will have to make decisions about what colors, fabric, threads and stitches to use. Any one of the latter elements could even be your initial inspiration – an unusual textured fabric or some exciting knitting yarns might trigger off an idea for a wallhanging worked freely in surface stitchery.

It is important to familiarize yourself with the range of categories within the craft of embroidery before you can fully realize the creative scope it offers. The narrow view of embroidery, as simply the application of decorative stitches to a background fabric, is an outdated one. Contemporary embroidery is regarded as a textile art form that encompasses wide-ranging techniques, most of which can be done in either a traditional or a more experimental way.

Surface stitchery, with its multitude of stitches, is the most obvious category; its scope today is virtually infinite, with the range of different threads available and stitches that can be worked as freely as you like. Metal thread embroidery, a surface stitch method that in the past was used only for ecclesiastical and ceremonial work, is today adapted for evening bags, belts and embroidered jewelry. The recent advent of sophisticated domestic sewing machines, incorporating numerous embroidery stitches, has created a technique in its own right. Free machining can produce with a needle an impression akin to drawing. Delicate lacy effects can also be achieved with one of the dissolvable agents such as vanishing muslin. Depending on your design, or how it is adapted, almost any of the embroidery methods can be employed in the creation of exciting pieces of work.

Designing your own embroideries not only allows you to produce original pieces – be they pictures, wallhangings, garments, or accessories to complement your home – it also gives enormous scope as a means of self-expression. The processes involved in the refining of a design idea – from the original inspiration and planning the composition to the selection of colors, fabric and threads – all help you to build confidence and develop a range of skills that will allow creative freedom. Working to your own designs is what elevates embroidery from the application of technique to a creative and expressive art form.

It is not necessary to go to great expense when collecting equipment to help you design your own embroideries—some of the best ideas have started life sketched on the back of an old envelope. As you progress, you can gradually build up the design equipment you need, buying the best quality that you can afford. You will probably find that you are happier working with certain media than with others—some people enjoy the freedom of working with charcoal, for example, while others may find it messy. If you enjoy working in color, a box of watercolors or some tubes of gouache may be ideal for you, or you may prefer a collection of felt-tipped pens and colored pencils.

The paper you choose for sketching or designing is also a matter of personal choice. If you find a large blank sheet of pristine white paper daunting, choose a sketchbook with smaller sheets, maybe of colored or textured paper. Keep all your reference material—cuttings, snippets of fabric and threads, sketches, stitch experi-ments, written notes or ideas—together in a folder or scrapbook.

Most of the items listed on these pages are available from stationery and art stores, or from specialist needlecraft stores. Experimentation with different media will enable you to acquire a reper-toire of design methods which will, in turn, broaden the scope of your embroideries.

DRAWING EQUIPMENT

Pencils of graphite are made in grades of hardness (8H—8B) for different effects. Hard pencils (H) produce fine gray lines; soft (B) make thicker, blacker marks. Experiment to see which you prefer. A plastic or a putty rubber is the best type of eraser. Colored pencils are available in a huge range of colors, as are felt-tipped pens, magic marker pens and colored inks. A waterproof fabric marking pen is essential for marking the outlines of a design on canvas and you will need either dressmaker's chalk (in block or a pencil form), or a water-erasable pen for transferring a design in surface embroidery.

If you use the pricking and pouncing method of transferring a design, you will need pounce powder. Pounce is a mixture of chalk and charcoal, both available in stick form from art shops. These need to be crushed to a powder. Depending on the color of the intended background fabric, use more or less charcoal. Powdered dressmaker's chalk, which comes in several colors, is a useful alternative.

Wax crayons give a soft-edged, semi-opaque effect; they are also used for making rubbings. Charcoal, usually made from willow, is good for bold, free work. However, it smudges easily and should be used with a fixative. You could also try conté crayons and pastels.

The two types of paint most popular with embroidery designers are watercolor and gouache. Watercolors, available in blocks or tubes, give a light, transparent touch; gouache, sold in tubes, is opaque and gives a more solid, bolder effect. Both types of paint are water-based and come in a wide range of intermixable colors.

Brushes are available in sizes 000–12, the last being the largest. The best brushes have sable hairs and are consequently extremely expensive. Cheaper varieties are made in materials such as squirrel, or synthetic fibers. When you are beginning to design, three or four brushes in a range of different sizes should suffice.

TYPES OF PAPER

Sketchbooks and pads, usually containing cartridge paper, can be bought in an extensive variety of sizes. Choose the size with which you feel happiest. Some people prefer working on a large scale, while others will make minute sketches. You can always alter the scale from the original drawing by enlarging or reducing it (see p. 21). A layout pad contains paper of a thinner quality, thin enough for tracings yet heavy enough to take crayons or paint.

Tracing paper is useful for copying, altering and adapting designs. It will assist you in making repeat, overlapping and mirrored images. Wax paper is a cheaper alternative and is better than tracing paper for transferring designs by the tracing and tacking method, since it tears away easily. Tissue paper will be useful in preliminary experiments for embroidery on transparent fabric. It is available in a range of colors, which will blend if overlapped.

Graph paper, in pads or large size sheets, will be needed for working out charted designs, such as cross stitch, Assisi work, Florentine and some geometric needlepoint. Squared dressmaker's pattern paper is good for large-scale projects and garments, as the sheets are very big. Other papers, such as sugar, colored self-adhesive, patterned craft, wrapping, corrugated, metallic finish etc. may be added to your collection for making collages, preparatory to appliqué designs. Those with interesting surfaces may help you make decisions about the use of texture in a design.

IMPLEMENTS AND ADHESIVES

Keep a special pair of scissors specifically for cutting paper as they will blunt rapidly. Alternately, use a craft knife with replaceable blades. In conjunction with a metal ruler or straight edge and a cutting board, a craft knife is essential for cutting mounts, stencils and geometric shapes.

Choose an all-purpose adhesive which will stick everything from paper to fabric, or miscellaneous objects such as buttons, beads and pieces of wood. Masking tape or transparent cellophane tape will be necessary for holding drawings or tracings in place while you work. Double-sided tape is useful for collage, mounting and for making bound mounts.

A ruler is invaluable, both for measuring and for drawing straight lines. The following drawing aids can be bought as the need arises: a pair of dividers for plotting points; a pair of compasses for drawing circles and arcs; a flexible curve; a set square for geometric designs; a protractor for measuring and dividing angles.

Embroidery is created simply by the decorative relationship between fabric and thread. These materials *are* the embroidery, so their importance cannot be over-emphasized. Your choice of fabric, thread and needle will depend to some extent on the embroidery technique you choose, as well as on the design and the planned subsequent use of the work.

Traditionally, certain fabrics were deemed to be suitable for a given method. While this still holds true, experimenting with fabric and thread will prove that almost anything is possible, provided you take into consideration any restrictions imposed by the inherent characteristics of the technique you propose to use.

NEEDLES

The needle is your most important embroidery tool, and it is essential to choose one that is suitable for the piece of work. The correct type and size of needle will be dictated by the technique being used, the background fabric and the yarn. Guidance is given under the individual techniques explained in the Embroidery Basics section of the book (pp. 62–141). Needle size is designated by number, the lowest number signifying the longest and thickest needle in each category.

As a general rule, if the needle is too small for the thread, it will make too small a hole, causing the thread to become frayed as it passes through the fabric. If you find it difficult to pull the thread through the fabric, change to a larger needle. Never use blunt, bent or rusty needles; they can damage the fibers of your fabric and thread.

Embroidery or crewel needles have long eyes to take one or more threads of stranded floss or yarn. (Sizes 1–10)
Betweens or quilting needles, traditionally used by tailors, are short with small round eyes. They are suitable for quick, even stitching, such as that used in hemming or quilting. (Sizes 1–10)
Darners and long darners are, as their name implies, longer than other needles and manufactured for darning.
Tapestry needles have large eyes and blunt points which slip easily between the weave of the fabric without damage. Apart from use in needlepoint, they are essential for work on evenweave materials, i.e. pulled work, blackwork, drawn thread and needleweaving. (Sizes 13–24)
Chenille needles are similar in shape to tapestry needles but have sharp points. They are short with large eyes, and were originally used for chenille work, which uses a furry yarn. Today they are ideal for embroidering with thick knitting or weaving yarns, ribbon, raffia etc., particularly on closely woven fabrics. (Sizes 13–24)
Beading needles are for threading beads,

sequins and pearls as they are extremely long and fine with long eyes. They tend to bend in use and should be replaced as soon as they do. They are also used in metal thread embroidery for threading metal purls (small coils of gold wire). (Sizes 10–15)
Leather needles are a specialist item used by glovemakers and leatherworkers. Use them if you are working with leather, suede, plastic or vinyl for appliqué, since their triangular points will pierce the fabric without tearing. (Sizes 1–8)
Bodkins, with flat or round eyes, are for threading cords, tapes, ribbons and elastic.
Circular needles, used by upholsterers,

THE RIGHT NEEDLE FOR THE JOB	
Technique	**Needle**
Appliqué (fabric)	Crewel
(leather/plastic)	Leather
three-dimensional	Circular
Beadwork	Beading or fine crewel
Counted thread	Tapestry
Cutwork	Crewel
Eyelet	Crewel
Free embroidery	
(fine)	Crewel
(heavy)	Chenille
Metal thread	Fine crewel, between or beading
Needlepoint	Tapestry
Quilting	Between
Shadow work	Crewel
Smocking	Crewel

Crewel size 7

Crewel size 3

Quilting

Darner

Long darner

Tapestry size 24

Tapestry size 18

Chenille size 24

Chenille size 18

Beading

Leather

Large-eyed wool

Bodkin

Circular

are good for awkward jobs, particularly for three-dimensional embroidery.

If you have poor eyesight which makes needle-threading a problem, either use one of the large-eyed needles in the range or try the easy-threading needles which have a slot-eye into which the thread is pulled.

YARNS

Thread or yarn is an integral part of any embroidery, and virtually anything that can be threaded through the eye of a needle can be put to use. The variety of yarns available can be overwhelming—not only are there plenty of specialist embroidery threads in a full range of colors but, with the continuing popularity of knitting and crochet, each season produces a whole new selection of versatile textured yarns.

For experimental and non-traditional work the use of bouclé, chenille and other novelty wool and cotton yarns can bring exciting possibilities to your designs. You can also experiment with other unconventional materials such as raffia, tape, ribbons and string—in fact anything with which you can sew. Fabric such as nylon, chiffon, jersey, suede and leather can be cut into strips. For a thread exactly matching the background fabric, it may even be possible to withdraw some of the weft (horizontal) threads and use these.

All the specialist embroidery threads, and some knitting and crochet yarns, are available from mail order suppliers, whose service is usually both quick and reliable. You can either purchase shade cards from these suppliers or they will send a returnable selection of these. (See list of suppliers at end of book). Some carpet and woolen mills sell their "thrums" (warp ends left over from weaving). These are usually sold by weight and can be incorporated in wall-hangings and needlepoint.

Apart from the aesthetic qualities of color and texture, you will need to choose your thread in relation to the weave of the background fabric. Bear in mind too, any constraints imposed by your chosen technique.

SPECIALIST EMBROIDERY THREADS
Stranded floss, available in a good choice of colors, both plain and shaded, is probably the most widely used embroidery thread. It has a pleasing luster and is adaptable in that the six strands can be split to produce a number of thicknesses. It is useful for traditional surface stitches and can be incorporated in needlepoint. In blackwork you can use it to achieve a change of tone by varying the thickness used. One drawback of stranded floss is that it can separate out when used in a long stitch. It is not a good idea to use it on smocking, for example.
Pearl cotton (perlé), a shiny, twisted 2-ply yarn, comes in both balls and hanks in three thicknesses, 3, 5 and 8, with 3 being

12

the coarsest. It is suitable for surface embroidery and needlepoint.

Coton à broder is a fine non-stranded thread with a slight sheen; it is good for counted thread embroidery and smocking, since there are no strands to separate.

Matte embroidery cotton is a tightly twisted, matte, 5-ply thread and is mostly used for couching or on coarsely woven fabrics.

Flower threads, 100 percent cotton and dyed with natural and vegetable dyes, are chosen for their high degree of luster.

Silk threads, available in twisted, twisted buttonhole and 6-stranded floss, can be used in most types of embroidery wherever a luster is required. It is the thread usually chosen for shadow work. Waxed silk thread is often used in conjunction with gold or silver in metal thread embroidery.

Linen threads are less widely available than cotton, but specialist shops stock them. They have a dull finish and are used in smocking and counted thread work.

Embroidery yarns are primarily manufactured for needlepoint but can be used on many other backgrounds, provided the weave allows. They include very fine 2-ply crewel yarn, 3-stranded loosely twisted Persian yarn, 4-ply tightly twisted tapestry yarn and the thicker rug yarn.

Machine threads, which can also be used for handwork, include ordinary sewing thread and the thicker button twist. There is also a large range of cotton and rayon machine embroidery yarns in several thicknesses and, more recently available, some metallized and textured examples.

Metal threads come in gold, gold plate, silver, aluminum or copper. They are most easily purchased by mail order. Most metal threads are laid on the background surface and couched. They range in thickness from tambour (very fine) to heavy cords and braids.

Top right to bottom left: matte embroidery cotton, linen thread, coton à broder, stranded floss (2 colors), sewing threads, pearl cotton (sizes 5 and 8), tapestry yarn, crewel yarn, Persian yarn, bouclé yarn, silk embroidery thread (2 colors), silver lurex thread (top); ribbon (2 widths) and beads.

The selection of metal threads includes: top —purl purl in three thicknesses; center—gold Russia braid, tambour, gold plate, imitation Jap gold cord; bottom—smooth purl in two thicknesses, gold check purl, white gold twist.

Purls consist of a length of wire coiled like a minute spring. Pieces can be cut off to the required length and then threaded and sewn down.

TRADITIONAL THREADS FOR EMBROIDERY

The techniques below were traditionally worked in these specific threads. However, experimentation with other yarns will provide exciting and unusual effects.

Technique	Thread
Appliqué	Cotton thread
Beadwork	Waxed cotton thread
Counted thread	Linen and coton à broder
Cutwork	Stranded floss and coton à broder
Eyelet	Coton à broder
Free embroidery stitches	Stranded floss
Metal thread	Gold, silver, with waxed silk thread
Needlepoint	Tapestry, Persian and crewel yarn
Quilting	Cotton thread
Shadow work	Fine cotton or silk thread
Smocking	Linen or coton à broder

13

Most needlework boxes contain general sewing equipment such as dressmaking pins, sewing needles, tape measure, seam ripper and dressmaker's chalk, several or all of which will come into use on any embroidery project. It is advisable to have two pairs of scissors, a small embroidery pair for snipping off the ends of threads and for cutting precise and intricate shapes or holes, and a larger pair for cutting out bigger pieces of fabric. Pinking shears, though not essential, enable you to cut decorative zigzag edges. Keep all your scissors sharp. A thimble is largely a matter of personal preference, but for certain techniques, and for working leather or very tough fabric, it will certainly prevent sore fingers.

Some specialist items, though they may have gone out of general use, are still essential for certain types of embroidery. They can be purchased in specialist stores or obtained from mail order companies specializing in needlecrafts. A stiletto, for example, is necessary for eyelet embroidery, but is also good for making eyelets and holes in a wide range of fabrics. Beeswax, which can be bought loose or in a plastic holder, is used to strengthen thread, particularly that used in quilting (see pp. 90–95) and metal thread embroidery (see pp. 96–99). A pair of tweezers or a small pair of pliers, though not normally embroidery tools, can be a useful asset in pulling thick threads through fabric and inserting quilting yarn for Italian quilting.

From top to bottom: sewing needles (assorted sizes), dressmaking pins, stiletto, fine pointed embroidery scissors, tweezers, seam ripper, tailor's chalk, thimble, tape measure, beeswax.

An assortment of fabrics in different weights, from upholstery fabric (bottom) to calico (top); batting (top), interfacing and vanishing muslin (bottom); fabric scissors.

FABRIC

Whether the fabric is principally the background to the embroidery or part of the applied decorative effect, choosing the right material is crucial. Each type of fabric has its own particular characteristics and you need to consider the design, the technique used and the practical use, if any, of the proposed work, when selecting a fabric. Firstly it is essential to know the properties of the whole range of fabrics.

Fabric can be categorized in different ways. Look first at its structure: is it woven, knitted, or non-woven? Woven fabrics made on a loom are structured, with warp threads running the length of the fabric and weft threads interweaving them at right angles. The weave can be plain or patterned and in any fiber. Evenweave fabrics, used for the counted thread methods of embroidery, have distinct, well-spaced warp and weft threads. To check whether a fabric you may have is evenweave or not, count the warp and weft threads over 2in—there should be an equal number.

Knitted fabrics, such as jersey, are constructed with a continuous yarn which gives elasticity. They are malleable and drape well but they tend to be difficult to use as a background fabric for embroidery unless mounted on a firm backing. If you are embroidering a garment made of knitted fabric you should back the area to be embroidered with a woven fabric first.

Non-woven fabrics include felt, leather, suede, kidskin, plastic and bonded interfacings. Their main advantage is that they do not fray and are firm to handle. This makes them particularly suitable for appliqué. The bulk of felt also makes it an appropriate fabric to pad motifs or shapes in appliqué and shadow quilting.

Having ascertained the structure of your fabric, now look at the fibers. Are they natural or synthetic? It is sometimes difficult to tell without reading the fabric content tag, since a vast range of manmade and synthetic fabrics are now produced to simulate, or made into fabrics mixed with, natural fibers.

The natural fibers include cotton and linen, both of which come from plants, and silk and wool, derived from animal sources. Materials made from these usually wash and iron well, are pleasant to handle and can be manipulated satisfactorily. They are also suitable for dyeing in either hot- or cold-water dyes and will readily accept fabric paints. Cotton dress fabrics, including lawn, poplin, terrycloth, voile, brushed cotton, velvet and corduroy can all be used as backgrounds for embroidery, or for hardwearing, washable clothes on which embroidery is worked. Household items such as placemats, throw pillows and quilts also work well in cotton.

Linen can be fine or heavy and either evenly woven or with a slub effect. Traditionally used for table and bed linen because of its fine washing and wearing qualities, it is also suitable for clothes and, depending on its structure, may be appropriate as a basis for counted thread decoration. Natural burlap and jute make good background fabrics (though the dyed varieties tend not to be colorfast).

Silk is available in various types and weights from fine Honan silk through to silk tweed, as well as the transparent organzas, chiffons and georgettes. Although expensive, it has a unique luster, will press into pleats and tucks yet also has good draping qualities. It is suitable for surface stitchery on fine garments and evening bags, for embroidered wall panels and for appliqué and smocking.

Wool, though traditionally rarely used as a background for embroidery, can be made into warm garments such as stoles and scarves, then decorated with surface stitches. Its soft texture can enhance a piece of appliqué, and fine woolens such as crêpe and challis can successfully be smocked.

Synthetic fibers are produced either chemically or from sources such as coal, wood and petroleum. Many need little or no ironing, which makes them suitable for easily laundered clothes and household items. Their visual resemblance to natural fibers means that they can generally be used in the same way as these, though some have a resilience which makes them more difficult to pleat or tuck crisply. They vary in their acceptance of hot- and cold-water dyes, depending on their content, but they can all take fabric paint.

Batting is a useful material made of synthetic fibers of polyester. It is sold by the yard in three weights and several widths and is both washable and dry cleanable. Its main use is in quilting or for padding and stuffing three-dimensional embroideries.

Interfacings are non-fray, bonded materials, produced to stiffen or give added support to fabrics. They are useful for appliqué and for backing finished embroideries. They can either be ironed or sewn on; the latter type can be painted and dyed.

Upholstery fabrics have either a natural or synthetic fiber content or a mixture of both. They are particularly good for wall-hangings and embroidered panels since they are wider than dress fabrics and heavier in weight, which gives the greater substance needed for large-scale embroideries. Upholstery sheers and loosely woven acrylics and linens are suitable for pulled and drawn thread work; net curtains can be pattern-darned or used for transparent effects.

Specialist embroidery fabrics, normally

Evenweave cotton fabrics in different densities of weave for counted thread embroidery

Canvas: 14-hole mono | 10-hole mono | 7-hole interlock | 6-hole plastic

24-hole (petit point) | 18-hole mono | 12-hole Penelope | 8-hole Penelope

fine-weave linen | coarse-weave cotton/linen | loose-weave slub linen | textured upholstery sheer

in cotton or linen, are available in a selection of different widths from 22in to 60in. Some are specially woven to lend themselves to a particular embroidery method. Evenweave cottons and linens are all intended for counted thread designs such as cross stitch, pulled and drawn thread work and blackwork. They come in varying densities of weave, from fine to coarse, and your choice of fabric for these techniques will depend on the size and scale of the design. Those plain weave fabrics produced with surface embroidery in mind, like fine linen, are most appropriate for traditional designs on such items as table linen.

Vanishing muslin and water-dissolvable fabrics are two materials used for making lacy effects in machine embroidery—the first disappears in contact with a hot iron, the second with boiling water (see p. 121).

Canvas is a specially woven material in either cotton or linen for the technique of needlepoint (canvaswork). Your choice of canvas will depend on the size and intricacy of the design (see pp. 122–123).

There are two types of woven canvas, mono and Penelope, each available in several widths from 23in to 39in and with a wide range of mesh gauges. Canvas gauge is given as the number of threads (or, in the case of Penelope canvas, holes) per inch. They range from fine petit point canvas with 24 threads per inch to coarse rug canvas with 4 threads per inch. Mono canvas is more useful than Penelope, since it is difficult to adapt the double variety for the large number of textured stitches used in needlepoint.

A recent innovation is a rigid canvas made of plastic with six holes to the inch. This can be used for such items as boxes, pencil cases, coasters etc.

In addition to the use of dress, upholstery and specialist embroidery fabrics, certain embroideries demand a more unusual approach. Wallhangings and pictures can include any type of textile. Some progressive embroiderers are even incorporating paper and plastic in their designs for decorative panels.

15

DESIGN/THE BASIC PRINCIPLES

Design incorporates the selection and arrangement of different elements to form a satisfactory composition, whatever the nature of the piece of work. In the case of embroidery, these elements include shapes and spaces, line, color, texture and pattern—all of which must be brought together with regard for any limitations imposed by the technique, as well as such practical considerations as time and cost involved or whether the item is washable. A successful composition will command notice unselfconsciously, and will avoid being a confused jumble of shapes or colors assembled in haphazard fashion. A pleasing design will be well-proportioned; it will have balance and a focal point or areas of interest, as well as lines of sight to draw your attention.

You may already have a natural talent for design—a sense of color, proportion and balance—and be able to draw and sketch well; or you may feel that you are lacking in these qualities and that you need some help in this direction. (Don't worry about your drawing skills for a start; there are other ways to put together a working plan.) Remember that you are constantly applying design principles in your daily life; you choose and coordinate your clothes, use cosmetics, decorate your home, hang pictures, arrange flowers or plan a flower garden—all of which require you to make decisions as to the final look of the job in hand. In the same way, when planning a design for embroidery you will arrange the elements in a way which pleases the eye, and as your design experience increases you will soon recognize if something is unsuitable.

When making a composition you should be aware of certain traditional design concepts which can serve as guidelines and may prevent errors from creeping in which cannot later be rectified. You need not follow the time-honored laws of composition slavishly, but like any artist you will be better off if you understand them before going your own way. They distill what the human eye has found pleasing over the course of centuries. Just as needlework itself possesses a venerable history, so do the basic principles of design.

PROPORTION AND SCALE
Proportion in a design refers to the relationship between the size of one element and another. It is important to get the proportions right at the beginning as it is difficult to make alterations to them at a later stage. You need the correct organization of amounts and areas to give your basic plan a satisfactory balance. Embroidery projects call for particular choices to be made in the matter of scale. The scale of a practical article is frequently dictated by its use or surroundings—a chair seat must

fit the chair or a garment the wearer; a wallhanging or picture should relate suitably in size to the space in which it is displayed. As far as the design itself is concerned, bear in mind that the scale of the embroidered area must relate in size to the overall shape, and that the undecorated background space should work effectively as part of the design.

BALANCE: SYMMETRY AND ASYMMETRY
The most well-balanced design (although not necessarily the most interesting) is one based on symmetry. A symmetrical design is one which, when cut through the center either horizontally or vertically, results in two mirrored halves. This makes for a rigidity and formality which might well have a place in border designs or samplers, or on household items such as table linen, with strong regular patterns. In terms of clothing, a symmetrical embroidery design would suit, for example, the fronts of a vest or jacket. Its effect is generally less satisfactory for embroidered panels and wallhangings.

If it is overused, this type of balance can be limiting and monotonous. However, symmetry can be relieved in a number of ways—for one, by retaining the outline exactly, but changing the details within (colors, stitches, fabrics, textures). This would be the more creative approach. Another way of altering symmetry is to work a counter-change design. An example of this would be where the motif in one half was black on a white background, and the reverse colors in the other half. A counter-change design has great strength and in repeat patterns can provide added interest. Although normally effected by the reversal of colors, counter-change can also be achieved by reversing stitches or qualities of texture.

Asymmetry (without symmetry) characterizes a design of unequal balance and tends to create a more interesting and lively impression than strict symmetry does. Although the halves of the design are not identical, they still need to be balanced. In an asymmetrical composition, you need, for instance, to offset dominant elements on one side with smaller components of a similar weight on the other to prevent the design from looking lopsided. The same applies to the tonal and textural qualities of the composition. For example, a heavily padded or brightly colored focal point placed on the right would need to be complemented with smaller areas similarly worked on the left so that it would not become isolated in space.

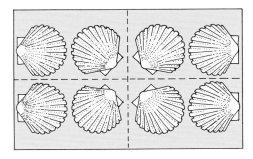

A symmetrical design: cut in half either horizontally or vertically one half is a mirror image of the other. The result is regular and somewhat formal.

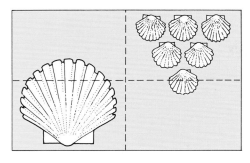

An asymmetrical design: the large motif in one corner is balanced by the arrangement of small units in the opposite corner. Such a design has an interesting and lively quality.

The large shell is undoubtedly the focal point, but it is balanced by other areas of interest in the design. Grid lines dividing the space into thirds and quarters help to plan out harmonious proportions.

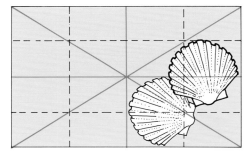

Do not be afraid of empty space – it can be an important part of the design if planned carefully. Taking a motif off-center prevents it from "floating" in space. The proportion of the total area filled works satisfactorily.

16

FOCAL POINTS/AREAS OF INTEREST

If a design has a focal point, it will form the heart of the composition—the most important, most colorful or largest textured area. In a symmetrical design, the focal point is most likely to be placed centrally with other less important elements surrounding it. In an asymmetrical design, if the focal point is moved slightly away from the center, a more interesting composition is possible.

The other areas of interest in a design, although secondary to the focal point, should relate to it in some way—by shape, color, texture or connecting lines. Sometimes a good design may consist only of isolated and unrelated shapes, but a more harmonious effect is likely to be produced if the elements are overlapped or connected somehow.

HARMONY AND CONTRAST

Harmony in a design can be achieved by using similar shapes and sizes, textures, lines and colors. A harmonious work is easy to understand and does not offend the eye. However, perfect harmony can produce rather uninspired designs: a small amount of contrast may be needed to provide a spark, enlivening the overall quality of the piece. The means for introducing contrast to an embroidery design include texture (such as beads or knotted stitches on an otherwise flat design); color (by using complementaries —see p. 40) or by using elements of shapes and sizes different from those in the main part of the design.

PRINCIPLES OF PATTERN

The arrangement and repetition of single motifs or units to form a pattern is an essential ingredient of embroidery design. The pattern's complexity or simplicity is determined by the designer, taking into account the proposed technique and the intended use of the finished article. Some techniques, such as needlepoint, lend themselves well to intricate patterns; others, such as quilting and appliqué, rely on different effects which are best kept uncomplicated. The elements of an all-over pattern can be arranged in a variety of ways—straight, brick, half-drop or random. Patterned borders are often made up of evenly distributed repeat or mirrored images (see pp. 58–59).

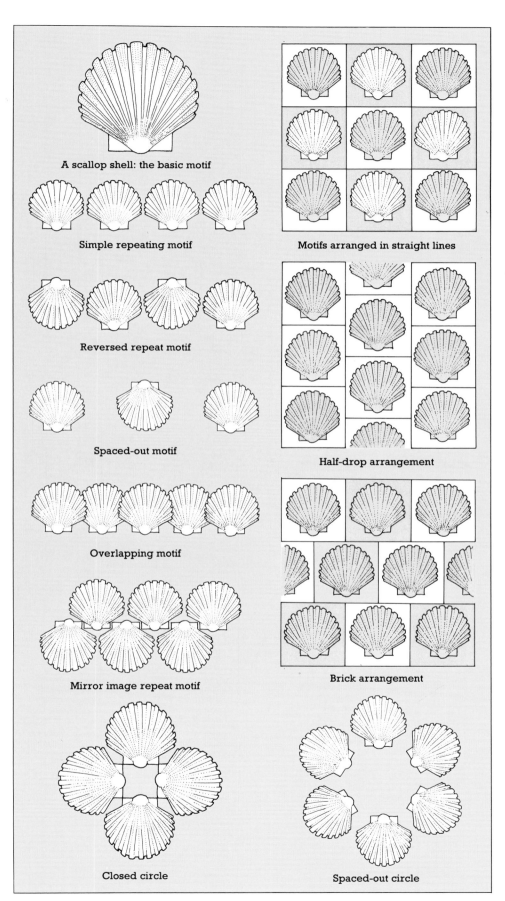

A scallop shell: the basic motif

Simple repeating motif

Motifs arranged in straight lines

Reversed repeat motif

Spaced-out motif

Half-drop arrangement

Overlapping motif

Brick arrangement

Mirror image repeat motif

Closed circle

Spaced-out circle

17

TYPES OF DESIGN

The type of design you settle on will depend both on your style preference and on the technique you intend to use; some methods lend themselves to realism, others to stylization or abstraction.

Realistic or naturalistic designs A realistic design is one which imitates as nearly as possible the form, color and texture of the subject. Naturalism is perennially popular because people enjoy producing instantly recognizable images—easy to relate to, but challenging in their fine details. There are several approaches to a realistic design. If you are skilled at drawing or painting, you can work from an existing sketch you like, or produce one with a specific embroidery technique in mind. As an alternative to drawing, borrow your idea from a photograph or painting (see pp. 22–23).

Do avoid copying other people's embroidery; there is never a shortage of original references from which to work. A landscape can be duplicated in surface stitchery with colors and textures faithfully reproduced; a picture can be recreated in appliqué with areas in high or low relief, padded to resemble the actual forms of the subjects.

Stylized or decorative designs Stylization is a deliberately altered view of reality in which the artist freely emphasizes those aspects of the subject she feels are most characteristic, while playing down the less important details. Lines may be straightened or exaggerated, plain flat areas given pattern and surface texture; elements may be eliminated to suit the technique or the materials used—but the subject never loses its basic identity. One method of stylizing a design is to trace from your original reference using a pencil and ruler, thus eliminating all the curves. The rather formal, rigid outline this gives you can be used for simple appliqué shapes or for counted thread methods. A bird, for example, would

assume a geometric outline; areas of head, breast and wings could then be divided and worked in whatever stitches you prefer, without the need to reproduce the exact look of the feathers.

A more ornamental method of stylization is to retain the original outlines of the subject, but add decorative features. How this will be done depends on the proposed technique. A butterfly motif could be completely covered in beads; a street scene stitched in blackwork patterns. Colors can be altered from nature—a seascape in black and white; a rose in gold or silver thread; a penguin quilted in color or a parrot in monochrome. Textures, too, can reverse reality—ballet slippers in bulky yarn or sheep quilted in satin.

Symbolic designs A symbolic design carries stylization a stage further, eliminating all superfluous decoration and detail so that the image is reduced to a minimum —purely an emblem of the original subject. A tree reduced to symbolic form, for instance, would be suitable for a cross stitch or Assisi work design.

Abstract designs The term abstract applies to a number of concepts. You can have abstractions of natural subjects, such as flowers, but these will be so far reduced in form as to be scarcely recognizable. The original flower is merely the inspiration for the abstracted shape. Abstract designs can also be based on geometric forms, lines or random shapes; on cut paper (see p. 24); on found objects and assorted accidental means (see p. 26). Abstract designs can also give expression to abstract thoughts or feelings—happiness, anger, warmth, loneliness, passion. There is scope for virtually every embroidery technique; the interpretation is in the hands of the designer.

DESIGNING FOR SPECIFIC TECHNIQUES

Whatever type of design you are embarking on, it is nearly always worthwhile to make a working drawing. This helps both to clarify your ideas and to eliminate any errors in the proportions of the design which might be difficult to alter at a later stage. You need draw no more than the design's essential elements; details can be added later. In any case, a totally worked-out plan leaves no room for any adjustments or embellishments. A design which is allowed to develop spontaneously as work progresses has more vitality and should give a more satisfying and original result. In any creative field from fiction to film-making the finished piece is more likely than not at variance with the initial working plan. Give your embroidery the same flexibility. The working drawing will need to be made with the embroidery technique in mind; some adjustments or simplifications may well have been incorporated already.

Surface stitchery Surface stitchery is probably the most versatile embroidery medium. The wide variety of stitches combined with the profusion of threads available in all colors, thicknesses and textures make it suitable for any type of design—realistic, stylized, abstract or symbolic. The success of the design hangs on the ideal selection of stitches and threads. When working a naturalistic design, try to make the direction of the stitch compatible with the subject—matching the upward thrust of growing ferns or the lateral motion of water, for instance. The stitch chosen will also need to interpret the texture of the original—such as satin stitch in silk for a smooth area, French knots in thick wool clustered together for a chunky effect.

Appliqué Appliqué generally calls for bold designs which take into account the cutting out of the applied shapes. If you choose to work with delicate and fairly intricate pieces, a double-sided bonding

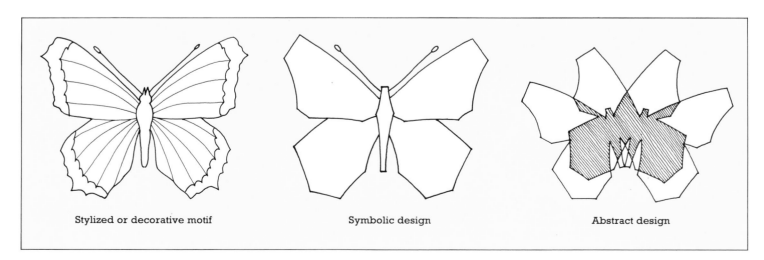

Stylized or decorative motif   Symbolic design   Abstract design

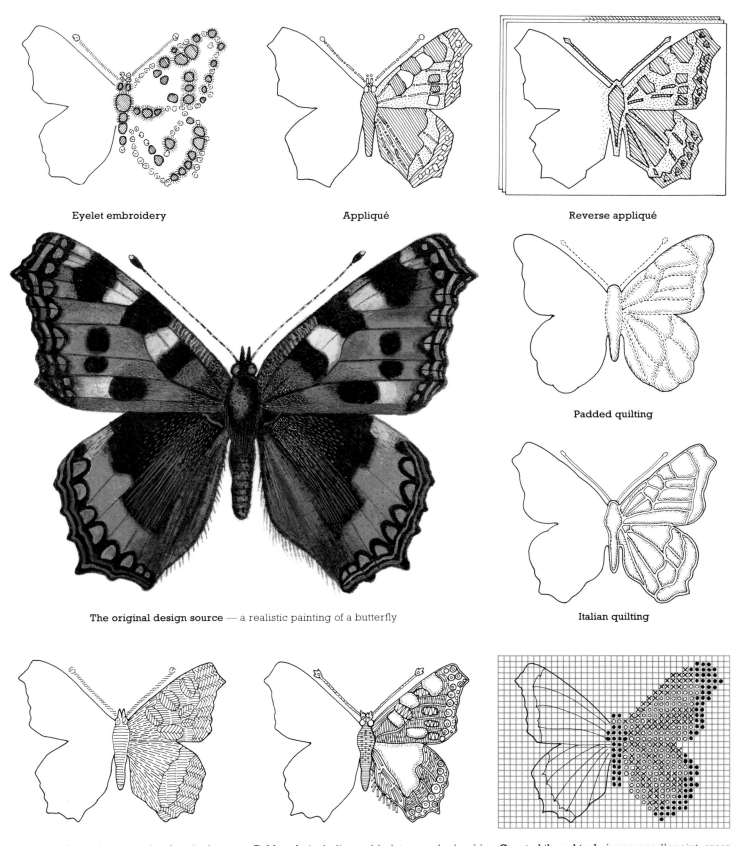

Eyelet embroidery

Appliqué

Reverse appliqué

Padded quilting

Italian quilting

The **original design source** — a realistic painting of a butterfly

Surface stitchery, incorporating herringbone, fern stitch, long and short stitch on the wings; padded satin stitch for the body; stem stitch and French knots for the antennae

Goldwork, including gold plate, couched gold thread, padded kidskin, bugle beads and sequins secured by a bead on the wings; padded couching for the body; gold cord antennae

Counted thread techniques: needlepoint, cross stitch and Assisi work

19

material helps; but care must be taken to prevent fraying or loss of definition of the outline. You will need to simplify your design slightly for most types of appliqué, paying particular attention to narrow shapes and points which are difficult to use satisfactorily. Cut paper designs make a good basis for appliqué methods as they rely on shape rather than line for their immediate impact.

Reverse appliqué requires special treatment. You separate the design into individual elements, rather like a stencil, working from the top down. These elements are then divided by a series of parallel lines to correspond with the several layers of fabric this technique uses, similar to contours, which will take the form of layers of fabric.

Quilting Designs which have been considerably simplified or reduced to outline work best with padded and stuffed quilting methods. Quilting relies for its effect on the shadows cast by the uneven surface, therefore it is essential that a large proportion of the surface is left unworked: the more quilting there is, the flatter the work becomes and the effect is diminished.

Designs which contain parallel lines are suited to Italian quilting. This method permits easy interpretation of, for instance, the trailing, sinuous curves of Art Nouveau or the interlaced patterns of Celtic art. Other subject matter would need to be adapted by breaking it down into a series of parallel lines which is the chief characteristic of this technique.

Metal thread Metal thread is a highly decorative technique, particularly suitable for stylized designs. Areas can be filled with textured purls or couching; the latter form lends itself to linear patterns in which the metal threads can be laid in long lengths.

Cutwork Cutwork relies on the correct distribution of the design's main elements; they must overlap or connect in some way, as the background area will ultimately be removed. This in turn creates a pattern of spaces which needs your careful consideration as it forms an important part of the overall design. Shade in the spaces on your working drawing to judge the effect.

Eyelet embroidery The special characteristic of the eyelet technique is that the design consists of the overcast holes. The holes must be close enough together to form a coherent pattern. To help plan your design, you can use small objects such as buttons, moving them about until you come up with a satisfactory arrangement.

Cross stitch and Assisi work Cross stitch and Assisi work operate on a grid principle and therefore the most suitable designs are simplified silhouettes or symbols which are easy to adapt in this way.

In both types of embroidery each stitch covers two intersections of the evenweave fabric. Cross stitch is used to create the motifs themselves; in Assisi work the stitches cover the background instead. For instructions on how to transfer your design to graph paper, see page 102.

Blackwork Blackwork relies for its success on the correct interpretation of the tonal values of the design. The most suitable designs are those based on spaces rather than lines, although line stitches can be added to the surface to delineate and emphasize the forms. The subject matter may be realistic or stylized. You can work from a collage made either of black and white photos or of cut or torn newspaper shapes carefully chosen for their tones.

Drawn thread designs The nature of the drawn thread technique limits designs to those based on vertical or horizontal bands, with or without adjoining squares or rectangles. When planning the work you may find it helpful to use strips of cut paper which you can arrange to form your design.

Pulled work Pulled work, like blackwork, is best executed using a simplified or stylized design. The pattern derives its impact from shapes, although outlines can be added at a later stage if essential.

Smocking Embroidered smocking designs are a decorative addition to smocked or gathered fabric. Traditional designs are based on a series of straight and zigzag stitches, such as honeycomb and chevron. You can experiment by working lines unevenly or by creating textured areas to contrast with unworked portions of your pattern.

Machine embroidery You can incorporate the automatic patterns for embroidery available on many sewing machines into your design. They provide useful decorative effects, particularly with stylized work. Alternately, free form stitching, which emulates drawing, is an excellent medium for realistic effects.

Needlepoint Needlepoint lends itself readily to geometric designs, based on the grid of the canvas. You can either work freely or plan your design first by making a line chart (see p. 29). Pictorial needlework does not require a detailed graph of the design. It is better to make a simplified plan of proposed stitch patterns; transfer only the outlines to the canvas and fill in the spaces accordingly, using compensating stitches (see p. 127) to cover any gaps. This will result in a stylized and decorative appearance.

For a more realistic effect, the entire design could be carried out in tent stitch, with precise use of color to depict the subject most naturally. For this, your original design should be either painted in oils (see p. 123) or worked out using a box chart (see p. 29). In the latter case, each

box would signify one stitch worked over one intersection of canvas. You do risk losing spontaneity with this type of design; if you prefer, you can disregard the grid of the canvas to some extent and rely on surface stitches added later to heighten realism. The intricacy of the design will determine the choice of canvas. A finely detailed piece will require a small mesh; a less intricate one, a larger mesh.

Design is choice: ask yourself the following questions to help you with your initial plan.
What shall I make?
Where will it go?
What will the size and shape be?
Which technique or combination of techniques shall I use?
What is my design source?
Which type of design—realistic, stylized, abstract, symbolic?
Which colors, textures, patterns, shapes, lines?
Which fabrics and threads?

ENLARGING AND REDUCING

Often the scale of your preparatory sketch or source material will need to be altered—enlarged or reduced—to make it practicable for your proposed design. You can do this in several ways: first, you could redraw it to the required size; or you could reduce or enlarge it using a photocopier. A third alternative, however complicated it might sound, gives you the option of incorporating a distortion or elongation that would improve the piece.

Using a large piece of paper, make a tracing of your original drawing and enclose it within a rectangle.

Make a grid of the rectangle by halving and quartering it, adding further equal divisions as necessary. The more complex the design, the more grid lines you will need. Number the squares vertically and horizontally.

To make your enlargement, draw a diagonal line from the bottom left to the top right corner, extending it well beyond the rectangle. Decide on either the height or width of your proposed enlargement and extend the right-hand side line or the top line accordingly. Draw a line at a right angle to this to meet the diagonal. Then join the remaining sides to form the enlarged rectangle. Divide the large rectangle into a grid containing the same number of squares as the original tracing. On both grids, assign matching numbers or letters to the vertical and horizontal lines. Copy the design section by section onto the larger rectangle, making sure that each part corresponds correctly to the original drawing.

To make a reduction, simply reverse the enlarging process by drawing a smaller rectangle. Again, divide it into the same number of squares as the original and make your copy.

To elongate or distort the scale, omit the diagonal line: decide on the size of the finished design and divide the grid into the same number of squares as the original, but make each one taller or wider, depending on the distortion.

To alter the perspective, you can change the grid in a variety of ways. Here the squares remain the same width but have been made less deep, so that the butterfly is foreshortened but appears wider.

DESIGNING FROM DRAWINGS AND PHOTOGRAPHS

The source material for embroidery designs can take many forms. But designs produced from your own sketches and drawings are likely to produce the most original embroideries. In drawing a subject you get to know it intimately—it will lead you to an intuitive feel for the essence of the piece, for which shapes, lines or forms you wish to play up or to eliminate.

If you are already a competent artist, this is of course a great asset. However, with some practice, most people can draw up a satisfactory working scheme for an embroidery design. In this instance you are not trying to paint a portrait, landscape or still life as a work of art in its own right, but to produce an adequate plan or pattern from which you can achieve a pleasing piece of work. Remember that it is the final embroidery that is all-important.

If you like the idea of sketching, carry a small sketchbook with you whenever you can; it will enable you to make thumbnail sketches as well as a few notes whenever appropriate. It is a good idea to include, in words, your impressions of mood, color and texture, since these will help formulate the prospective design as well as your choice of fabric, thread and technique.

The materials you use for drawing are largely a matter of personal choice and you should try out different media;

colored pencils, paints, wax crayons and charcoal all have different qualities, some of which may suit your way of working better than others.

In addition to a sketch pad of your own drawings or paintings, it is a good idea to make a scrapbook of items which intrinsically appeal to you. Pictures invariably spark off ideas for embroidery designs. Postcards from well-loved holiday places or visits to museums and art galleries all provide tangible reference as well as abstract images. Some birthday and greetings cards provide interesting sources of reference for decorative embroidery.

Books are a rich source of inspiration, too. If you enjoy outdoor pursuits such as gardening, birdwatching or walking, you will probably have books relating to your hobby which will be full of nature reference. It is well worth looking in children's books, since they often contain detailed or decorative illustrations suitable for interpretation in stitchery, or bold oulines which could be adapted directly for appliqué. Your local library will of course provide much more material. Whatever your idea or inspiration, it can be interpreted realistically, or adapted to stylization or abstraction.

Magazines and color supplements are another good source of ideas. Look at

advertisements that use interesting photographic images—distortions, reflections, shadows—whose unusual effects could well be exploited in embroidery. Medical journals, as well as books on biology and botany, often include photographs of highly magnified subjects, which make exciting foundations for abstract ideas. At the other extreme, aerial photographs eliminate all detail, but reveal distinctive pattern and shape.

In some ways it is better to use your own camera, if you have one, to gather original source material, since you can select the exact subject for a specific design idea. If you do own a camera, always take it with you on excursions; do not limit its use to special occasions and your annual holiday. Treat it as a useful tool to help you record impressions, without worrying too much about the artistic merits of the photograph.

Photographs are the most authentic reference for portraits, which can successfully be carried out in several embroidery techniques, especially surface stitchery and needlepoint. A close-up lens will help you to record detail—the center of a flower-head, the ridges and indentations on tree bark, the pattern and color of lichen on a rock, the texture of moss between paving stones.

Very often a part of a photograph or drawing can be taken out of context and successfully used. To do this, cut L-shaped pieces of paper as shown opposite and use them to form rectangles or squares of varying sizes, selecting and isolating different areas of interest. Look carefully at the composition before arriving at a final decision: consider the possible focal points and the distribution of pattern and texture and evaluate these in the context of the technique used. Unnecessary background spaces can always be left out so that the focus is directed to more interesting parts of the design.

If you make a tracing of your source material, you can interpret it freely: some unexpected areas can be shaded in and accentuated, or background shapes and spaces can be made more important than foreground elements; certain parts of the design can be eliminated, others emphasized. The removal of detail, leaving only the main lines, will reduce the subject to a symbol (see p. 18) and this is a sound basis for simple appliqué, Assisi work or cross stitch. Repeat patterns and overlapping images can all be made from your original source, using tracing paper as an aid.

Remember that your source material, whether magazine cuttings, drawings, photographs or slides, should be used as a starting point only. Do not try to reproduce it exactly in embroidery. It is better to consider it as an initial source of inspiration, which can then be adapted to your needs and to that of the embroidery technique.

Slides, though not generally as useful as color or black and white prints, have an advantage for designing large-scale embroideries such as wallhangings and large panels. The advantage of a transparency is that it can be projected onto a sheet of paper (as long as it is vertical) enlarged to any size, and the design drawn in. It is essential that the projector is placed correctly to insure that no distortion occurs.

Slides, if projected onto objects such as boxes, bags or garments, can give unexpected and unusual effects which could develop into highly original work. Projecting a letter onto a box produces an interesting three-dimensional distortion which can be exploited in an exciting embroidery design.

Cut L-shapes out of paper or cardboard and move them around to "frame" different areas of a photograph.

Your choice of embroidery technique will influence which portion of the photograph you isolate as the basis for a design. This area might lend itself to appliqué or shadow appliqué, whereas a detail from the foreground might be more suitable for surface stitchery.

Taking a drawing from a photograph, or from part of it, blurs the edges and makes it more abstract. Though the photograph may be your initial inspiration, the drawing might translate more readily into a working design for embroidery.

Abstract effects can be made by cutting photographs or drawings into strips and moving them up and down to create a sense of movement. The strips can also be rearranged in a different order, or reversed, for a more complex design. Though these strips are interspersed with blank strips of paper, they still form a coherent whole.

23

DESIGNING WITH PAPER

In addition to the obvious use of paper as a background for drawing or painting (see p. 23), different qualities of cut or torn paper can be a valuable aid to embroidery designs, particularly for those who are nervous or inexperienced at drawing. Every needleworker is adept with a pair of scissors, and paper is cheap, expendable and easy to use.

There are many types of paper available, from art suppliers or more general stores, ranging from those manufactured for specific design purposes, such as graph and tracing paper, to the decorative variety sold for collage, wrapping or display.

Tracing paper is one of the most versatile design materials, and has many uses in addition to transferring designs to the fabric. It can be used for adapting and altering designs, repeating and overlapping motifs, producing mirror images of drawings and sketches, or as a design element cut from paper.

Paper designs have the advantage of immediacy; they are quickly executed, can be altered or adjusted without endless rubbing out and give bold, strong designs —a great advantage for the timid designer. They are particularly suited to those types of design in which shapes need to be filled in, rather than those which rely on lines for their effect; included in this category would be blackwork, needlepoint, pulled work, appliqué, padded and trapunto quilting.

COLLAGE
For a first experiment, cut out a few random shapes of different sizes from paper and move them around on a contrasting background. They can be pushed close together in a group, with some overlapping, or gradually scattered over the surface. They can also be arranged to fill a specific shape relating to that of the finished project—a rectangle or circle for a pillow, an oval for a table center, or a square for an embroidered pocket.

Paper that has been torn gives a softer-edged effect. This can translate well into designs based on natural forms—landscapes, hills, bushes. A collage of tree forms made from pieces of torn paper in different tones could easily become a design for surface stitchery. Use striped wrapping paper to represent lines of band stitches or needlepoint or see how metallic papers can lend themselves directly to designs for metal thread embroidery. Brightly-colored torn tissue paper can interpret skies or water; newsprint could be used for the same features on a darker or stormy day.

When areas of colored tissue paper are overlapped, an additional color is produced, and a third shape also. In arranging the pieces, look carefully to make sure you have a well-balanced composition. In addition to a delicate appliqué panel, this material could lead to a design using shadow work or shadow quilting.

A collage made with carefully selected cut-out shapes from a newspaper can provide inspiration in a technique such as blackwork, which relies for its effectiveness on the tonal values of the design. Black and white photographs and newspaper cuttings can also be enlarged and used as a basis for blackwork designs.

FOLDED AND CUT PAPER
Cut paper designs of the sort children create for friezes can be a good source of ideas for borders, worked in different techniques ranging from cross stitch and Assisi work to appliqué.

A variation on this theme is to fold a square or circle of paper into eight and cut out a shape against the central folded edge, which will produce the type of design known as Hawaiian appliqué. It is suitable for a pillow or for a repeated block to be made into a quilt. If your cut-out design contains a number of large holes rather than a single shape, it could adapt well to a cutwork design for a camisole top, for example.

REPEAT MOTIFS
The effect of repeat motifs can be clearly seen if you cut out several identical paper shapes. These can then be arranged to form a great variety of patterns: straight, brick or half-drop arrangements (see p. 17); they can be reversed, placed at an angle in rows or in circles; they may be scattered or overlapped to suit your purpose. They will lend themselves to numerous interpretations in embroidery, and are particularly suitable for border designs (see pp. 58–59).

EXPLODED DESIGNS
The principle of exploded designs is that, since all the elements have been cut or torn from a single piece of paper, they will be harmonious shapes that will relate well to one another. Place the cut shapes together on a contrasting background like a jigsaw puzzle. Now gradually draw the pieces apart, without altering the direction in which they lie, until you have a pleasing arrangement. Look carefully at the spaces left between the cut shapes, bearing in mind that the background area is part of the design.

For designs to fit specific areas, for example the flap of a handbag, cut out two pieces of paper—one for the background the exact size and shape of the finished work, and a contrasting piece in the same shape but considerably smaller. The smaller shape can be cut and exploded, and the pieces juxtaposed to form a well-balanced design. Exploded designs translate well into many embroidery techniques, including quilting, appliqué, stitchery and needlepoint. In needlepoint, you would also need to fill the background areas with contrasting stitches.

STENCILS
All types of stencils lend themselves readily to use in repeat designs, since only a single motif needs to be cut and the stencil can be repositioned for subsequent use. Such designs can be quilted, embroidered with surface stitchery, or painted with fabric paint, using a stencil brush or spray-gun (see p. 33).

The use of a stencil of paper or, preferably, of cardboard, can be directly applied to the method of reverse appliqué, since its fragmented elements reflect the type of design necessary for this technique.

To adapt a design for a stencil, it is necessary to simplify the original motif and to separate each element of the design from its neighbor.

Draw the design on thick paper or cardboard, then carefully cut out each shape with a craft knife, using a cutting board.

One advantage of tissue paper is that when two colors are overlapped a third is produced. In embroidery terms, this can be exploited through an appliqué design using transparent fabrics such as net, organza or chiffon.

Hawaiian appliqué motifs are made by folding a square of paper into quarters and again diagonally from the center into eight, and cutting a shape against the folded edge. Use the resultant paper pattern to cut out a motif in lightweight cotton.

If you fold a strip of paper accordion-style and cut holes or shapes in it, it can result in an interesting repeat motif, suitable for a border.

For an exploded paper design, select a shape such as a circle and cut it into pieces; the cuts can be straight or curved. Replace the cut circle on a contrasting background paper in different ways. Whatever the arrangement, it will have an inherent unity.

For a newspaper collage for a blackwork design, choose newsprint in as wide a range of sizes and densities as possible, and arrange the shapes to coincide with those of your original sketch or inspiration.

Strips of paper can be woven together, perhaps with strips of a contrasting paper, to form an abstract design. The textural qualities of these papers could be interpreted in corduroy and heavy satin, or in surface stitchery using, for example, lines of couching with long and short stitch or split stitch.

25

ABSTRACT DESIGNS

Abstract designs can evolve from almost any source; even a realistic image can be adapted, or reduced to its bare outline, so that it becomes pure pattern or design, barely distinguishable from its original form. Abstract patterns can also be based on geometric forms, lines or random shapes. However, one of the most direct routes to an abstract design is simply to play around with a pen, pencil or with found objects such as buttons or shells, until you create, almost by "accident", a pleasing pattern.

If you are visually receptive, there is potential for abstract design all around you. A heightened visual awareness will help you to register unexpectedly interesting effects as you look around. Notice, for example, the rainbow colors and fluid patterns of oil spilled on the road, of cream poured on stewed raspberries, or of raindrops trickling down a window pane. Such ideas can all be adapted for embroidery design, so make sketches and notes or take photographs whenever possible. Save ideas so that when you are looking for inspiration for a specific project, you can turn to your reference material and adapt it accordingly.

Studies of shadows and reflections can result in interesting embroidery designs; the shadow cast on a wall behind an object could be developed into a design using repeat images or overlapping shapes in transparent fabrics. Reflected images can also be worked as a counterchange design in different colors, or one technique could be juxtaposed with another to represent the reflection. For example, an embroidered picture depicting a lakeside scene could have the top half done in needlepoint, and the bottom half in cross stitch or Assisi work on linen. Alternately, the top could be carried out in appliqué with the lower half in shadow quilting.

DESIGN BY ACCIDENT
A simple way to make a mirror, or reflected, image is through an ink or paint blot. Make a large blob of ink on a piece of paper, fold the paper in half and press the liquid away from the fold. Weird insect and butterfly shapes will emerge, which can be adapted for the technique you have chosen to embroider. If you try this with tissue paper, the design produced will have indistinct feathery edges suitable for a delicate treatment.

You can make a transfer printed blot in the same way. Iron the print onto a piece of fabric made of synthetic fibers, such as polyester, and embellish the design with stitches, quilting or beads. Paint or ink can be splashed, dripped or blown with a straw across the surface of paper; try out different types of liquid and paper but remember to protect the surrounding surfaces.

Doodles sometimes produce sketches that can be adapted for use in embroidery. Doodles depend on your mood and personality; some are flowing and rhythmic, others more rigid and geometric. Flowing lines could well be interpreted successfully as a design for stitchery or Italian quilting. A geometric pattern may well be adapted to one of the counted thread methods such as pulled or drawn thread work, blackwork or needlepoint.

Accidental methods will, by their very nature, tend to produce random, free designs, lacking in control. The asymmetric, uncontrolled quality may be part of the appeal, but, in most cases, the blot, splash or doodle will need some form of adjustment before serving as your embroidery design. This is best done before committing the design to fabric, though it may sometimes be possible to make alterations at a later stage as long as you are aware that this needs to be done.

Once you have chosen the embroidery technique to use, the blot or doodle can be altered accordingly to accommodate any restrictions or characteristics imposed by that technique. In any case it will be neccessary to take a tracing of your accidental source material, simplifying and eliminating any areas or elements that you think need improvement. Decide on a focal point or areas of special interest and colour or shade these in; thicken some lines to add emphasis.

Most accidental designs can also be made into repeat motifs, borders or mirror images; they may be charted for counted thread techniques, padded for quilting or cut away in cutwork or eyelet embroidery.

PATTERN MAKING FROM FOUND OBJECTS
Many inexperienced designers find it difficult to draw a design on paper. One way around this problem is to arrange "found objects" into patterns. Make a collection of small, everyday items such as buttons, beads, nuts and bolts, paper clips, matches, seeds, pasta of different shapes. Choose a background paper or fabric, and make a window mount to coincide with the size and shape of the finished design. This could be a rectangle, square or circle for a pillow or an abstract panel, or could take the specific shape of the article you are designing—handbag flap, glasses case or garment, for instance.

Select three or four different types of object from your collection and begin arranging them in a design. This may take the form of a repeating all-over pattern, a border, a circular, swirling design or a symmetrical or asymmetric scheme. Decide on points of interest and, as you move the pieces around, take into account the spaces between them. Look at the overall shape and make sure that the

arrangement of the objects relates to the entire area. Once you feel satisfied with the plan, the items can be glued down to paper and then traced or photocopied.

Certain objects, such as small beads, would make a good basis for an eyelet embroidery design, the beads representing the characteristic holes. Curtain rings or coins of different sizes could be the inspiration for a surface stitchery design using buttonhole or woven wheels, spiders' webs or circular couching; alternately, the design could be interpreted in circles of appliqué.

Making a seed collage—with beans, peas and lentils as well as fruit and flower seeds—is fun, and the collage can be the starting point for flowing designs based on natural forms, both realistic and abstract. Seeds can also be dropped en masse to form exploding designs or random patterns. These lend themselves to interpretation in embroidery using a mass of French knots or beads. The effects made by an arrangement of pasta shapes could be exploited in quilting or even metal thread embroidery.

String, if cut into various lengths, arranged into patterns and stuck down, can also be manipulated to suit your purpose. Alternately, it can be left in a length, and dropped at random on a background for a flowing, linear design. This also works well with strings of beads, and could be developed into an Italian quilted design or a line stitch sample.

An ink or paint blot is one of the simplest ways of achieving a symmetrical design for embroidery. The shape could be filled in with surface stitchery or blackwork patterns, or its outline simplified in a tracing in order to use it for appliqué.

Blowing paint through a straw across a paper surface will produce an abstract, fluid shape which could be transferred to the fabric using transfer paints. This type of design is appropriate for a technique such as quilting.

Buttons of different sizes can be arranged alongside each other to work out a scalloped edge, for example. Depending on their shape, they might equally represent the circular or teardrop-shaped holes of eyelet embroidery.

A pleasing arrangement of seeds, peas and beans could create a design suitable for beadwork or for surface stitchery, combining massed French knots and a variety of band and filling stitches.

A pasta collage might suggest an interesting basis for metal thread work, using a combination of purls and braid.

String stuck down in well-ordered lines could inspire a design for Italian corded quilting or surface stitchery, using mainly line stitches. A more representational shape, as here, could be interpreted in goldwork, with the metal threads couched down.

27

GEOMETRIC DESIGNS

Pattern-making—or the planning of abstract designs from geometric shapes —is a simple method that can be applied to many embroidery techniques from surface stitchery and appliqué to needlepoint and drawn thread. Inspiration can be taken from natural objects as well as pure geometric forms and adapted for a variety of embroidery methods. Some natural phenomena, though not obviously geometric in form, may contain circular or spiral shapes—as seen in shells or pine cones; concentric circles can be seen in cross-sections of logs or onions, as well as appearing when a stone is dropped in water. Snowflakes are hexagonal. Many manufactured items, such as cogs, wheels and plates are circular, while straight-sided rectangular shapes occur in a diversity of man-made forms such as furniture, buildings and fences.

Almost any design source broken down to basic form or outline will result in the evolution of a geometric shape capable of being modified for embroidery design. One of the simplest geometric arrangements is the stripe, which often appears in printed and woven fabrics. Stripes could be translated into bands of surface stitchery, drawn thread or needlepoint rows.

Rectangular shapes are suitable for bold pieces of appliqué, while circles could be treated similarly, or, on a different scale, could be developed into a design using stitches which naturally form circular shapes—buttonhole and woven wheels, spiders' webs and circular needle-weaving. Straight-sided geometric shapes (squares, rectangles, triangles, diamonds and so on) will integrate well together in one project as will circles and ovals in another. It is, of course, possible to combine curved and angular elements in a single work, but more care will be needed in their placement if a well-balanced result is to be achieved.

Use a ruler and set square to draw squares and rectangles and a protractor for triangles, diamonds and parallelograms of specific angles. All these shapes will introduce a quality of strength and regularity to a design. They can be drawn precisely and arranged to form a pattern or a border; they can overlap or repeat. For a symmetrical design you will generally need an even number of shapes of each size; for a more interesting asymmetric design, choose an uneven number.

Circles are intrinsically harmonious and restful shapes; a circle draws the eye to the area it encloses. Circles have a gentle movement and rhythm, in contrast to the strength and angularity of the straight-sided forms. There are many ways to draw circles, the simplest being to draw around circular objects such as saucers, lids, buttons or coins. (You can also use a selection of these items for pattern-making, as shown on pages 26–27, for direct interpretation in embroidery.)

Another method for working out ideas is to use a compass, setting the distance between the point of the compass and the end of the pencil to the radius of the intended circle. To divide the circle into petal shapes, place the point on the circumference and draw arcs. Concentric circles can be drawn by steadily decreasing the radius to make a series of different-size circles inside each other. These two ideas can be combined or adapted with limitless possibilities. Radiating lines, like the spokes of a wheel, can also be introduced. To divide the circle into equal-size segments, use a protractor and measure off the divisions, keeping the number of degrees at the center constant.

Circles make good designs if several different sizes are used together; cut out a selection of paper circles and move them about, overlapping some, until you have a pleasing arrangement. Arcs can also be incorporated to "reflect" the images.

COUNTED THREAD AND NEEDLEPOINT

The counted thread embroidery techniques of cross stitch and Assisi work are done on evenweave fabric and their designs need to be drawn on graph paper in the form of a box chart. The standard cross stitch covers two intersections of the evenweave fabric, and each square on the graph paper represents one stitch. Needlepoint designs worked only in tent stitch are also charted in this way.

To transfer your design, either use squared tracing paper or trace the design directly on the graph paper by taping it to a window. Then redraw the design outline in steps, following the lines of the grid. Some curves may need accentuating; otherwise they will flatten out when the embroidery is worked. Fill in the squares with appropriate colors or, in the case of Assisi work, fill in the squares of the background area with one color and outline the motifs (which are left blank) in a contrasting tone.

The scale may need to be adapted to suit the finished design by enlarging or reducing (see p. 21).

Needlepoint lends itself readily to geometric designs, based on the grid of the canvas. If you wish to plan a design completely and not work freely, you will need to make a line chart. This differs from the box chart in that the lines on the graph paper signify the threads of the canvas, as opposed to the stitches to be worked. The actual stitches are drawn by pencil strokes, between the grid of the graph paper.

The form and structure of each stitch must be carefully shown; make sure the lines cross the graph paper as they would the canvas threads. If you are using a selection of stitches, each requiring a different thread count, use a versatile module of 12 threads. Each module can incorporate stitches which cover multiples of two, three, four or six.

For pictorial needlepoint designs it is not necessary to plan a detailed chart; a freer way of working is explained on page 18. A design to be worked entirely in tent stitch, using different colors, is best represented by a box chart.

Bargello embroidery, with its characteristic zigzag patterns, is based upon a repeating stitch unit and is one of the simplest forms of embroidery to design yourself. The pattern of bargello embroidery is established by means of Gobelin stitches, usually over an even number of threads, placed in step formation. To form a curve or a less sharp zigzag, blocks of two or more stitches are stepped instead of single stitches.

Once you have worked out your unit of design, this can be repeated horizontally along the row and subsequent lines in different colors worked in exact repeat formation. Alternatives such as motifs or four-way bargello designs can also be tried, with the help of mirrors.

For this type of needlepoint, you need to draw your design as a line chart, with the actual stitches drawn between the grid of the graph paper. If the design does not specify an exact width, start in the center of the row and work horizontally toward one edge, repeating the pattern unit as many times as you wish. Then return to the center and exactly mirror the row already worked, on the other side. If a precise width and number of units is stipulated, the threads of the canvas used for the entire design should be counted and the pattern unit calculated to fit exactly. For example, a width of 48 threads could be divided into four patterns, each based on 12 threads.

An attractive variation on the row design is one containing motifs. The effect of this can be seen if an upright mirror is placed along the original horizontal pattern, thus producing a reflected image of medallions, lozenge shapes or diamonds. The resultant central spaces between the rows can be filled with bargello or other straight stitches.

A further elaboration of this type of design is four-way bargello, which consists of four identical triangular quarters, placed at right angles to each other along diagonal lines. You will need mirrors to help you formulate this type of design.

To chart the four-way design, draw horizontal and vertical lines on the graph paper to establish the center. Then draw diagonal lines at 45°, intersecting the center. Only a quarter of the design needs to be copied on the chart, since this is repeated in the three remaining areas. Compensating stitches (see p. 131) will be needed to complete the diagonal edges.

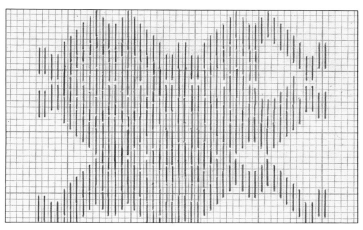

To establish a bargello motif design, slide two mirrors along a row of charted bargello stitches, placed at right angles to each other and to the stitches. When you find a part that mirrors well to form a suitable motif, draw the perpendicular center lines on which the mirrors lie, and mark the end of the pattern also.

On a piece of graph paper, chart the stitches between the marked lines, then repeat them as a mirror image on the other side of the vertical center line. Chart the lower row to mirror the top row. Draw another motif next to the first and part of a second row underneath. The open areas between motifs may form secondary motifs.

For a four-way bargello design, place two mirrors on the row of charted stitches, one parallel to the stitches and the other at a 45° angle to the first; move them along the row to select the most appropriate part of the design.

The design for the corners of a continuous border can be worked out by placing a mirror at 45° diagonally across the proposed pattern. This will show a reflection at a right angle. Move the mirror along the border design to select the most pleasing part for a corner.

To chart a design for needlepoint, place the canvas over the drawing and count the number of threads it covers in each direction. Measure these on graph paper (any gauge); mark the center lines. Transfer your design to the graph paper, square for square.

In a box chart, each square on the graph paper represents a stitch; the squares are filled in with the intended colors in different areas. Box charts are suitable for needlepoint designs worked in tent stitch only, as well as for cross stitch and Assisi work designs.

In a line chart, the chart is an exact duplication of how the different stitches will be laid over the canvas threads; draw the lines in the colors to be used. Use a line chart for bargello patterns and for needlepoint designs worked in a variety of stitches.

CREATE YOUR OWN BACKGROUNDS

Once you advance beyond the simple application of decorative stitching to a plain fabric, your embroidery can become truly inventive. To achieve an original look, you should take advantage of the enormous design potential of backgrounds. As a visual dimension, the background is far too important to be left to chance; it can make or break a design even when playing a supporting role, and is so versatile it can assume an equal or even dominant character in relation to the other elements in your composition.

There are various subtle liaison techniques you can employ to pull your scheme together. Effective links between background and foreground can be made with pattern, color or texture. The medium for a link might be a form of stitching—machine embroidery, pulled work or the application of a transparent fabric in harmonious colors, for example; alternately, it might be a combination of fabric paints and/or dyes planned to team with the embroidery. Modifying the background as you like allows for totally original results.

Paint can be incorporated at any stage of the project—at the start, before embroidery begins; to highlight areas as the work progresses; or as a finishing touch. Paint can also be used to decorate the unworked areas of a needlepoint panel. In combining painting or dyeing with embroidery, always bear in mind the following points. The color you apply should contribute something to the design which could not be achieved by embroidery alone, and the two methods should be carefully balanced in order to harmonize agreeably.

FABRIC PAINTS
You should find fabric paints quite simple to use. There are three categories: all-purpose fabric paints, silk paints and transfer paints. Colors within the range for each category may be mixed, making possible infinite tonal variations. The paints are water-based and are generally made fast to washing and light by pressing with a hot iron. They can be applied either direct by brush or sponge; spattered, using a toothbrush; or sprayed on with a mouth spray diffuser or spray-gun.

All-purpose fabric paints All-purpose fabric paints are suitable for every type of fabric. First wash and iron the fabric, then mount it in a ring or stretcher frame, or fix it with masking tape to your work surface. Protect the work surface by putting paper beneath the fabric, and if working on a two-layered item such as a T-shirt or pillowcase insert cardboard or heavy cartridge paper between the layers.

For small-scale and detailed designs use a fine brush and as little water as possible to avoid seepage along the grain of the fabric. For large areas of background, paints should be applied with a sponge; either the paint must be considerably watered down or the fabric must have been dampened first.

Silk paints Silk paints are specially manufactured for fine fabrics such as silk, thin cottons and synthetics. Choose the type made fast by ironing, rather than by the more complicated steaming process. As silk paints are far more watery than the all-purpose fabric paints, they will spread by capillary action along the fibers of the fabric, giving a transparent watercolor effect. Beautiful backgrounds, such as sunsets, can be created by allowing different colors to blend together.

Transfer paints Only materials containing synthetic fibers can accept transfer paints. These paints are applied first to paper, allowed to dry and then ironed off on the fabric. Be sure designs such as lettering and asymmetric motifs are painted in reverse, mirror-style, so that they appear correctly when transferred. Transfer crayons have similar properties.

SPATTERING AND SPRAYING
You can use any of the different fabric paints to create a spattered or sprayed effect for a background; however, silk paints tend to spread as their consistency is more watery. Those areas you do not intend to spray should be masked or shielded with cardboard or paper; secure it to the fabric with masking or double-sided tape. Self-adhesive film, of the type sold for covering books, makes a good alternative to paper masks as it adheres to the fabric.

Spattering can be done with a toothbrush or mouth spray diffuser (see below). Guns for spraying are available in a wide range of models and can be used either with an aerosol can of airbrush propellant or with a more expensive compressor. Assemble and fill the gun according to the manufacturer's instructions, watering down your paint carefully to a milky consistency; make sure there are no paint lumps to block the nozzle. Holding the spray-gun about 8in away from the surface, apply the paint with constant even pressure on the button, moving the gun back and forth at a steady rate. Most spraying is easily done with the work in a horizontal position (except when using a mouth spray diffuser).

Spraying or stippling with a stencil brush through a variety of different meshes will provide an interesting negative image. You can try rug canvas for a chequered pattern representing buildings or brick walls; or wire mesh of varying sizes for a texture and pattern unobtainable by ordinary painting methods.

Gutta resist helps to control watery silk paints for more detailed or clear-edged designs. First iron the fabric, then tape it to a work surface covered with plastic. Apply the gutta resist to the fabric before painting to prevent seepage from one part to another; use the special applicator to insure that the fabric is penetrated completely.

Use a toothbrush to get a spattered effect. Dip the brush into diluted or undiluted paint and, holding the head away from you, draw a piece of stiff cardboard toward you over the bristles, at the same time directing the paint toward the fabric. The work can be in either a vertical or horizontal position. Practice to get correct coverage. Mask the areas not to be spattered with paper or self-adhesive film.

The mouth spray diffuser can be used with a stencil. Keep the work vertical. Put one end of the diffuser in paint watered to a milky consistency and put the mouthpiece in your mouth. Keeping the nozzle about 8in from the work, take a deep breath and blow steadily and hard. Practice first. Mask the area beyond the stencil with paper or cardboard stuck down with double-sided tape or self-adhesive film.

Blending occurs readily with brush- or sponge-applied silk paints. Their watery tints spread by capillary action through fine fabrics.

Sponging can produce a mottled effect like this when the paint has been dabbed on with a piece of plastic foam.

Gutta resist, a rubber-based solution, penetrates fine fabrics to prevent paint seepage, allowing for clear-edged designs.

Transfer paints, which bond with synthetic fibers only, are applied to paper first, then reversed on the fabric and fixed by ironing.

Some fabric crayons can be applied direct and fixed with an iron. Masking tape gives the clean edges which contrast with the grainy color.

Two-tone toothbrush spattering combined with the same mask used in two consecutive positions creates this special star-center effect.

Use a mouth spray diffuser if you prefer a coarser, grainier spattered effect than is normally obtained by the toothbrush method.

Working with a stencil brush, use your chosen fabric paint sparingly and at full strength, applying it with a stabbing motion.

The rectangular motif of the stenciled and spatter-painted background is echoed by the outline-stitch quilting applied afterward.

31

CREATE YOUR OWN BACKGROUNDS/TIE-DYEING

Dyeing colors fabric in a way that is fundamentally different from painting, and home-dyed materials generally display tonal qualities of softness and luminosity quite distinct from the more strongly dyed hues of commercial fabrics. If you are working with a natural fiber cloth, ordinary cold-water dyes are suitable for home use. You can mix them to produce original shades; just follow the manufacturer's instructions.

In addition to dyeing in solid colors, you can create unique background patterns by employing one of the resist methods. A resist method of dyeing is one that treats a portion of the fabric in such a way as to resist the penetration of the dye. Batik does this with wax; gutta resist uses a rubber solution; and tie-dyeing simply exploits the tight folds in the material which block the even spread of color to create a variety of pleasing random-effect patterns.

The usual procedure for tie-dyeing is to tie the fabric with string, which prevents the dye from penetrating those areas most tightly bound. As well as different types of yarn, you can use rubber bands, paper clips, bulldog clips and clothespins to hold the fabric firmly and to produce characteristically different patterns. In tie-dyeing, chance always influences the final result. Exact repetition is impossible to achieve, but similar effects can be reproduced by repeating a prescribed technique.

If you are aiming for a specific tie-dyed effect, do allow time for experimentation. Keep comprehensive notes on the methods of folding and tying and on the length of dyeing time for future reference.

BASIC DYEING METHOD

To dye small quantities of fabric with the minimum of trouble, use cold-water dyes. A good range of colors is widely available and you can always mix your own new ones from these. Cold-water dyes are the rule for both natural fibers and viscose rayon; most synthetic fibers require hot-water dyes. Always follow the printed instructions faithfully, taking note of the amount of dye and water—particularly if you intend to repeat the color in future. Dissolve every particle of powder completely, stirring the solution at each stage, and use the dye immediately since it will remain stable for only two to three hours after the salt and soda have been added.

Tie the fabric in the desired way, leaving a length of string with which to lower the bundle into the dye; this can be looped over the edge or tied to the handle, if you are using a bucket. First wet the bundle with plain water, then immerse it in the solution; stir continuously for a few minutes to insure even distribution of the dye. Check for depth of color frequently,

bearing in mind that it will be considerably paler when rinsed and dried. When you are satisfied with the shade, remove the sample from the dyebath, rinse thoroughly, untie, rinse again, dry and iron. If you like, the sample can then be re-tied and re-dyed in another color to produce a greatly enhanced, multicolored effect.

FOLDING AND TYING

The method used to fold the fabric will determine the nature of the pattern you get. There are numerous folding techniques. The simplest is to fold the cloth in half and bind it, which will result in a mirror image when dyed. Fabric can be folded in quarters, diagonally or accordion-style. Remember that the fabric on the inside of the sample will be the least likely to accept the dye, so ascertain which areas of the piece you would prefer darkest in color and arrange these on the outside of the folded sample.

One of the easiest and most useful techniques is **marbling.** The random patterns produced are suitable for a variety of embroidery backgrounds. Voile and muslin can be marbled to evoke skies, vegetation or watery scenes; the effect can also be used simply to add interest to otherwise bland fabrics of different types.

To get a marbled effect, simply crumple the fabric in your hand and tie it securely by binding it with string, raffia or strong thread, criss-crossing the entire surface. Fasten with a knot.

You can use the folds and tying to control the pattern shape. For example, a **chevron** design can be made by folding a square of fabric in half lengthwise, accordion-pleating diagonally and binding straight across. Bulldog clips produce **rectangular** areas of resist which form interesting and regular geometric patterns on squares of fabric folded in different ways.

Circular motifs in a variety of shapes and sizes can be produced with the aid of such objects as buttons, pebbles and thread spools. Just wrap the fabric around them and either bind with yarn or secure with rubber bands. The results are often flowerlike dots, suitable for a garden scene, or for cutting out and embroidering individually on an appliqué panel. If you intend to make a regular pattern, plan the positioning of the objects and mark the fabric with a pencil before beginning. It will then be possible to see where each one should be placed even when the fabric has become distorted in the course of the binding.

A **sunburst** design can be produced by wrapping up an object such as a large button in the center of a piece of fabric. The remaining bundle can then be bound at intervals with string to give concentric circles. If the sample is dyed a second

time, bind the string in the areas between the original bindings to produce a richer image. Experiment with fabrics of different textures, such as satin or transparent chiffon, and enhance the design with surface stitchery by hand or machine.

Individual, **stemmed flowers** can be created by proceeding as for the circular or sunburst motifs, using a small button for the center of each flower. To make the stems, fold the fabric vertically just beneath the center of each flower head and clamp a piece of wood with a bulldog clip along the edge of the fold.

Tritik is an interesting variation on the tie-dye theme. The resist is achieved by means of needle and heavy thread, rather than by clamping or binding. It suits a fine fabric such as cotton lawn or muslin, which you stitch in your own choice of gathers, tucks, pleats or overcasting; finish by pulling the thread very tight before dyeing and unpick it afterward. Tiny dots can be made by binding with thread, and outlines for designs can be made with a double row of tiny running stitches, or by oversewing along the line. Alternately, you can stitch the outline in a zigzag stitch through two or more layers of fabric if you would like to create a repeat motif.

Discharge dyeing, or tie-bleaching, will produce any of the patterns described above in reverse, leaving you with a positive image on a bleached background. Simply use non-colorfast dyed fabric with any brand of color and stain remover, or experiment with a weak solution of household bleach and water using a 1:6 ratio.

Rectangular patterns like this with the look of Indian Madras cotton are produced using bulldog clips on accordion folds. Plastic kitchen wrap was also bound around the middle to prevent too much black dye from penetrating.

Marbling is one of the simplest effects to achieve. Simply crumple the fabric in your hand and bind it with string, criss-crossing the surface.

Chevron designs result when fabric squares are folded lengthwise and accordion-pleated diagonally, then bound straight across.

For sunburst patterns wrap an object such as a large button in the center of the cloth and bind the remainder at intervals to form concentric circles.

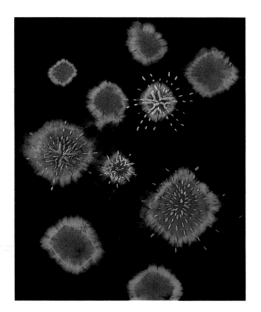

The tritik method is similar to tie-dye, but uses pulled thread instead of binding to achieve the resist. Fabric is gathered, tucked, pleated or overcast before dyeing.

Circular motifs that sometimes look like the heads of flowers are made by securing pebbles or buttons in the fabric with string or rubber bands.

33

EXPERIMENT WITH LINES AND SHAPES

The basis of almost any embroidery design, when reduced to its essentials, is the use of line and shape: whether the design is pictorial, stylized or abstract it will depend for its success on the proportions of shapes and spaces, together with the direction and use of line.

USING LINES
Lines in all their forms constitute potent elements of embroidery, from the jagged zigzag lines of bargello to the gently curved contour lines used in quilting.

Lines are ever-present in natural forms. They can exist as pure pattern—think of the stripes on tigers and zebras, as well as on shells, pebbles and leaves—or in delineating shape, as in the linear elements of a landscape: imagine rolling hills with lines of plowed fields converging toward the skyline, the lines of streaky cloud formations or of flowing water. Man-made forms also produce strong linear effects —for example, the curving structure of a road bridge contrasted with the parallel lines of the highway.

Lines appear in many forms—straight, curved, wavy, broken, zigzag, parallel. Horizontal lines in a design give a sense of calm and tranquillity, while vertical lines, by contrast, are stronger and more aggressive. Flowing curves usually depict gentle rhythms, whereas the angularity of zigzags suggests vigorous movement of a very different nature.

Subjects that are made of related lines, rather like contours—wood grain, rock strata, an avenue of trees, corn blowing in the wind, the folds on a garment or a draped fabric—can all be translated into harmonious embroidery designs. Such a subject could also be taken out of context, by isolating part of it in a window mount (see p. 23) to make an abstract project.

Several embroidery techniques rely particularly on linear forms. Many surface stitches naturally create lines (see pp. 69–75). Those such as backstitch or stem stitch produce thin lines; some, like Pekinese, are fairly narrow but decorative; others, such as buttonhole and loop stitch, make wide borders and bands. Their effects can, of course, be varied considerably, depending on the sort of yarn used as well as the way in which the stitch is worked (see pp. 50–57).

Running stitches, which make broken lines, have a much more tentative or subtle effect than broad chain stitch, which produces strong, solid lines. A dotted line can be achieved with coral stitch or couching, whereas bullion or French knots would make dotted lines with spaces between the dots. Lines that expand or diminish in width are easily made by using chain stitch combined with open chain.

Band stitches, when worked conventionally, form broader lines than line stitches. Wide, openwork stitchery can be achieved with up-and-down buttonhole or feather stitch, and very decorative effects can be made by juxtaposing several rows of complementary band stitches, such as double herringbone, chevron and open Cretan. Textural borders can be created using raised chain band or rosette chain.

Many quilting designs are based on intersecting lines or, like Hawaiian quilting, on concentric contour lines. Italian (corded) quilting, being made up of narrow padded parallel lines, lends itself to continuous curving lines. Stems and stalks can be depicted effectively in this type of quilting; interlaced patterns will make interesting border designs.

Many metal thread designs depend on the use of line, since the method of couching gold cord or threads plays a large part in the technique (see pp. 96–99).

Drawn thread work is composed of vertical or horizontal bands of threads withdrawn from the ground fabric. In its traditional form, this technique can be used either for borders or to execute formal, grid-based openwork designs. You can experiment with drawn thread work by varying the width of line or by using the openwork areas as part of a stylized pictorial design: for example, as upright tree trunks with the foliage carried out in surface stitchery or pulled work.

Smocking designs are usually composed of a series of parallel lines worked in stem, cable and double cable stitch to form rows of different widths. Experimental effects could be tried by using lines which separate and then converge, or which are wavy rather than straight.

Machine embroidery, by its very nature, consists of rows of stitching, used to create thin linear effects. The width of line can be altered by adjusting the stitch-width control, and thicker, more textured lines can be produced by couching wool, braid or handmade textured yarns. Some automatic patterns will make decorative lines, particularly suitable for dress embroidery or for table and bed linen.

Lines can be used to build up shapes. In this experimental form of needlepoint, in which the canvas is allowed to show through the stitches, long lines of thread are worked in different directions to form a multilayer grid-based design. The juxtaposition of primary colors adds a further dimension to this geometric embroidery.

34

The type of needlepoint known as bargello relies on the structure of the related lines of stitches to form the wavy or zigzag patterns characteristic of this technique. The blocks of stitches stepped to establish curves can be combined with zigzags of single-stepped stitches for an infinite number of different patterns. Try experimenting with one basic unit in as many ways as possible (see pp. 128–129). Make a mirror image to create a medallion shape (see p. 29); alter the placing of the colors to give unusual effects; work the unit as a four-way sample.

USING SHAPES

When adapting a three-dimensional subject to a flat embroidery design, it will be necessary to reduce the object to basics, so that you are left with an outline which encloses a shape. It may help to classify a shape—is it geometric or free-form, simple or involved? Can it be broken up further into smaller areas?

Make a selection of items that attract you purely for their shape—it might include a hand-crafted pot, a piece of sculpture, or a handful of smooth pebbles—and try to analyze the reasons for your choice. It may be the perfectly regular form of the pottery, the asymmetric curves of the sculpture, or the related shapes in the pebble collection. A design that uses related shapes is easier on the eye than one containing a number of unrelated elements. For example, a geometric design made up of squares and triangles, or one developed from an exploded shape in cut paper (see p. 25) would be harmonious.

Both natural and man-made subjects can involve similar shapes. Circular motifs are inherent in many flower-heads and fruit, as well as appearing as manufactured wheels, coins or plates. When considering shapes in relation to embroidery design, remember that the background is part of the design. When drawing or arranging pieces of cut paper or fabric, look carefully at their distribution and make sure that the areas of background form satisfactory and harmonious shapes.

The theme of filling spaces in a decorative fashion constitutes a major part of many embroidery methods. Filling stitches, as their name implies, cover the surface fabric in a fairly solid way. Those such as satin stitch, Roumanian and Bokhara couching, can cover the ground completely; others, such as wave and cloud filling and trellis couching, will leave some of the fabric showing. Single unit stitches such as seeding, detached chain and fly stitch can be sprinkled lightly over an area or the outlined shape, producing delicate pattern and texture, while band stitches, if worked closely together in rows, will fill a solid shape.

Appliqué is a method that uses cut-out

shapes. They make a bold impact, so it is important to plan the original design carefully. The various motifs must be complemented by the intervening spaces.

English quilting should be composed of well-chosen and defined spaces, as these will constitute the raised areas between the lines of stitching. These shapes should not be too small or the effect of the padding will be lost. In cutwork designs, it is the spaces between the elements that form the design, so the main motifs must be carefully placed with this in mind.

In metal thread embroidery, shapes are often filled with closely worked lines of

Appliqué is primarily concerned with the use of shapes, which make a bold statement in an embroidery design. Combined with machine work in this embroidered panel, it is easy to see how the harmonious composition of the design, based on flower borders in a garden, relies on the successful use of lines and shapes. The large appliqué sun motif at the top is echoed in the smaller repeat motifs used as a border around the edges.

35

EXPERIMENT WITH LINES AND SHAPES

The full potential of embroidery is shown when a pictorial design is successfully worked in a single stitch. Needlepoint done in tent stitch is the most obvious example, but in this picture of the site of a wartime airfield, couching, an essentially linear stitch, is worked vertically in single-strand silk thread down the grain of the fabric. The elements of the scene—the Lancaster bomber, the airman, the cows, the clump of trees and the aircraft flying overhead— are clearly delineated through change of color. Even quite strong horizontal lines, as well as the subtle formation of a cloudy sky and the color graduations in the meadow, are all suggested visually.

couched thread, in basket, brick or *or nué*. Some parts of a design can be padded with gold or silver kid, or filled with purls.

All the counted thread techniques, except drawn thread which is mainly made up of lines, are very much concerned with the decorative filling of spaces. The various pulled work stitches will cover an area with patterns containing holes of different sizes and shapes. The decorative nature of blackwork patterns makes it somewhat difficult to achieve realism. However, if outlines are eliminated and tonal values taken into account, a pleasing result can be achieved. Shaded effects can be created by gradually altering the density of a stitch, by changing the thickness of the thread, and by adding or subtracting elements of the pattern.

Both cross stitch and Assisi work are primarily concerned with shape—the regular nature of these techniques relies on the use of harmonious filled-in areas combined with well-proportioned background spaces. In making box charts for these two methods (see p. 29 and p. 102), look carefully at the shapes to insure that they are immediately recognizable. If not, you may need to accentuate or redefine some outlines.

BORDERS AND EDGINGS

A border is an extension of the linear theme; whether it comprises a repeating motif from the embroidery design itself, a row of band stitches or a few lines of pulled work or withdrawn threads, the formation is either a single line, four lines or the perimeter of a circle. Some embroidered pieces, such as pictures, require a border or edging to finish them off. Certain types of embroidery, like drawn thread work, virtually incorporate borders within the technique itself.

The border decoration on table and bed linen may well form the total or a major part of the design. Hems, edges or sleeves of garments all offer scope for borders to be worked in a variety of techniques; pillows or panels could have border designs, either as a surround to a central motif or as a series of embroidered stripes. It is essential that borders are worked out at the planning stage rather than added as an afterthought. They should be considered in proportion to the whole; the width, in particular, needs careful consideration.

Items worked in drawn thread, pulled work, cross stitch and Assisi work on evenweave fabric can be greatly enhanced by neatly finished hems and decorative borders. A drawn thread border or edging looks well with any of the counted thread methods; for a sampler in cross stitch, it is appropriate to have a border of the same technique or maybe one in Assisi work; some needlepoint may need a "frame" to set it off attractively.

For each of these methods, the threads

of canvas or evenweave fabric should be counted and the length of the border measured, marking the center with a thread. A box or a line chart can then be drawn on graph paper (see p. 29). If you use a repeat motif, always include the surrounding area as part of the unit to insure that the correct spacing is allowed.

For a one-edge border, or one in which corners do not have to be considered, divide the length of the edge by the number of threads needed for the unit to ascertain how many units will fit in. A motif pattern can be centered, giving an uneven number of motifs, or spaced from the center to produce an even number. For drawn thread borders the hemstitching can usually be adjusted. If the number of threads in the total length does not divide exactly, the extra one or two threads can be incorporated within adjacent groups.

The easiest way of making a four-sided border fit a given space is to start by working the corners and gradually move toward the center of each edge. This will give a mirrored design which, when the midway point is reached, can be adapted to form a central motif; or a few compensating stitches can end the pattern.

Border designs can sometimes be taken out of their original context and used to form geometric patterns in themselves— they can be arranged as stripes, diagonals or in a trellis.

Blackwork designs are based on regular shapes decoratively filled with stitches. Blackwork relies for its effectiveness on tonal contrasts between blocks of stitching, some being worked densely and others to form more lacy, openwork patterns. Borders and edgings based on geometric motifs are characteristically worked into the design.

Blackwork combines well with other counted thread techniques, especially pulled and drawn thread work. In this embroidery the border of the left-hand panel is created with pulled work. The same technique has been used for the flower heads and the pale crosses and diagonals in the right-hand panel.

37

CONSIDER COLOR

Before embarking on any embroidery project you need to give careful thought to the colors you will use. The color theme may even be your starting point, if you are designing a pillow or a chair seat or even a picture to complement a particular room scheme. Many people have an intuitive sense of color, and indeed everybody expresses their personality in the colors they wear and with which they decorate their homes. Becoming more color conscious will, however, enhance your abilities as a designer. To this end it's worth knowing the essentials of color theory. Understanding the principles will enable you to develop more successful color schemes and to create tonally well-balanced embroideries.

THE COLOR WHEEL
In the graphic device known as the color wheel, the colors of the rainbow are depicted arranged in a circle; the colors appear in the same order as in the spectrum but the red and violet from the ends are joined together.

The basic color wheel shows only hues, but each segment of the wheel in fact represents a vast range of shades. The hue gives a particular color its name (such as brown, purple, orange) and defines its position on the wheel, but shades of color are scientifically defined by two other characteristics. Its value, or lightness, tells you how much white or black a color contains, or whether it is light or dark. A tint is pale, i.e. the color mixed with white, and a shade is dark, i.e. the color mixed with black. Finally, a color's saturation is a measure of its purity or intensity. For example, a pinky, dove-gray is low in saturation, high in value, whereas crimson is highly saturated, medium in value.

When planning any color scheme, all three elements play a part, and it is important to understand their relationship. The tonal value, that is, the lightness and saturation of the colors you choose, is as important as the actual hue in achieving the harmony or calculated contrast that you want. A color that is subtly grayed, for example, may be discredited next to a clear, bright tone, whereas it could look perfect with other colors of similar value.

As a general rule, related colors, that is, those which appear next to each other on the color wheel, will blend together well and create a harmonious scheme. Contrasting colors, which appear opposite each other, are known as complementaries. Thus red is complementary to green, yellow to purple and blue to orange. Black and white are of course contrasting. Contrast can also be achieved by using wide tonal differences in a monochromatic design, for example a dark or strong pure color like royal blue placed next to a tint or muted shade such as a pale sky blue. Using contrasting colors together will produce vibrant, exciting designs. The palest pastels all blend harmoniously, even those derived from opposites on the color wheel.

In embroidery design the warm, advancing colors (reds, oranges, yellows) are best placed in the foreground, or in some way used as a focal point, while the muted or cool colors (blues, greens, purples) lend themselves to achieving an effect of distance or depth in a design.

Colors can also be considered to have "personalities". Reds, for instance, are bold, warm and friendly, sometimes provocative, while browns are homey and restful. Yellows are cheerful and sunny, as compared to greens which can be crisp, cool and fresh. Blues usually evoke calm and serenity. Packaging designers exploit these characteristics to the full, using, for example, pale, clear greens to convey freshness and browns for a nostalgic country style.

How can you apply these color principles to embroidery? First of all, *use* the color wheel. Test out your proposed color choices against the theories of harmonious and contrasting combinations.

To increase your awareness of color,

38

The color wheel, embroidered here in satin stitch, shows the relationship of color families: which are harmonious and which are contrasting. Use it to explore tonal values also: the inner ring shows tints, with 50 percent white added to the basic hues, while the outer ring is made up of shades, with 50 percent black added.

The primary colors are the pure hues of red, yellow and blue from which, with black and white, all other colors derive. The primaries are equidistant on the color wheel and divide it into three.

The secondary colors are achieved by mixing two primaries together in equal amounts. Thus red and yellow make

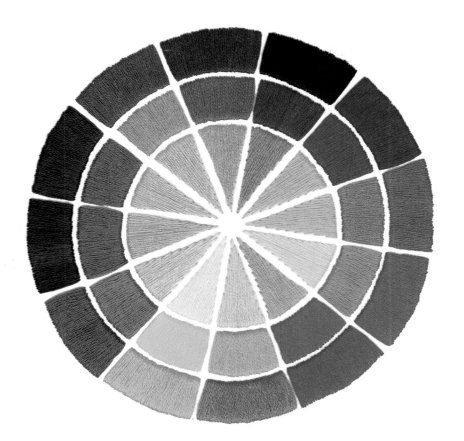

orange, yellow and blue make green, and blue and red make purple. These appear between the primaries on the color wheel; each secondary color is the complement of the one primary not used in its make-up and appears opposite it on the wheel. Additional colors are interspersed. These tertiary colors are mixtures of each primary color and its adjoining secondary.

Achromatic colors, which do not appear on the wheel, are those made from a mixture of black and white, i.e. grays and neutrals. Mixing all three primaries, plus black and white, in different proportions create grays and browns.

start to look at the color combinations used by professionally trained people: textile designers, window dressers, florists and interior designers, and analyze what makes a successful scheme.

Make your own color collection, starting with color charts from paint shops, color swatches of fabric and sample cards of threads; these are usually arranged in color families which blend well together. Collect clippings from magazines, commercial packaging, photographs, postcards and scraps of fabric and wallpaper. You might also include natural objects which are attractive to you purely for their color, such as shells, pebbles, leaves or dried flowers.

Keep your collection on a bulletin board or in an old shoe box and study them. This will teach you a lot about how color works. It will show the dynamic range of the main color groups and the unexpected shades and hues within each one.

It's worth doing a few embroidery-related color exercises before you begin a specific project, particularly if you are a beginner at design. Several are outlined on the following pages. Experimenting in this way brings new possibilities and combinations to mind, and makes you more aware of the way colors react. You will need a wide selection of scraps of different colored fabric and thread, as well as paint, brush and some white cardboard.

39

CONSIDER COLOR

TONAL VALUE
The importance of tone in a composition is paramount. Bear in mind that darker tones will recede and lighter ones advance.

These basic monochromatic exercises use paint, threads and fabric.

1 Start with paint of a pure hue, such as blue, and add different amounts of black to produce five graduated shades; then add different amounts of the blue to white to produce at least five graduated tints.

2 From your selection of threads, choose those of one color family, in this case blue, and grade them from palest sky blue to deepest navy.

3 Alter the tone of a blue piece of fabric by overlaying it with organza or net, first white, then gray, then black.

A further tonal exercise (not illustrated) is to dye several lengths of white cotton threads, taking them out of the dyebath at intervals for a graduation of tone (see p. 52).

HARMONY
Harmonious colors, that is those in close proximity on the color wheel, are easy on the eye and generally work well together.

1 Paint several squares in a group of harmonious colors—say orange, orange-yellow and yellow. Do not add any black or white, as this will alter the tonal value.

2 Make a harmonious scheme, using threads in the same oranges and yellows (or, say, red, pink and lilac). First, use equal amounts of each color; then try to make it more interesting by varying the proportions of each color used.

3 Make a collection of wallpapers or printed fabrics which employ basically harmonious colors. Notice how the additional contrast (blue-gray) adds interest to the middle fabric, while the splashes of bright orange pep up the color scheme in the top fabric.

CONTRAST
Contrasting color schemes employ the complementaries; they are strong, lively and make for vivid and interesting designs.

1 Using primary colors, either in fabric, paint or colored paper, make several contrasting schemes by trying them in differing proportions.

2 Make a complementary color scheme with threads in, say, red and green. Notice how vibrant and cheerful it is. Try using different amounts of each color and analyze your reactions to the result, then add some gray threads and see how the vibrant contrast is subdued.

3 In a strongly contrasting scheme using fabric, add an achromatic color. Notice how the vividness is subdued; the achromatic shade has a neutralizing effect and reduces the contrast.

40

COLOR IN NATURE

Interesting schemes can develop from observing natural objects. Take a ready-made color scheme from nature, using a shell (or a leaf, a piece of mineral or bark, or a flower).

1 Examine the colors of the shell and choose threads of stranded floss or yarn in exactly the same shades. Wind them around a piece of cardboard in similar proportions.

2 Using the same color threads, make a second and a third sample, altering the amount and proportion of each color or shade. Study the differences and see which you prefer as the starting point for an embroidery design.

Working through some of the exercises opposite and above will provide further insights into the subject of color. You then have to consider the practical ways to use color.

Some embroidery techniques, by their very nature, will be best carried out in monochrome—many of the counted thread methods, such as whitework and blackwork, look best in one color. Quilting, which relies for its effect on light playing on the uneven surface, is often stitched in a thread that matches the fabric. Eyelet embroidery and cutwork are traditionally carried out in monochromatic color schemes, since the effectiveness of those techniques relies on the pattern and position of the holes and spaces in the design.

Color in embroidery can be applied in several ways; stitching with colored yarns is the most obvious, but you can also make colored areas by adding fabrics, by painting and by the use of ribbons or beads. You can create areas of vibrancy with solid stitches in bright colors, or pastel delicacy with lacy threads and a more open stitch. In addition, color and tonal changes can be varied by interspersing stranded threads in cotton or wool; by placing stitches closer together or farther apart or by shading threads from dark to light. Shading can also be achieved by "optical mixing" in which two different colored threads are interspersed to make a new color. This is a useful device when only a limited color selection is available.

Colored or patterned pieces of fabric applied to a background will make immediate impact—appliquéed children's clothes in bright colors are extremely eye-catching. Transparent fabrics on an embroidered panel will give infinite

varieties of tone, as shown in the Tonal Value exercise opposite.

The background of an embroidery is a vital part of the design. It should be chosen in conjunction with the proposed threads and fabrics. If you have already selected these, try them out on different backgrounds. When the background color is already dictated by other factors, such as its position in a room setting, experiment with different shades of that color to achieve the best effect.

Fabric paints can be applied to background fabrics of any fiber, creating color without additional texture. Dyeing your fabric to harmonize with threads in exactly the way you wish is another possibility. The practicalities of both these are explained on pages 30–33.

Ideas for subject matter may strongly influence your choice of color, but don't feel too constrained by naturalistic representation. Your observation of natural objects such as butterflies, gems or shells may well be a starting point for an embroidery design, but the work itself can be carried out either by reproducing the natural colors exactly, or altering them to suit your purpose.

A reassuring aspect of taking your design idea from nature—whether it is flowers, or a landscape or a piece of bark—is that colors in nature are always harmonious. But this may not always insure a sufficiently lively or exciting color scheme for an embroidery. You might need to introduce deliberate areas of contrast.

Once you have the initial inspiration, be prepared to develop the idea: an apple does not necessarily have to be depicted in red or green, it could be worked in gold metal thread. Equally, a tree could be stitched in purple and a design of shells on

a vest could be appliquéed in black and white satin.

Your choice of color for an embroidery may well be dictated by the intended use of the proposed work. Pillows, for example, will be planned to match, harmonize or contrast with the other home furnishings in the room, and the color of an embroidered belt for a ready-made dress will have to balance the overall effect of the garment. For an embroidered panel or wallhanging, these criteria may not be of prime importance, so your choice of colors is more open.

For many, choosing the colors for such a project is the easiest part of the design process. You may have already been inspired by the purchase of a beautiful background fabric or some appealing yarns. Then you need simply to choose a color scheme which you find interesting and with which you feel at ease. This does not mean that you should play safe and use only neutral or harmonizing colors—some areas of contrast could possibly enliven the whole embroidery.

When designing, try to keep an open mind about color. Consider all the aspects of tone, harmony and contrast at the planning stage, but always be prepared to alter and rearrange some colors as the design progresses.

EXPERIMENT WITH TEXTURE

Texture is an integral aspect of all embroidery, not least because the application of stitches to a surface immediately adds a further textural dimension to it. The appeal of the different embroidery techniques varies from the smoothness of satin stitch worked in silk to the rough chunkiness of tweed and burlap incorporated into a piece of appliqué.

Contemporary designs, particularly those for embroidered panels and wallhangings, are unlikely to restrict the embroiderer in terms of texture, nor are there usually any implicit practical limitations, except on items of clothing. Threads can be twisted, braided and superimposed on one another; additional components such as beads, glass or shells can be stitched to the surface; fabrics can be added, padded, manipulated; or the background fabric can be removed to form decorative holes.

Texture is enhanced by contrast, that is, when any rough area is juxtaposed with a smooth one. Imagine, for example, the tactile quality of tweed next to cotton, velvet juxtaposed with silk, or a cluster of beads surrounded by the silk finish of long and short stitch. A mixture of techniques in a simple design is another way of intro-

ducing contrast in texture. Try leather appliqué with crewel embroidered needlepoint, for example. Change of texture on dress and household items can also provide exciting possibilities. A plain knitted sweater could be transformed to a luxury evening garment with the addition of beads, sequins or satin or appliqué motifs; a chintz-covered armchair could be complemented by a monochrome pillow worked using an interesting texture such as quilting or needlepoint in pearl cotton.

CREATING TEXTURE WITH STITCHES

The textural effect created by an area of stitching depends on the stitch and on the type of thread used. Satin stitch, for example, is usually worked in a smooth thread, but the same stitch worked in a hairy wool yarn produces an entirely different texture. As a rule, flat stitches, when used in an orthodox way, create a smooth texture. Such stitches include split, stem, back, long and short stitch, as well as couching and satin stitch. By contrast, all the knotted stitches — including French and bullion knots, coral, twisted chain, raised chain band, spider's web and rosette chain — produce knobbly effects.

One of the simplest ways of adding an

unusual texture is by using thick thread — bouclé, chenille and chunky knitting yarns will all produce effective results, almost regardless of stitch. A textured area can also be built up by superimposing one layer of stitches on top of another, using a variety of thick and thin yarns.

A change of texture can be achieved by contrasting solid areas of filling stitches with the more open, lacy type of stitch; Roumanian or Bokhara couching would contrast well with wave filling; closely worked line stitches such as stem or chain could be combined with trellis couching.

The texture of conventional machine embroidery is mostly rather flat; the automatic patterns of this technique result in a smooth satiny finish. Incorporating a thick, contrasting thread is a means of adding extra textural diversity; bouclé or slubbed knitting and weaving yarns can also be couched down, using the normal zigzag stitch. Delicate, lacy patterns can be created by using one of the dissolvable methods of machine embroidery, such as vanishing muslin. These methods allow areas of open work to be added as decoration on garments, or can form backgrounds in themselves for filmy hangings and similar embroideries. You can use them to produce freestanding motifs such as butterflies or skeleton leaf shapes.

Goldwork (see pp. 96-97) has an extravagant appeal which can be exploited in a design in combination with the texture of the threads themselves. When gold threads are applied over string as a padding, for example, it forms a bumpy woven surface; gold plate can be crinkled over a screw to reflect the light; rough, smooth and check purls are all in themselves highly textured and, if padded or stitched in loops, create a "crunchy" effect.

ADDING ON

The addition of beads and/or sequins to embroidery is both decorative and textural. Such additions are made to evening garments and bags or used on embroidered pictures. As well as these conventional additions, you can also use a wide range of "found" objects to create exciting textural effects. These could include washers, curtain rings, plastic and wooden tubing, dowels, coils of wire; or natural objects such as shells, bark, minerals, pebbles, feathers, dried flowers, dried leaves and driftwood.

Any of these objects, if incorporated into an appropriate design with suitably chosen threads and fabrics, could give your embroidery new scope. To work effectively they must, however, integrate well with the surrounding areas of texture. For a more subtle approach, many are best covered in some way or stitched with decorative threads. Those with an inherently attractive appearance can be attached unobtrusively with invisible thread and a spot of glue.

Beads can be sewn onto an embroidery individually, or couched down on a connecting thread. To provide more prominent texture, thread several beads on a previously waxed thread and re-insert the needle into almost the same spot on the fabric from which it emerged. This will result in a loop of beads that stands away from the background. Repeat this process for a thickly encrusted texture.

Shisha glass, which has for centuries decorated Asian mirror embroidery, needs to be sewn on in a special way with crossed stitches, firmly buttonholed, to hold it securely in place. Jewels and small stones or pebbles can be attached in a similar fashion. A spot of glue will help to hold these in place while stitching.

A variety of textural effects, based on contrast, is created by stitches alone or with additional decorations. A selection is shown in the embroidered sample below.

1 Satin stitch and line stitches (split, stem and running) worked first in stranded embroidery floss for a smooth effect, then in angora yarn for a rough, more textured result.

2 Filling stitches worked in a combination of contrasting yarns (crewel yarn and pearl cotton): seeding, fly, bullion knots, detached chain.

3 Overlapping stitches worked in pearl cotton: spider's webs and buttonhole and woven wheels; Cretan stitch and French knots; seeding and herringbone stitch.

4 Solid stitching combined with open, lacy stitches: Roumanian stitch with wave filling; closely worked chain stitch and trellis couching.

5 Shiny sequins create a brittle texture; they are attached in a diversity of decorative ways, including beads and French knots.

6 Beads and bugles attached singly and in groups for delicate or denser effects.

7 A three-dimensional, highly-textured flower motif is created with shells, pearl beads, shisha glass (simulated here by foil-covered cardboard), beads covered with needleweaving, plus buttonhole and detached chain stitch.

8 The goldwork includes padding over felt and string; a variety of smooth purl and purl purl; Russia braid; and circular couching with rough purl.

EXPERIMENT WITH TEXTURE

Texture is an element of every environment. Using a similar approach to the subject of color (see pp. 38–41), start by becoming aware of the textural qualities of natural and domestic objects. Look at the roughness of a wooden fence, the bricks of a wall or house, the bark of trees. Compare the smoothness of the front of a leaf with the ridged effect on the back.

When designing your own embroideries, think about how you might recreate some of these textures, in terms of the fabric and thread you might use, as well as the stitches themselves. The garden wall, for example, might be translated into a design using thick wool yarn on a rough-textured fabric; a collection of smooth pebbles might be the basis for a picture worked in quilted satin with areas enhanced by fabric paint and silk stitchery; a carving might evoke a three-dimensional soft sculpture in padded appliqué and manipulated fabrics.

A practical exercise that will heighten your awareness of texture is to make some rubbings, using wax crayons and thin paper. Select a surface which you think might be interesting, such as the weave of a basket or the ridges on frosted glass. Rubbings of the backs of leaves, with their prominent vein formations, could inspire a composition which might decorate an appliquéed garment, with the addition of Vandyke, fishbone or fly stitches depicting the ridges.

MANIPULATING FABRICS

Altering the existing texture of a fabric can add a new dimension to your work. It is possible to exploit the inherent textural qualities of the fibers and the weave by manipulating the fabric in a number of ways. Soft fabrics such as georgette, chiffon, and crepe will drape and gather well, but would be difficult to pleat, except in unpressed folds. Crisp fabrics, such as poplin, linen, silk organza and cotton organdy, do not drape satisfactorily, but they can be tucked and pleated precisely. Gathered and draped fabrics could be incorporated in a garment or could add an area of texture to an appliqué panel. A ruffled, scalloped hem can be made by gathering a row of tiny stitches in zigzag formation, producing an unusual edging to lingerie or babywear. Ribbon or narrow lengths of fabric can be similarly treated.

Smocking is a traditional technique which involves gathering fabric into regular folds and subsequently decorating it with stitches. Although most frequently used for dress decoration, the method can be adapted successfully to more sculptural effect.

Pleats and tucks are dressmaking techniques that impart a linear or geometric aspect to a piece of work. Lines of tucks or pleats can be interspersed with

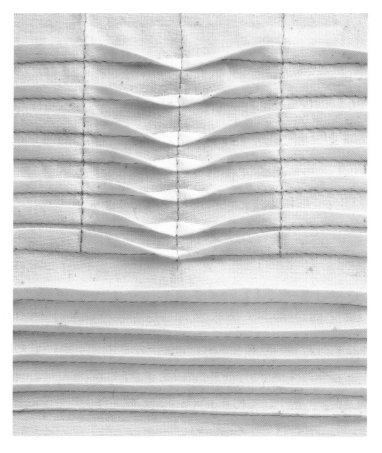

Wood's rough texture is recorded in a rubbing (above) and depicted in pearl cotton and stranded embroidery floss, used in single- and six-strands. The stitches include stem, satin, fly, Cretan and French knots. Alternately it could be developed into an Italian quilting design.

A solid fabric can be tucked or pleated by machine to add textural interest, or the tucks can be used as a grid, with embroidered motifs decorating the spaces.

44

rows of automatic machine embroidery, or hand embroidered band and border stitches, to embellish a pillow, for example. In an embroidered picture, these linear effects could be used to interpret architectural features or the natural lines of a landscape.

Quilting methods involve the manipulation of the surface by padding, and usually without additional color. The all-over padded effect of English quilting relies for its visual impact on the play of light and shade on the surface. It is therefore essential to choose a fabric that is able to create this effect and to avoid dull, dark colors as these will absorb the light and the quality of texture will be lost.

The characteristic channels of Italian quilting can add lines of texture, either in the traditional coiling and interlaced quilting patterns or by reinforcing a linear aspect of the design such as an outline. The padding of trapunto quilting will throw some areas of a design into high relief. This will create focal points or simply strengthen the overall textural quality.

Appliqué is an embroidery method which concerns itself with the addition of texture. Padded and three-dimensional appliqué, in particular, can vary the surface of a design in a way that will produce exciting results. Using batting will create a soft, squashy texture compared with the firmer effect of felt.

ALTERING THE BACKGROUND SURFACE
To create textural interest, the actual background fabric can be cut, slashed, pulled apart or have threads withdrawn.

The traditional techniques of reverse appliqué, cutwork and eyelet embroidery rely on holes and spaces to emphasize the design. These techniques all require firm, closely woven fabrics that will not fray. The first involves slashing the top layers to reveal those underneath. For cutwork methods, the spaces between the main elements of the design are first surrounded with buttonhole stitch, then the enclosed area is cut away with sharp scissors. In eyelet designs, the holes are overcast.

Pulled and drawn thread work also create holes and spaces. A loosely woven, evenweave fabric such as linen is traditionally used, but you can experiment with any material whose weave allows the threads to be appropriately manipulated. For pulled work, the weave is pulled apart and stitched, usually in matching thread, to form decorative filling patterns, borders or abstract designs. By using fabrics such as upholstery sheers or linen scrims, you can create much less rigid textural effects.

Withdrawing threads, as in drawn thread work, produces horizontal and vertical openwork stripes. These can be bound together with needleweaving or decorated with hemstitched patterns.

Suffolk puffs (left) are made by gathering around the outer edge of small circles of soft fabric and pulling up the thread (see p. 89). They can simulate circular objects, or be used in an abstract way.

Vanishing muslin allows the creation of lacy effects by machine. The stitching is worked freely and the muslin later "burnt out" with a hot iron or dissolved in water.

45

EXPERIMENT WITH FABRICS

Using fabrics in a creative way is one of the most challenging and exciting aspects of embroidery. Fabrics may be patterned or plain, shiny or dull, rough or smooth and made of any kind of fiber. To the embroiderer, all fabrics have both tactile and visual appeal, from the pile of velvet and the flimsiness of chiffon to the profusion of pattern and color in everyday dress materials. Whatever the project, the fabrics need to be chosen carefully. You need to consider their visual impact, in terms of both color and texture, as well as any practical considerations such as wear and washability.

The way a fabric behaves is also an important factor in embroidery design, and the properties of woven and non-woven, natural and synthetic fabrics are discussed fully on pages 14–15. Ideas for embroidery can often be inspired by the pattern or weave of a material—a woven tweed may be suitable for depicting buildings or architectural features in appliqué, for example. In addition, the fabric structure may suggest a technique.

The motifs on a printed fabric can be used in appliqué and quilting. In simple, padded quilting (above, left) the main lines are hand-quilted for an overall textural effect. The penguin motif is recreated (above, right) in white satin and black leather; it is appliquéed on a felt background and embellished with surface stitchery. The edges of the satin are overcast with blanket stitch and the feet and beak worked in satin stitch.

A bonding web is used to attach re-arranged, cut-out motifs on the felt background (left, top); without bonding; the raw edges will have to be turned under or overcast with blanket stitch (left, below). Trapunto quilting is used (far left) to pad the front of the penguin: batting is inserted from behind and the outlines are hand-quilted.

46

PRINTED MATERIALS

One of the simplest ways of using patterned fabric is to cut out motifs or areas of the design and appliqué them to a background. The quickest method is to use a double-sided bonding material, which will attach the motif to the background and will stand up to washing and a good deal of wear, particularly if the edges are sewn down firmly or satin stitched by machine. When positioning the pieces, make sure that the spaces between the cut-out shapes are harmonious and that the size of the motif is in proportion to its surrounding area. It is a good idea to spend some time cutting up a number of shapes, moving them about, overlapping some and studying the relationship between them and the background.

A simple use of this method would be to decorate a tablecloth and napkins, cutting out, for example, large flowers or other motifs from a patterned fabric. Very often motifs of different sizes appear in a printed design which would be suitable for this type of project. The idea could also be used in reverse, appliquéing shapes of a solid fabric on a decorative background. Similarly, motifs can be stitched to children's wear, such as sweatshirts and jeans, or incorporated into an embroidered picture.

Do not overlook the possibility of using the back of a fabric in contrast or preference to the front. The reverse side of printed material is usually paler in shade than the right side and this could well be exploited in an appliqué landscape, to soften the tone and achieve an effect of receding into the distance. Patterned, mainly geometric fabrics, such as striped or checked silks and cottons, can be used to provide direction or atmosphere in an appliqué design. Stripes could be used in a realistic way to portray awnings in a street scene or deck chairs on the beach, for example.

Altering the pattern of a printed fabric with the addition of stitches can be an interesting experiment. Choose a fabric with a simple design, such as spots or widely-spaced repeating motifs, and add stitches to transform the pattern—spots can be enlarged, turned into different shapes, such as stars, triangles or flowers, or can be embroidered to join up with each other.

You can achieve interesting results through smocking a printed fabric. Some of the design will disappear in the folds, so that, with a degree of forethought during the gathering process, you can plan for particular effects. If you use checked gingham, take care that it is smocked with flair and sensitivity, or it can look out-of-date or ordinary.

WOVEN FABRICS

Fabrics in which the weave is an important characteristic will give plenty of opportunity for experimentation. Loosely woven evenweave materials, such as the specialist embroidery linens and cottons shown on page 15, are suitable for the traditional counted thread techniques of pulled and drawn thread work. The regular warp and weft make it easy to count the threads, thereby leading to the many patterns and designs which are a feature of these methods. The stitches, usually worked in thread to match the background, will alter the surface of the fabric in different ways.

In pulled work the stitches pull the weave apart, creating a pattern of holes. Traditionally this would have been done only in regular geometric designs but today a freer approach, using less rigid and regular stitches, can produce exciting results. Drawn thread work is less easy to use in a contemporary style, but both these methods can be adapted in a more experimental approach if you use non-traditional fabrics such as loosely-woven sheer upholstery fabrics.

Frayed and fringed effects made by unraveling woven materials can be incorporated in all kinds of embroidery. For example, you can finish a set of linen table napkins with a simple fringed border, or make a decorative edge to an embroidered wrap or cape. Frayed fabrics can also provide a textural feature in an embroidered panel to give feathery or wispy effects—frayed silk could suggest feathers or ferns, for example.

Shot fabrics are usually shiny silk or synthetic fibers simulating silk, the warp

Striped fabric can be tucked, pleated or folded to eliminate one color or to accentuate another (top left). Spots and stripes can also be smocked to good effect by manipulating the fabric in a particular way when gathering and when smocking.

threads being in one color, the weft in another. Thus an orange fabric will be made up of a combination of red and yellow, a lilac one from pink and blue. This property can be exploited by using the fabric in such a way that the light playing on the fibers accentuates the iridescent effect.

In an appliqué design, place some pieces of fabric with the warp running horizontally and others with the warp running vertically, to produce a distinct change of color. Shot fabric will produce a fringe of one color if frayed horizontally and the other color if the fraying is done vertically.

The color of pile fabrics such as velvet, velveteen or corduroy will alter depending on the way the fabric is placed. If the pile runs upward on a garment or hanging, the effect is darker and richer than if it runs downward. On some fabrics the back may be entirely different from the front, both in color and texture—some rayon curtain fabrics have a pale, very shiny reverse side compared with the darker, more matte right side. You can choose which is the more suitable or combine both in a design.

The characteristics of a firm, closely woven fabric will invite experimentation by means of cutting through the surface, for such techniques as cutwork, eyelet embroidery, inlay and reverse appliqué. The effects created in cutwork and eyelet (both whitework techniques) are opposites. In cutwork, the holes cut in the fabric are part of the background area between the main elements of the composition, while in eyelet embroidery the pattern of holes actually forms the design. Both these techniques are suitable for lingerie, for babywear such as christening gowns, and for traditional bed and table linen. They can be updated and used in conjunction with surface stitchery.

Reverse appliqué requires a fine, closely woven fabric such as lawn, in order that the various layers can be cut away and hemmed satisfactorily. A much less difficult way of achieving a similar effect to reverse appliqué is to use layers of felt or leather which will not need to be turned under.

Transparent fabrics offer scope for new dimensions in embroidery, both in technique and design. Chiffon, georgette, organdy, organza, cheesecloth and net are some of the materials with which you can experiment to create subtle effects of water, skies and dark shadows in an appliqué or mixed-technique panel. Overlay other fabrics with them to alter the tonal value or to change a color completely. Gray organza, for example, will darken an area for the effect of shadow; red chiffon placed on top of yellow satin will produce orange.

Shadow work, a technique that probably orginated in India, makes use of transparent fabric. Double backstitch (see p. 73), is worked on the reverse side of the fabric to produce the desired shadow effect. The thread chosen needs to be much brighter than the intended finished color, since the fabric overlay will soften the hues considerably. The same applies to the colored yarns and fabrics used for shadow quilting (see p. 95), a technique which produces a most delicate result.

An experimental sample of drawn thread work on a loosely woven furnishing gauze combines hand and free machine embroidery (top right). The hand embroidery includes hemstitch and herringbone stitch as well as needleweaving, whipping, buttonhole wrapping and interlacing. The eyelets are worked by machine to create a more solid effect.

Exploit the many inherent characteristics of individual fabrics in embroidery as shown in the panel on the right. Try juxtaposing contrasting weights (top left); varying the direction of the grain so that the light plays on a shiny fabric in different ways (bottom left); withdrawing the warp threads and fringing both warp and weft of a shot silk fabric to reveal its two-color composition (top right); using the back as well as the front of a fabric to achieve both variety and continuity (bottom right).

48

NON-WOVEN FABRICS

Materials such as felt, leather, suede and interfacings, which are not woven, can play an interesting part in your experiments, mainly in appliqué. Their virtue is that, when cut into shapes, they do not become distorted and do not fray.

Felt is often used in appliqué for this reason, but you should choose it as much for its matte textural quality or its color as for its ease of application. It could give an otherwise sophisticated piece of work an unwanted naïvety. However, for some designs requiring bold areas of flat color, felt may well fit the bill: an embroidered panel for a child's room, for example.

Leather and suede, unlike felt, can add a touch of luxury to a design if the shapes are applied to garments or accessories using stitches that suit the subject. Double-sided, padded, three-dimensional shapes such as leaves and flowers in one of the non-woven fabrics can also be incorporated in a decorative wallhanging. Gold and silver kid have a strong brilliance and are often used in association with metal thread embroidery. It is conventional to pad this type of work, either with layers of felt, or with batting for a softer effect.

An unusual application for bonded sew-in interfacing is to treat it as a fabric in its own right. It can be painted or dyed and used for padded or three-dimensional work in the same way as felt or leather. A soft flimsy type can be used for flower petals; the stiffer quality can depict something more rigid and freestanding.

Modern decorative and experimental techniques also employ paper and plastic in combination with embroidery, particularly machine embroidery. Paper of all types and thicknesses can be tried; plastic sheeting of different grades, though not durable, can offer scope for experimentation. Automatic patterns (see p. 116) work well on typing, tissue and cartridge papers as well as on the more unusual and expensive handmade varieties. Free machine techniques (see p. 119), with the paper or plastic held firmly in a frame, can also be used, but take care not to stitch too thickly or it will tear.

Some of the subtle and varied effects in the use of transparent and semi-transparent fabrics are demonstrated in this panel on white silk.

In the Italian quilting (top) the yarn is revealed at intervals to show how the strong colors are muted by the silk.

In the examples below, the techniques of reverse appliqué, shadow appliqué and cutwork are combined with machine stitching using layers of felt, organza and silk.

Layers of chiffon in different shades are placed on top of one another and cut away to produce subtle color variations.

A thick tissue paper forms the experimental ''fabric'' in this example of hand quilting and hand embroidery.

49

EXPERIMENT WITH THREADS

To anyone interested in textiles, a basket containing hanks of colorful yarns tumbling in profusion or of skeins of embroidery thread lying neatly in serried ranks in a box have an intrinsic attraction. This attraction can often lead to a purchase which will, in turn, spark off inspiration for an embroidery. Buying some balls of unusually textured knitting yarn in the colors of fall could develop into an idea for an embroidered panel depicting harvest-time; a skein of silver thread could be the inspiration for decorating the yoke or hem of an evening dress.

Although by tradition certain threads are deemed correct for specific embroidery techniques, the modern view of the craft allows plenty of room for experimentation—as techniques are adapted in scale and form, so the accompanying threads can be altered to suit the aesthetic quality or the practical needs of the design. It is essential to experiment with different qualities, colors and textures of yarn to provide the widest possible choice —ideas will then develop for their use.

If the intended project has a practical use, such as clothes, accessories or table linen that would need to be washed, then the fiber content and the thickness of the yarn should be taken into consideration in planning and executing the design. For example, the yarns traditionally used for needlepoint have been crewel or Persian yarns; these were chosen particularly for their hardwearing qualities, appropriate for uses such as for chair seats, kneelers and footstools. Today this tradition still holds good, but if needlepoint is used for pictures and other decorative pieces, these materials can be supplemented with any other yarn which will pass through the canvas without distorting it and which will cover it. This means that textured knitting yarns, as well as ribbons, raffia, tape, string, strips of leather and fabric can all be incorporated if you wish.

Surface stitchery is usually worked in conventional embroidery threads, as well as those manufactured for knitting and crochet. But almost anything that can be threaded through the weave of the back-

ground fabric can also be incorporated, provided the practical use allows. Very coarse threads may have to be couched down to the surface (see p. 71).

TEXTURED THREADS
The thickness of the thread can usually be altered to suit your purpose. Some embroidery threads, such as stranded floss and yarn, are manufactured with this in mind, allowing the strands to be divided and used individually or as a combination of any number together. Some yarns, such as pearl cotton and carpet thrums, will not divide satisfactorily, however, since they rely for their strength on being twisted.

For a subtle change of color, two lengths of yarn of different hue can be split and re-formed to produce a range of tones. Using a six-stranded floss in yellow, for example, remove one strand and replace it with another in, say, blue; twist them together slightly, if appropriate. Take another length, remove two strands of yellow and replace them with two of blue. Continue in this way until you have replaced all the yellow with blue. Stitching with these threads will give subtle graduations of tone to a filled area of embroidery.

Most yarns can be doubled or trebled if a thicker version is needed, though some care may well be needed to make sure the tension of the stitch is satisfactory, and that the yarns do not separate untidily. Threads of different textural qualities can also be combined—a shiny rayon used with a matte wool will add a glint of light to an otherwise dull surface.

Textured threads can be made from most yarns by knotting, plaiting and twisting. These will generally need to be couched to the surface, since the knots and the thickness will prevent the thread from penetrating the background fabric, unless the latter is very loosely woven. The simplest textured thread can be made by tying knots in a single or doubled length of yarn, at regular or irregular intervals—the knots themselves can be pulled tight or left loose. Or two contrasting yarns can be knotted together to form a thicker thread.

Simple three-strand braids can be made with either a single type of yarn or a variety of yarns. Such braided yarns can be used as a textured line, as a braid to cover an edge, or to make a decorative border. Different thicknesses and types of yarn can be twisted together to form cords suitable for decorating pillows, bags and household items. You may need to make an occasional invisible stitch to maintain the twist.

ALTERNATE YARNS

Ribbons, tapes and strips of fabric, suede or leather can be combined with embroidery—as, indeed, can any other material cut or torn into lengths. Ribbon and tape are available in a number of widths from $1/8$in upward. The narrow type can be threaded through a needle and used exactly as a normal thread, for a variety of stitches from simple running stitch to French knots. In combination with other yarns it will add texture and interest to a piece of needlepoint, or it can even replace more conventional threads when smocking.

The photograph below shows the experimental diversity possible with threads.

1 French knots using stranded floss (6, 2 and 4 strands), pearl cotton and tapestry yarn.

2 Rows of satin stitch in stranded floss, color-graded from blue to yellow; satin stitch blocks in different directions, in 1 down to 6 strands; stranded floss, blocks of satin stitch in matte embroidery cotton and shiny pearl cotton.

3 Twisted and braided threads: twisted cord in matte embroidery and pearl cotton; knotted matte embroidery cotton; braided pearl cotton; slubbed knitting yarn with knots; twisted cord in pearl cotton with knots; 2-color, 3-strand braid in pearl cotton; twisted cord in pearl cotton, diagonally couched; matte embroidery cotton, couched in a brick pattern.

4 Wrapped piping cord and thin cardboard, couched down; threads woven through fabric, leaving fringed ends.

5 Ribbons and braid: blue ribbon threaded with cotton tape; 3-color braided ribbon; French knots in narrow ribbon; running and backstitch worked in bias binding; nylon string, twisted and couched; knotted ribbon; raffia braided with yellow matte embroidery cotton and blue yarn; crocheted ribbon couched down. **Interwoven** strips of shot silk with frayed edges; ribbon weaving.

51

EXPERIMENT WITH THREADS

By tradition, ribbons are threaded through whitework edgings for babywear and lingerie. Drawn thread work, cutwork and eyelet embroidery all incorporate holes through which either traditional or more innovative threads can be woven.

Ribbon weaving is currently popular for articles such as pincushions, glasses and needle cases as well as decoration on clothes. This technique can also combine the use of fabric strips, lace and braid for a more varied texture.

DYEING THREADS

It is well worth experimenting with dyeing threads, since this will add both scope and individuality to your work. Some embroidery threads are produced in a limited range of colors, in which case dyeing is the only way of extending the tonal range within a piece of work. Threads can be dyed at the same time as a background fabric, in order to match it exactly, can be shaded to achieve a range of tones, or can be space-dyed in different colors.

Yarns of natural fibers—cotton, wool and linen—as well as some blends, accept both hot- or cold-water dyes satisfactorily. Follow the manufacturer's instructions on the packet of dye to prepare the dyebath. You will not need to use all the solution unless dyeing large quantities of yarn, so adjust the amount of dye, fixative and water accordingly.

Wind the threads into a skein or cut them into manageable lengths before dyeing, otherwise they will tend to become tangled in the dyebath. Secure each skein at the top with a long thread which can be used for lowering it into the dye and can be tied to the handle of the dyebath or looped over its edge. If the skeins are left in the dye for different lengths of time, they will take up the dye accordingly and you will achieve a wide range of tones.

Remember that after rinsing and drying, the depth of any dye color will be considerably reduced. If dissimilar yarns of different fibers are placed together in the dyebath, they will accept the dye to a different extent, giving a variety of shades. Used in an embroidery, these will produce an inherently harmonious color scheme.

Space dyeing is a tie-dye method (see pp. 32-33). This method produces a two-colored thread. The process can be repeated by re-tying and re-dyeing in another shade for a multi-color result.

As well as threads, ribbons and tapes can also be space-dyed; fine fabrics such as chiffon, muslin and even nylon pantyhose, cut or torn into narrow strips, can be treated in the same way.

To apply fabric paint, wind the thread around stiff cardboard. Then paint on both sides with a fine, soft-haired brush. Fix the color by ironing across the threads when dry. **Left** Hand-painted, multi-colored threads (silk twist, wool, pearl cotton and stranded floss).

For space dyeing, the skeins of thread are bound or knotted firmly with string or thread at even or random intervals, then put into the dyebath. The dye will not penetrate the bound areas.
Left Multi-shaded lengths of thread in one color, dyed for different periods of time; yarn and matte embroidery cotton treated in the same dyebath for the same duration.

Dyed threads and alternative yarns (below left) couched down by machine using space-dyed thread.

To bind a mount Apply double-sided cellophane tape to the back of the mounting board. Peel $3/4$in from the backing of the tape, then fasten the end of the binding thread to the sticky side. Continue binding in this way, peeling off the backing as you go. The corners can be painted or left uncovered.

WRAPPED THREADS

Wrapping is a technique traditionally used to bind the warp ends of woven garments and rugs, or is used for making the decorated tassels that edge ethnic embroideries. Wrapped threads can be incorporated in modern embroidery in exactly the same way, or the method can be adapted for more unusual possibilities.

Simple binding involves winding another yarn around a central core of string or cord. The ends can be knotted and taken through under the binding when completed. If you are using fabric, the ends can be sewn invisibly. In addition to changing its color and texture, binding a piece of string or cord with yarn will cause it to become much more rigid.

Wrapped effects can also be produced with a sewing machine. The easiest method involves the use of an embroidery, or, better still, a braiding foot. Thread the yarn to be wrapped through the hole in the base of this foot, and set the stitch width to coincide with the thickness of the yarn. Ordinary zigzag and decorative automatic stitches can be used to cover the yarn with differing effects. If you do not have these particular machine attachments, the yarn would have to be fed by hand: hold it taut both behind and in front of the machine needle.

Wrapped frames and inserts or mounts can add an individual finishing touch to an embroidered panel (see left). The threads can be chosen to match or contrast with those used in the embroidery. These frames and mounts can then be glued on, to surround the whole embroidery or to enhance a particular area or focal point.

MAKING FRINGES

Textured or knotted threads or cords can be made into a fringe to complement the design of a wallhanging, household item or garment. Attach them by looping them through the edge of the embroidery on, for example, a wool shawl or needlepoint cushion. On a hanging, you might need to sew them to the lower edge. They can hang freely or be formed into loops.

Ribbons and tapes can be manipulated to twist or curl; wind them around a piece of dowel and spray them with a fabric stiffener such as that sold for use on window shades. For a slightly gathered effect, you can machine-stitch a line either along one edge or down the center of a length of ribbon. The edges of cut or torn bias strips of fabric can be zigzagged to make a fringe for a wallhanging, or bias-cut loops of silk will make a frothy edge for a luxury garment. Strips of shot silk will produce a two-color fringe if some are frayed horizontally and some vertically. Such finishing touches can lend embroidery of all kinds an individuality absent from manufactured articles.

A variety of decorative fringes, incorporating knots and wrapped threads. The "fabric" is made of threads, laid on vanishing muslin (see p. 121) and machine embroidered. Textured linen threads (left) have a tuft of blue silk threads bound into each tassel.

Smooth blue silk threads are tightly bound into tassels with yellow silk thread; each tassel is then divided into two and each half knotted together with the adjacent tassel to form a fringe.

A combination of silk, linen, slubbed and other threads has an elaborate fringed edge; each tassel is held in a bound tube like a bead. To make such "beads", wrap a small piece of paper around a pencil, then bind it tightly with colored threads. Remove the pencil, cut away any excess paper and push a bundle of threads through each wrapped bead.

EXPERIMENT WITH STITCHES

Stitches are the very essence of embroidery. They can decorate almost any textile from simple garments, pillows and table linen to elaborate wallhangings intricately stitched with textured yarns. If you are prepared to experiment, there are effects which imaginative stitchery can create, irrespective of color and texture. Embroidery stitches can delineate shapes, make patterns, fill in areas and introduce mood and individuality. They direct the eye of the viewer and give movement and rhythm to a design.

The scope of stitchery is infinite: meticulously worked formal stitchery can have a quality of precision and order. Uneven, haphazard work will produce a livelier, less formal effect.

Surface stitches can be categorized in many ways—some form lines, for example, while others produce a single unit. Yet others are categorized as border stitches or as filling stitches. Stitches that produce lines, including running, back, stem, chain, broad chain, coral and couching are essential for outlining or emphasizing a shape; single unit stitches, like tête de boeuf, detached chain, detached twisted chain, seeding and fly, can create an overall texture or pattern. Some stitches are ideal for circular motifs and dots. Examples include French knots, buttonhole and woven wheels, spiders' webs and circular couching. Openwork stitches that will still reveal the background fabric

include wave and cloud filling, trellis couching and buttonhole stitch.

Border and band stitches, such as chevron, herringbone, feather and raised chain band, lend themselves to edgings and striped designs. However, although a stitch may be put into a certain category, these groups are always arbitrary, and should not prevent you from using a stitch as you please. A chain stitch will make a line, but it can also fill a solid space, form an openwork lacy pattern, or be worked as individual detached chain stitches.

Instructions and illustrations for working stitches are usually given for the orthodox method. This is fine if you want to create a precise, regular effect, but you will find, if you experiment, that most stitches can be adapted or modified. Try altering the scale and direction of a stitch, work it unevenly or use varying thicknesses and types of yarn. The textural variations created by using unusual or improvized yarns are explored in the sections on Texture (pp. 42-45) and Threads (pp. 50-53).

MAKING A SAMPLER
A useful way to start experimenting with stitches is to make a one-stitch sampler. Choose buttonhole stitch, for example, and work it in as many ways as possible. Initially, do not include any additional distractions such as change of color or thread; you can move on to these variations later.

1 Using stranded wool or floss, work a neat, even row conventionally, with each stitch the same size and evenly spaced.
2 Now make the effect more random. Still maintaining the essential method of stitching, make some stitches large, some small, some upright, some slanting.
3 Try to create a change in tonal value in the following way. Stitch one row with the stitches close together, trying to cover the background completely. Space the stitches of the second row a little farther apart, and with each subsequent row gradually increase the amount of background fabric showing.
4 Allow the stitches to encroach upon each other; they can overlap or be worked on top of each other. Try building up a highly textured area in this way.
5 Experiment further to make twists, spirals and circular motifs.

COUNTED THREAD EMBROIDERY

Experimentation with any of the counted thread methods usually involves a change of scale or direction of stitching. Bargello embroidery, for example, can be worked in different directions (see four-way bargello design, p. 128), or a more random approach could be adopted with uneven lines of varying length stitches meandering over the surface.

Instructions for most techniques worked conventionally state that a stitch should cover a specific number of threads and be executed in a certain direction. However, a little trial and error will prove that many stitches can be modified to suit your design. Thus, in needlepoint, cushion stitch can be made to cover a larger or smaller square. The direction of stitching can also be altered and extra stitches can cover those already worked. Of course, not all needlepoint stitches can be altered in this way, so try them out on a spare piece of canvas or fabric, bearing in mind any practical considerations, such as the need to cover the canvas totally.

If experimenting with the scale of drawn thread and pulled work, particularly for table linen, remember that washing and ironing will tend to weaken the ground fabric. For this reason, do not withdraw too many threads or make large stitches which might catch when in use or being ironed. Traditional blackwork can also be altered in scale, and the tonal values of the design can be diminished by gradually omitting parts of the pattern.

All counted thread methods can incorporate the use of surface stitches if you so desire. These can add another texture— French knots combine well with pictorial needlepoint for example. Surface stitches can also establish or emphasize lines – adding a row of whipped chain or couching to pulled work or blackwork, for instance, can reinforce a curve that is otherwise difficult to distinguish.

TRADITIONAL TECHNIQUES

Never feel restricted to a precise stitch. Even an embroidery method such as cutwork, which employs traditional stitches for legitimate practical reasons, may be open to freer interpretations. Buttonhole stitch undoubtedly secures the cut edge satisfactorily, but you could experiment with one of the variations of buttonhole stitch such as tailor's or up-and-down, working them either precisely or to uneven lengths.

Smocking traditionally incorporates those stitches which will best hold the gathers in place—stem, cable, honeycomb or chevron. Besides using these orthodox stitches in regular formation, try a more random approach with uneven curving lines of other stitches such as feather and double feather, and by adding some surface stitches such as French and bullion knots in between the pleats.

Using wool yarn gives an embroidery an exciting, unusual quality. This sample (above), worked on linen scrim, uses conventional line stitches but some are pulled tight and others worked more loosely. This variation in the tension creates a swirling effect and gives the work a sense of movement.

Samplers of buttonhole stitch (below left) and Cretan stitch (below right) worked in no.5 pearl cotton show the diversity possible within a single stitch.

55

EXPERIMENT WITH STITCHES

Cretan stitch used as an outline

Blocks of satin stitch worked in different directions to catch the light

Cretan stitch super-imposed with fly stitch

Detached buttonhole stitch worked in a "ladder"

Encroaching Cretan stitch, with fly stitch interspersed

Roumanian stitch

Surface stitchery lends itself readily to being worked freely. The detail of the above picture depicted in surface stitchery has a lively quality that comes from the imaginative use of stitches. The stranded embroidery floss is used in varying thicknesses; going down to a single strand and allowing more fabric to show through toward the right conveys the impression of receding into the distance. Juxtaposing the direction of stitches, and allowing stitches to encroach densely, builds up an interesting surface texture.

SURFACE STITCHES

To depict	Suggested stitches
Circular motifs, including flower centers, flower blooms, etc.	Buttonhole wheels, spider's webs, woven wheels, French knots with tails, bullion knots in rose formation and with tails, circular couching, radiating fly stitches, straight stitches in star formation, Turkey work for a fluffy center, Cretan and rosette chain in circular formation.
Leaves	Detached chain, buttonhole (several variations), close herringbone, Cretan, Vandyke, raised chain band, quill, feather, fly, long and short, satin, tied satin.
Petals	Smaller versions of leaf stitches.

To depict	Suggested stitches
Grasses	Straight, Cretan, herringbone, fly.
Outlines, including stems	Line stitches including chain, back, stem, broad chain, coral.
Trees and bushes	French knots, bullion knots, rosette chain, herringbone, satin stitch, fly, feather, buttonhole.
Sky or water	Line stitches—split, stem, chain, wave, couching; Cretan.
Architectural features, paths and walls	Brick, satin stitch blocks, couching, laid work, Bokhara and Roumanian couching, cloud filling. Raised chain band, herringbone, chevron.

56

Two shades of gray stranded together for a speckled effect

Jacquard stitch

French knots worked in two colors

Mosaic stitch

Tent stitch in two colors

Long and short slanting satin stitch

Cross stitch

Diagonal satin stitch

Alternating oblong cross stitch

Lighter gray thread for highlights

Small checker stitch

Tent stitch worked in reverse direction

Needlepoint is a technique which imposes certain restrictions through the regular canvas grid, but a great variety of different stitches can successfully be incorporated in a single picture, as seen above. An impression of texture is created by varying the number of threads over which a stitch is worked, by changing the direction of stitching and by the use of French knots. Juxtaposing different stitched areas creates a patchwork effect in the background. Stranding colors together adds to its subtle complexity.

NEEDLEPOINT STITCHES

To depict	Suggested stitches
Flowers and leaves	Leaf stitch and Gobelin (altering direction and scale); eyelets, diamond eyelets, rice.
Skies	Tent, slanted Gobelin, fan, fern.
Clouds	Tent, velvet.
Architectural features	Cushion, brick, Scotch, Brighton, Parisian, Moorish, Byzantine, rice, Hungarian, Gobelin, checker.
Backgrounds	Tent, diagonal, mosaic, Gobelin, Hungarian.
Geometric	Square stitches: Rhodes, rice, leviathan, Smyrna, Scotch, cushion.

57

BORDERS, MOTIFS AND ALPHABETS

Borders and motifs have always been an important feature of embroidery designs. Borders effectively "frame" a piece of embroidery. Whether the border elaborates a simple design or creates a neat edging to a more intricate one, it must be in scale with the composition as a whole; it should not overwhelm the central design.

A border can be basically linear and continuous – sometimes split up into sections to add interest – or made up of repeating motifs. The motifs may be geometric or pictorial and worked as a straight, reversed or mirror-image repeat. A mirror can help to resolve the corners of a border (see p.29), or the border can be interrupted and a suitable motif used to fill the angle of the corner.

Lettering has also played a historic part in embroideries, either in the form of samplers, in which the whole alphabet was worked as a stitching exercise, or as initials and dates on household linen. Embroidered initials can still turn an everyday item or garment into something personal and special. Letters and numbers can be arranged to form a design in their own right, as in overlapped or interlocking monograms. You can adapt a non-embroidered alphabet for an original approach: look at magazine and television graphics for inspiration.

It is essential to use a smooth thread and to select an embroidery stitch that will make well-defined letters; satin stitch is the most popular in surface stitchery, though chain and stem stitch lend themselves to curved letter forms, the latter being especially good for script lettering.

This page shows an alphabet and several motifs and border patterns suitable for surface stitchery. Those on the facing page are all designed on a regular grid for counted thread embroidery. They may all be traced and used actual size or enlarged or reduced (see p.21).

58

ADAPTING A DESIGN THEME

Eight embroideries: interpretations of a simple design theme using different techniques

Needlepoint, using tent stitch, diagonal satin stitch, Scotch stitch, mosaic stitch, cross stitch and French knots

Cross stitch and Assisi work (counted thread techniques)

Shadow quilting, using fabric paint to enhance the effect

Appliqué, using bonding web, with the embellishment of surface stitchery

Pulled work, using mock faggot filling for the background and needle-weaving for the stalks; the solid cherries are stitched on the back to create slight padding

Surface stitchery, using satin stitch, stem stitch, backstitch, leaf stitch and split stitch

Cutwork, using buttonhole stitch

Free machine embroidery, using layers of straight stitch

EMBROIDERY BASICS

The amazing diversity of modern embroidery design is made possible by an equally varied range of techniques. Some of these techniques are centuries old: the metal thread embroiderer, for example, uses methods that have not changed significantly since the Middle Ages. Others, such as experimental smocking, are modern adaptations of traditional techniques. A few are recent innovations—an example being machine-embroidered lace worked on dissolvable fabric. Imaginative embroiderers are continually inventing new stitches and new ways to use the rich variety of materials at their disposal.

In the past, mastery of embroidery techniques was often considered an end in itself. Young girls spent long hours learning to stitch correctly. Precision was of paramount importance; experimentation was not encouraged. Today, a more relaxed attitude prevails. Embroidery is taken up as a satisfying pastime, a means of self-expression, and is an art form in its own right. The techniques you choose to acquire are mainly a matter of following your inclinations. Those who like to work methodically may be attracted to counted thread techniques, such as cross stitch or blackwork. For those who most enjoy working with fabrics, appliqué will have a strong appeal. Needlepoint has tactile qualities and a pleasant rhythm which help to give it wide appeal. Embroiders with less patience may prefer the speed and the impromptu nature of free-form machine work. Some techniques lend themselves to both meticulous and spontaneous ways of working: surface stitchery, for example, can be as precise or as bold and free as you like.

Whatever type of embroidery you choose, it is important to acquire a thorough understanding of its materials and methods and to be able to use them effectively. In some cases experts disagree on the best method of working a particular stitch or achieving a certain effect; try different methods and decide which you prefer. You might even devise a new method of executing a stitch that works better for you.

Do not be afraid to branch out and try different types of embroidery. The more techniques you have at your disposal, the more scope you will have in interpreting your design ideas. And the greater your mastery of those techniques, the more successful your original designs are likely to be.

The success of any piece of embroidery depends not only on the skill with which you work the stitches (and, of course, the quality of the design) but also on your preparation. The design must be transferred to the fabric in the most appropriate way, and the fabric must be mounted in a suitable frame. There are several methods of transferring the design, explained below.

Before cutting the fabric for the embroidery, make sure – if the item is to be washable – that the fabric is pre-shrunk. If you are in any doubt, immerse it for a few minutes in hand-hot water, then let it dry naturally and press it.

Cut the fabric at least 2in larger than it will be after finishing to allow for seams and/or hems. (Depending on the type of frame you are using, you may need to increase these margins.)

Positioning the design is normally a simple matter and can be done by eye, especially on tracing paper. But in some cases, such as working a motif in the center of a tablecloth, it may be necessary to position the design precisely.
1 Mark the center of the fabric by folding it into quarters, pressing after each fold. Or use basting.

2 Similarly, mark the center of the design with two pencil lines. When transferring the design, superimpose the marks.

DRESSMAKER'S CARBON

This method can be used on any smooth-textured fabric and is suitable for fairly complex designs, as well as simple ones. On rough-textured fabric the lines tend to be distorted.

Dressmaker's carbon paper can be purchased in notions departments and usually comes in a package containing several colors, suitable for different fabrics. Do *not* use office carbon paper, which would leave indelible marks on the fabric. Even better than dressmaker's carbon paper (which may leave a faint smudge on some fabrics) is artist's tracing paper; this can be obtained from some art stores. You will also need a ballpoint pen (a worn-out one will do). Positioning the design is easier if it is on tracing paper, as shown here, although this is not essential.

1 Tape the fabric to a smooth, hard surface (or fix it with thumb tacks). Place the design, right side up, on top of the fabric, making sure that it is positioned correctly. Secure it with weights or masking tape.

2 Slip the dressmaker's carbon paper between fabric and tracing, colored side down. Using the ballpoint pen, go over the lines of the design firmly. Carefully lift the paper and carbon to check that you are pressing firmly enough.

DIRECT TRACING

This method is best suited to sheer or translucent fabrics, although it can be used on a light-colored, medium-weight fabric, provided the design is fairly simple.

You will need a fabric-marking pen or dressmaker's marking pen, available in notions departments, which makes a mark that should wash out with water (test it on your fabric first). One word of warning: some experts fear that these pens can in fact rot the fabric. If the item will not be washed, a hard pencil can be used.

Tape the design to a flat surface. Place the fabric over it, right side up, and tape or weight the fabric to secure it. Trace the design with the fabric-marking pen or pencil.

If the design is not easily visible through the fabric, attach it and the fabric to a window with masking tape, making sure there is enough natural light coming through. Then trace the outline onto the fabric.

Going over the lines on the paper first with a heavy black felt-tip pen may also help to make the design more easily visible through the fabric.

If you like the tracing method, you may want to invest in a light box. Available from graphic designers' suppliers, it consists of a shallow box containing fluorescent tubes, covered with frosted glass.

TRANSFER PENCIL

Make sure that the transfer pencil you buy is of the non-smudge type. There are various transfer pencils on the market, and they differ considerably in quality. The best type resembles an ordinary lead pencil; others have a waxy texture and must be applied with a very light hand in order not to leave a thick line. Before using any transfer pencil for your design, test it on a scrap of the fabric.

You will also need some tracing paper and an iron.

1 Trace the design onto tracing paper with an ordinary pencil. Turn the paper wrong side up so that the design is reversed, and retrace the design on the back, using the transfer pencil.

2 Pin the fabric to the ironing-board or another flat, heatproof surface, and position the tracing, right side up, on top. Using a dry iron, at a temperature appropriate for the fabric, iron over the paper to transfer the design.

THE PRICKING METHOD

This transfer method is well suited to any kind of design and can be used with any fabrics except highly textured ones. It is a particularly good method to use if you need to repeat a motif, since the tracing can be reused several times.

You will need: fairly stiff tracing paper, a medium-size, sharp-pointed needle, a cork, a small piece of felt, pounce powder (see p. 11) or tailor's chalk, and either a fabric-marking pen or a fine brush and watercolor paint in a shade slightly darker or lighter than the fabric.

To speed up this process, you could use a sewing machine to make the holes, if the design permits. Remove top and bobbin threads and, using the longest stitch length, stitch along the design lines.

1 Trace the design and turn the tracing wrong side up to reverse it. Place it on a padded surface, such as a folded towel. Use the needle to prick holes along the lines. Make the holes about $3/4$in apart, or closer for a complex design. The needle is easier to handle if the blunt end is first inserted into a cork.

2 Lay the tracing right side up on the fabric and secure it in place. Fold the felt into a small pad, dip it into the powder and rub the powder through the holes with a circular movement.

Then carefully remove the tracing. Using the fabric-marking pen or brush and watercolor, connect the powder dots.

BASTING

This is the method to use on highly textured fabric. It is also ideal if you want to work the embroidery freely and spontaneously. The lines of basting serve as a guide for positioning the main lines and shapes, and you can then add details or build up textures without being restricted to a permanently marked line.

You need lightweight tracing paper and ordinary sewing thread in a shade slightly darker than the fabric.

Before transferring the design, mount the fabric in the appropriate frame (see pp. 66–67).

1 Trace the design and pin the tracing, right side up, to the fabric. Using the sewing thread, work running stitches (see p. 69) along the lines through both paper and fabric. Secure the thread at beginning and end with a couple of backstitches (see p. 69).

2 When the basting is completed, run the point of a needle along the lines of basting to score the paper and gently pull it from the fabric.

Depending on the embroidery technique you are using, you can either cover the basting completely or remove it as you go.

Some kinds of embroidery can be worked without a frame, but, for most kinds, a frame is essential. A frame not only keeps the fabric smooth but also helps to ensure that the thread is kept at the correct tension – neither so tight that it puckers the fabric nor so loose that the stitches lack definition.

Several different kinds of frame can be used for surface stitchery. A ring frame, also called a hoop, is the most common. A simple ring frame is useful for practicing stitches and is easily portable. The disadvantage of a ring frame is that, unless the project is fairly small or the embroidery well scattered, you will need to move the fabric in order to reach all the areas of the design, which may entail pressing the ring over previously worked stitches and possibly flattening or damaging them. In some cases this can be prevented by placing tissue paper or cheesecloth over the fabric before fixing the outer ring, then tearing the paper or cutting the cheesecloth away to reveal the working area.

A better solution, if the work is too large for a ring frame, is to use a scroll frame or stretcher frame of a size to accommodate the work. Such a frame not only avoids damaging the embroidery; it also permits you to see the whole area at once – enabling you to make adjustments in the design, if necessary.

Dressing each type of frame, that is, mounting the fabric in it correctly, is explained below.

BACKING THE FABRIC
Many pieces of embroidery benefit from the use of a backing fabric. If the embroidery fabric is lightweight or loosely woven, it should be backed to give it body and to prevent the underside of the stitches and threads from showing on the right side. In some cases – where an extra layer is not wanted but stitches need to be strengthened – it may be desirable to use a backing fabric, then carefully cut it away around the stitching when the work is completed.

Choose a natural fiber fabric for the backing. Lawn, calico and organdy are suitable for backing a lightweight fabric. If you need a heavier backing, choose muslin or curtain lining.

If the work is smaller than the frame available, or if it is an awkward shape, first stitch it onto a backing of the necessary size. Then either work through both layers, or cut the backing away under the embroidery fabric from inside the frame before you begin stitching, as shown here.

DRESSING A RING FRAME
Ring frames come in various sizes and styles. Whatever size you get (and you may want to have several), make sure that it has a screw for adjusting the tightness of the outer ring for a snug fit. There is also a spring-type ring frame whose inner ring automatically grips the fabric against the outer ring. The portable ring frame, though convenient, will not permit you to stitch with both hands (see p. 68). But other models of ring frame are designed to stand on a table or on the floor, to clamp on a chair arm or table, or to rest on a chair seat, held in place by the embroiderer's body. All of these do allow you to work with both hands.

Adjust the screw so that the outer ring fits easily, but not loosely, over the inner ring. Remove the outer ring, without loosening the screw, and place the fabric over the inner ring. Binding the inner ring will protect a delicate fabric and give a better grip (see p.118).

Press the outer ring firmly and evenly down over the fabric. The grain should be straight and the fabric should be as taut as a drumskin; if it is not, remove the outer ring, tighten it slightly and try again. Do not attempt to tauten the fabric by adjusting the screw or pulling on the fabric once it is mounted; this will distort the weave.

DRESSING A STRETCHER FRAME

A stretcher frame consists of four wooden strips with mitered corners. To assemble the frame you simply slot the corners together. You may want to sand the frame slightly if it is rough to the touch, but this is not usually necessary. The stretchers can be purchased at art shops and come in a wide range of sizes, enabling you to form whatever shape you need. Remember, however, that the width of the stretchers will reduce the size of the stitching area. If your design measures 12in square, for example, the assembled frame should measure at least 16in square on its outer edges. The fabric should be cut slightly larger than this to allow for attaching the edges to the frame.

To work on a stretcher frame, prop it against the edge of a table or other firm support, with the lower edge in your lap.

1 Mark the center point of each side of the frame and the fabric with a pen or pencil.
2 Align the center marks of the top edges of fabric and frame, and fasten the fabric to the top edge of the frame with a thumb tack.
3 Fasten the rest of the top edge, inserting the thumb tacks at $3/4$in to $7/8$in intervals.

4 Fasten the opposite edge in the same way, pulling the fabric very taut.
5 Fasten the center marks on the side edges.
6 Fasten the side edges alternately, inserting a pin on one side, then fastening the corresponding point on the opposite side, working outward to the corners.

DRESSING A SCROLL FRAME

The main advantage of a scroll frame – also called a square or slate frame – is that the fabric can be re-tightened while the work is in progress. The frame consists of two adjustable rollers held together by battens. The top and bottom edges of the work are sewn to strips of webbing attached to the rollers; the sides are laced to the battens.

Scroll frames come in various sizes, and some are designed to fit on a floor stand, which makes them especially convenient to use. The maximum width of the embroidery is limited by the length of the webbing on the rollers, but the length can exceed the length of the battens, if necessary. The excess length is simply rolled up on one of the rollers, then unrolled and rolled onto the other as the work progresses.

1 Baste along the vertical and horizontal center lines of the backing. Press under a $3/4$in hem on the top and bottom, then the side edges.
2 Cut two fairly long lengths of string; place each inside a side hem and machine stitch to form a casing over the string.

3 Mark the center of each strip of webbing. Pin the bottom edge of the fabric to one webbing strip, matching centers, and overcast them together, using doubled button thread. Work from the center to one side, then to the other. Join the top edge to the other strip of webbing in the same way.

4 Slip the battens through the rollers and fasten them with the pegs so that the fabric is fairly taut. Tie the string ends around the rollers.
5 Mark the center of each edge of the embroidery fabric. Pin it to the backing, matching centers, and overcast it as shown, alternating long and short stitches to distribute the tension.

6 Using a large-eyed needle and string, sew the side edges of the backing to the sides of the frame, taking the string over the battens and sewing through the fabric over the side strings, at $1\frac{1}{4}$in intervals. Pull firmly to tighten the fabric, and tie the string ends around battens and rollers.

The term "surface stitchery" embraces a great variety of embroidery styles. The simple floral motifs often worked on table linen, the swirling, fantastic forms of Jacobean crewel work, and the rich, delicate silk embroideries that decorated eighteenth-century costume are some types of traditional surface stitchery. Modern surface embroidery uses many of the same stitches but uses them in new, experimental ways, producing highly individual effects.

The one thing that all types of surface stitchery have in common is that the stitches' formation is independent of the fabric weave – unlike counted thread types of embroidery, such as blackwork and pulled work. Because surface stitchery can be worked in any direction, it is sometimes called free stitchery or free embroidery.

MATERIALS AND EQUIPMENT

As a general rule, the fabric should be firmly woven and opaque; sheer fabrics can be used – and in fact are required for shadow work (p. 73) – but keeping the wrong side sufficiently neat can be difficult. And until you gain some experience, it is best to stick to fabrics made mainly of natural fibers, which are easier to work on than most synthetics.

Another general rule is to match the weight of the fabric to the weight of the threads. Embroidery worked mainly in fine cotton thread, for example, would not be effective on burlap. Threads for surface stitchery include the whole range of embroidery threads (see p. 13) and many more besides. The best needles are crewels and chenilles, both of which have sharp points. The eyes of chenilles are larger, to accommodate thicker threads.

STITCHING TECHNIQUES

To achieve the best results with hand embroidery, you need to learn to use both hands properly and to manipulate the needle in a specific way to create each stitch. In the following illustrations showing how to work the stitches, the needle is often shown as if it is used horizontally, as in ordinary sewing; but this is simply to make the construction of each stitch clear.

When you work on a frame you should stab the needle vertically through the fabric, using both hands if possible. In some cases the 'underneath' hand must be brought to the top of the work – for example, when one hand holds a loop of thread in place while the other one stitches.

For embroidery stitches that are worked partly through each other, so that the needle does not penetrate the fabric, it helps to take the needle through eye first.

To begin work you can either make a small, neat knot at the end of the thread or take it under some existing stitches on the wrong side, then work a backstitch over them before bringing the needle to the right side. Backstitches can simply be worked into a backing fabric, taking care not to catch in the main fabric.

To end a line of stitching, take the needle through some stitches on the underside and anchor the thread with a backstitch.

Fastening the thread is also greatly facilitated if a backing fabric is used.

Using both hands may seem awkward at first, but it will become easy with practice. Using your right hand under the fabric (or your left, if you are left-handed) will facilitate the work. A thimble is normally unnecessary unless the fabric is very thick.

Threading the needle Various techniques can be used to make needle-threading easier. Moistening the thread will smooth it; a cotton thread can be flattened slightly with your teeth. Or a needle-threader can be inserted through the eye and used to pull the thread through, as shown.

Wool threads are often easier to thread if you first loop the end around the needle, then pinch the loop tightly between thumb and forefinger and press the eye of the needle down over it.

A NOTE TO LEFT-HANDED READERS
Some of the stitches shown in this book are worked naturally (by a right-handed person) from left to right or from right to left, and are illustrated accordingly. In some cases, a left-handed embroiderer will find it easy enough to work in the same direction, provided the two-handed method of stitching is used. If this is not possible, the direction of working should be reversed. (The finished effect will be the same.) Holding the illustration up to a mirror may help to make the method of working clear.

References to "right" and "left" in the text have been kept to a minimum. Where they do occur, left-handed readers may prefer to reverse the directions.

LINE STITCHES

When worked in the simplest way, stitches designated "line stitches" produce the effect of a thin line. Between pages 72 and 75 you will find stitches that characteristically form bands or narrow motifs; between pages 76 and 81, those used for round motifs or to fill larger areas of a design.

These distinctions are, however, somewhat arbitrary, since most surface embroidery stitches can be used in a variety of ways. Lines of chain stitch worked close together make an attractive texture for depicting leaves, flower petals and other objects.

Many of the basic stitches also have variations, some of which appear quite different from the "parent" stitch. Chain stitch is again a good example: five variations of chain are described here and others can be found among band and filling stitches.

RUNNING STITCH

This is the simplest of all stitches, used for outlining and for hand quilting. Take the needle in and out of the fabric at regular intervals, working several small stitches at a time.

Running stitch is a surprisingly versatile stitch. It can be worked in rows in a regular pattern to form a solid filling stitch (see Darning, p. 78), or less regularly to form textured areas within a design.

Whipped running stitch Work a line of simple running stitch. Then, using a tapestry needle and contrasting thread, take the thread under the stitches (not through the fabric). Do not pull it tightly.

Interlaced running stitch Work a line of even running stitches. Then, using a tapestry needle, take another thread – contrasting, matching or toning – alternately up and down under the stitches.

Take a third thread under the stitches in alternating directions as shown.

BACKSTITCH

Backstitch This is useful for thin lines, as in lettering. Bring the needle up at B, a short distance from the starting point (A), then take it down at the starting point. Bring it up the same distance ahead of A, at C.

Whipped backstitch Work a line of backstitch. Then, using a tapestry needle and contrasting thread, work under each stitch as shown, without going through the fabric.

Pekinese stitch Work a line of backstitch. Then, using a tapestry needle and contrasting thread, if desired, work loops under the stitches, without going through the fabric. The loops may be worked tightly or loosely, depending on the desired effect.

STEM STITCH

This is arguably the most useful of all line stitches. It forms a smooth, ropelike line which can be thin or thick, depending on the angle at which the needle is inserted. Thin lines of stem stitch are ideal for flower stems or lettering. They may also be worked close together to fill a shape and produce a satiny texture.

It is important always to bring the needle up on the same side of the stitching line. When working around a curve, bring the needle up on the inside. Shorten the stitches slightly when working sharp curves.

Bring the needle up at A. Take it down at B, then bring it up halfway between the two, at C. Take it down at D, forming the same length stitch. **For a thicker line,** work the stitches across the stitching line, rather than along it. The two methods may be combined to produce a line varying in thickness – useful in script lettering.

Split stitch This stitch produces a thin line. It can also be used to fill a shape with a matte texture. Bring the needle up at the beginning of the line (A), take it down at B, then bring it up halfway between these points (C), splitting the thread. Repeat.

CHAIN STITCH

Basic chain stitch produces a medium-thick line consisting of a series of loops shaped like teardrops. The thickness can be adjusted, to some extent, by drawing the thread loosely or firmly; however, it should not be pulled so tightly that the chain effect is lost.

When using chain stitch to fill a shape, work all the lines in the same direction to achieve a smooth effect. If the lines are long, fasten off at the end of each line; if they are short, take the thread back under the wrong sides of the stitches to the starting point.

Variations of chain stitch can be used for different effects. For a thick, solid line, use broad chain stitch; for a more textured line, use twisted chain. Many other decorative effects can be produced with the stitches shown here and with other forms of chain (see pp. 75 and 77).

Bring the needle up at the beginning of the line (A) and take it down at the same point, forming a loop (hold the loop in place with your thumb or index finger). Bring the needle up at B and take it over the loop, to form the first stitch. Repeat.

Backstitched chain stitch First, work a line of chain stitch. Then, using contrasting thread, work backstitch (see p. 69) through the center of the chain.

Zigzag chain stitch Work as for basic chain stitch, but with the stitches placed diagonally between two parallel lines. (These can be marked with basting first.) On the second and following stitches, insert the needle through the center of the thread to hold the loop firmly in position.

Twisted chain stitch
1 Bring the needle up at A, on the stitching line. Form a loop, as for basic chain, but take the needle down at B, crossing over the loop. Bring it up at C, and then down again over the loop.

2 Work the following stitches in the same way, always inserting the needle to the left of the stitching line, slightly below the point where the thread emerges. (When practicing this stitch, it may be helpful to mark the stitching line on the fabric.)

70

Open chain stitch

1 Bring the needle up at A, take it down at B, and bring it out at C, just below A.

2 Pull the thread through, but leave a wide loop. Take the needle down at D, inside the loop on the opposite side, then bring it out at E, forming the next loop in the chain.

Broad chain stitch

1 Work a single small running stitch (A – B) at the beginning of the stitching line.

2 Bring the needle up a short distance below (C) and take it back up and under the running stitch (not through the fabric) then bring it down again at C.

3 Bring the needle up at D, slightly below the first chain. Take it back under the chain and down again at the same place. Repeat step 3 until the chain is the desired length.

For a thick, braided effect, use a thick or double thread and keep the chains fairly short.

CORAL STITCH

Coral stitch consists of a line of small knots, which can be placed close together or farther apart as desired.

Lines of the stitch worked close together make an interesting rough-textured filling. Stagger the positions of the knots on alternate rows.

Coral stitch is most effective if worked in double thread.

1 Bring the needle up at the beginning of the stitching line (A). Lay the thread along the line and hold it with your thumb or index finger. Take a small vertical stitch under it (B – C), and loop the thread under the needle.

2 Pull the thread through, forming a knot, as shown.

SIMPLE COUCHING

Couching is a means of attaching a thread to the surface of the fabric by working a series of small stitches over it, using another thread. Here, couching is shown in its simplest form, as a line stitch, but the basic technique can be varied to produce some interesting filling stitches (see pp. 80-81).

Couching is used mainly for attaching threads that are too thick, too highly textured, or too expensive (such as gold threads) to be stitched through the fabric in the usual way. It greatly expands the range of threads you can incorporate in your work.

For the couching stitches themselves, you can use a fine thread in a matching color for an almost unbroken line; or you can use a thicker, contrasting thread to make a feature of the stitches, perhaps working them in a pattern as shown right.

1 Bring up the thread to be couched (called the "laid thread") to the right side of the fabric; remove the needle and hold the thread in place with your thumb or index finger. Thread another needle with the couching thread and bring it up on the stitching line (A). Take it down over the laid thread (B), and bring it up again at C.

2 Work another stitch a short way along the line. Repeat to the end of the stitching line; fasten off.

3 Re-thread the laid thread into a needle and take it to the wrong side. Secure it with a few stitches worked in a fine thread.

Varied effects can be produced by using different stitches to work the couching and by making them larger. Pairs of diagonal stitches, worked side by side or to form a cross, are two of the many possibilities.

BAND STITCHES

When worked in the conventional way, the band stitches shown on the next four pages form relatively wide bands. These stitches are also extremely versatile. Many can be used effectively as filling stitches, others for small oval shapes such as leaves.

Buttonhole stitch is one of the most useful of all embroidery stitches, and can be varied in many ways to produce quite different effects (see the worked sample on p. 54). If the stitches are worked a short distance apart the effect is like that of the edging on a blanket, but when worked close together, the stitches make a solid band with a firm lower edge, a form most often used for cutwork (see p. 100). Buttonhole stitch can also be worked in a circle to make small wheels (see p. 77).

When embroidering band stitches, it may help to work between marked lines.

Buttonhole stitch — Fern stitch — Tailor's buttonhole stitch — Chevron stitch — Up and down buttonhole stitch — Tied herringbone stitch — Loop stitch — Double herringbone stitch

Buttonhole/blanket stitch Bring the needle out on the lower stitching line (A). Insert it on the upper stitching line a short distance to one side (B), then bring it out on the lower line (C) and pull it through, over the thread. Finish by taking the needle down on the lower line.

Double buttonhole stitch This makes an attractive border for the cuff of a sleeve or the hem of a child's dress. Work a line of blanket stitch, then turn the fabric and work another line, interspersing the new stitches between the first ones as shown.

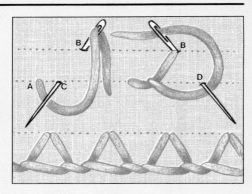

Closed buttonhole stitch
1 Work a narrow buttonhole stitch (A–B–C), but place it diagonally as shown.
2 Work a second diagonal stitch, inserting the needle at the top of the first stitch (B) and bringing it out on the bottom line, over the thread (D).
   Repeat steps 1 and 2 to form a row of interlocking triangles.

Tailor's buttonhole stitch
1 Bring the needle up on the lower line and form a small loop. Holding the loop in place with your index finger, insert the needle on the upper line.
2 Bring the needle up through the loop and draw the thread through gently, forming a small knot at the base of each stitch.

Up and down buttonhole stitch
1 Work an ordinary buttonhole stitch but do not pull the stitches tightly.
2 Take the needle down opposite the point where it emerged, but do not pull the thread through.

3 Bring the needle up alongside the first stitch and pull the thread through the loop.
   Repeat steps 1–3.
   Up and down buttonhole makes a pretty border, but it is even more effective as a filling, with each row overlapping the one above.

Loop stitch
1 Bring the needle up at A.
2 Insert it at B and bring it up at C.
3 Take the needle under the diagonal stitch thus formed and over the working thread and draw it through gently, easing the knot into place with your free hand. Repeat steps 2-3

Fern stitch As its name implies, this stitch is useful for suggesting fernlike foliage.
1 Work three straight stitches, bringing the needle up first at A, then C and then D, and taking it back down at B each time.
2 Make a straight stitch from E to F, another from just below B to F, and a third from G to F. Repeat step 2 as required.

Chevron stitch This stitch is most effective when worked evenly as a decorative border.
1 Make a small stitch from A to B. Bring the needle up at C, between A and B.
2 Take the thread to the upper stitching line at an angle. Take it down at D and bring it up at E. Now take it down at F and up again at D. Repeat step 2 on alternate lines.

Herringbone stitch This is most commonly used for edgings and fillings.
1 Bring the needle up on the lower stitching line at A, take it up diagonally to B and bring it out again at C, making a small backstitch.
2 Take the thread diagonally down to the lower line and work a backstitch (D–E) as before. Repeat steps 1 and 2.

Tied herringbone stitch This is a simple way of embellishing the basic herringbone stitch. The tying stitches are normally worked in a contrasting color.
Work a row of herringbone, then make a small stitch over the crossing points, taking the needle up on the outside and down on the inside.

Double herringbone stitch
1 Work a row of herringbone, but take each downward diagonal stitch under the upward one rather than over it.
2 Using contrasting thread, work another row as in step 1, but, when taking the thread up, take it under the downward stitch of the first row; use the blunt end of the needle if preferred.

SHADOW WORK
This type of stitchery, in which the stitches are seen through a sheer fabric, makes use of herringbone stitch. In this context it is also called shadow or double backstitch. The stitches are worked closely on the underside of the fabric to create a more or less solid band of stitching that shows through on the right side.

The stitching may be worked in the same color as the fabric, but more interesting effects can be created by using a colored thread on a white fabric. The thread color will be softened by the fabric, except at the edges, where it forms the backstitch.

There are two alternate ways of working shadow stitches. For method 1, transfer the design to the wrong side of the fabric, using the direct tracing method (see p.64). For method 2, simply trace the design onto the right side of the fabric.

Method 1 On the wrong side of the fabric, work a few running stitches on the stitching line to fasten the thread. Then work herringbone stitch between the marked lines, working the stitches close together for a solid effect, and making sure that each backstitch touches the one before it.

Method 2 On the right side of the fabric, work backstitches as shown, working on alternate stitching lines to form the herringbone stitches underneath.

CRETAN STITCH

This versatile stitch is used extensively by modern embroiderers, since it can create many varied and interesting textures. Its simplest form, open Cretan stitch, looks like a more graceful version of herringbone. When worked irregularly in overlapping rows, this stitch makes an attractive filling, ideally suited to depicting grasses; it is also useful to create areas of abstract texture. The use of threads of different thickness, different colors, or both, offers even more possibilities. If worked vertically, the stitch is excellent for suggesting water.

Closed Cretan stitch looks completely different from the open, spiky version, but it is formed in basically the same way. This version is well suited to stylized leaves and other motifs, but can also be worked to form a solid band.

Open Cretan stitch
1 Bring the needle up at A, take it down at a slight angle, at B, and bring it up directly below, at C.
2 Pull the thread through, but not too tightly. Take it over the first stitch, and insert it at D, bringing it up at E. Pull the thread through and take it over the stitch as before.

Closed Cretan stitch The stitches are formed in basically the same way as for open Cretan, but are usually worked vertically and with the central crossed area proportionately smaller. To fill a shape evenly, mark both the edges and the center line where the stitches will cross with basting or with a hard pencil.

Feather stitch This stitch makes an attractive border for clothing. Mark four evenly spaced stitching lines, as shown.
1 Bring the needle up at A and take it down at B. Bring the needle up above the loop at C.
2 Take the needle down at D and bring it up again at E, keeping the thread under the needle.
3 Work the third stitch to the right and work alternately to right and left in this way.

Double feather stitch This variation forms more pronounced zigzags, by working two or more stitches to the right and left alternately. Mark five stitching lines on the fabric.
1–2 Work as for steps 1–2 of feather stitch.
3 Take the needle down at F; bring it up at G.
4 Take the needle down at H and bring it up at I.
5 Take it down at J and bring it up at K.
Repeat steps 2–5.

Quill stitch This variation of feather stitch has a spiky appearance that is useful for depicting certain kinds of foliage, such as pine branches.
The stitch is worked in the same way as feather stitch, but you must change the spacing and proportions of the stitches as shown.

Closed fly stitch This stitch is ideal for leaves. Before working it, mark the center line.
1 Bring the needle up at A, then take it down at B and bring it up at C.
2 Insert the needle at D, bring it up at B, holding the loop down with the finger or thumb, and take it over the working thread.

Vandyke stitch This stitch is used for foliage.
1 Bring the needle out at A, take it up diagonally and insert it at B; bring it up at C, and down at D.
2 Bring the needle up at E, take it up diagonally and slide it under the crossed threads (eye first if this is easier). Take it down at F.
Repeat step 2, always sliding the needle under the last pair of crossed threads, and taking care not to pull the thread too tightly.

Flat Vandyke In this variation of Vandyke the center braid is worked right through the fabric, not merely through the crossed threads, which makes it easier to maintain the V-angle on a curve. The texture is slightly flatter than ordinary Vandyke stitch.
Work throughout as in step 1 of Vandyke stitch, taking care not to split the stitches.

Open Cretan stitch

Double feather stitch

Quill stitch

Rosette chain stitch

Detached slip chain stitch

Closed Cretan stitch

Feather stitch

Vandyke stitch

Flat Vandyke stitch

Raised chain band

CHAIN BANDS

Many of the chain stitch variations form attractive textured bands. One of the prettiest, rosette chain, makes an attractive edging on clothing, and can also be worked in a ring, with the rosettes pointing outward. It is less complicated than it looks, but always take care to space the rosettes evenly. Marking the stitching lines will help to keep each rosette the same size. Avoid pulling the thread tightly.

Detached slip chain stitch is ideal for a vertical border, worked down the front of a blouse, for example.

Raised chain band is extremely versatile. It can be worked evenly or freely. Several lines together create a pleasing "crunchy" texture. A foundation of cross threads of varying lengths can be worked at random to create an interesting pattern, as shown above.

Rosette chain
1 Bring the needle up at A, take it down at B and bring it up at C, looping the thread under the needle as shown.
2 Keeping the needle inside the loop, pull the thread through gently.
3 Slide the needle under the upper strand of thread, ready for the next stitch.

To work rosettes in a ring First mark the inner circle on the fabric, then indicate the positions of the rosettes with short radiating lines. After working the last rosette, take the needle down into the first one, as shown.

Detached slip chain stitch
1 Work an ordinary chain stitch (see p.70) and anchor the loop with a small vertical stitch.
2 Bring the needle up to the left of the chain loop at A, and slide it under the vertical stitch without piercing the fabric. Take the needle down at B.
3 Bring the needle up at C to work the next chain.

Raised chain band
1 Work horizontal stitches down the length of the stitching line.
2 Thread a tapestry needle with contrasting thread, and bring it up just above the center of the top stitch.
3 Bring the thread over and slide the needle up, under the horizontal stitch to the left.

4 Pass the needle down under the horizontal stitch to the right of the thread, forming a loop stitch, and pull the needle through the loop.

Repeat steps 3 and 4, taking care to keep the tension even and not too tight. Do not pierce the fabric.

FILLING STITCHES

Stitches that are ideal for filling areas of embroidery fall into several groups: detached stitches, which are scattered or clustered on the fabric to create texture or shading; small round motifs, which can be used individually or massed together; solid filling stitches, which cover the fabric completely or almost completely; and patterned fillings, which cover relatively large areas with a network of threads.

Detached fillings include some of the most useful stitches: French knots, seeding and straight stitch, for example. The single French knot is commonly used as a flower center or the eye of a bird, but massed French knots have a wonderfully tactile quality. Both seeding and French knots combine well with beads. Straight stitches, the simplest of all fillings, can be used for cross-hatching, as in a drawing.

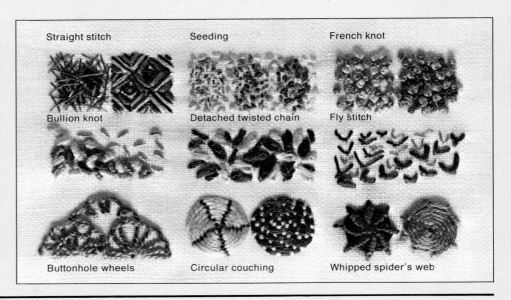

Straight stitch   Seeding   French knot

Bullion knot   Detached twisted chain   Fly stitch

Buttonhole wheels   Circular couching   Whipped spider's web

Straight stitch To work a straight stitch, simply bring the needle up where required, and take it down the desired distance away. Use long stitches for tall grass, blocks of short ones for cross-hatching or basketweave effects. To make a simple star or flower motif, work the stitches around a central point.

Seeding Worked in graduated density, seeding creates interesting speckled effects of shading and texture.

Work a small straight stitch, then work another stitch diagonally over the first one. If a thick thread is used, more or less the same effect can be achieved with only one stitch. Beads can be sewn on individually to echo and contrast with the texture of the stitches.

French knot
1 Bring the needle up at the chosen position. Wind the working thread once around the needle. (For a larger knot, use thicker thread.)
2 Holding the thread taut, but not too tight, insert the needle close to the starting point, and draw the thread smoothly through the loop.

For knots on stalks, take the needle down a short distance away.

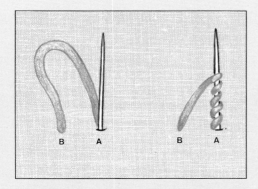

Bullion knot These knots give a curly, textured effect.
1 Bring the needle up at A and take it down at B, leaving a loop of thread, then bring just the point back through at A.
2 Wind the loop of thread around the needle point until the closed-up coil measures the same as the distance from A to B.

3 Gently holding the coil in place, bring the needle and thread up through it. Pull the knot toward B, and continue pulling on the thread so that the knot rests on the fabric. Use the needle to adjust the coil and smooth it if necessary.
4 Take the needle down at B.

Detached chain stitch This stitch is often used to make leaf or flower shapes. Work individual chain stitches (see p.70) as desired over the fabric, fastening each loop with a small tying stitch. Or work them in a circle to make "lazy daisy" stitch.

Free chain loops can be produced by working the anchoring stitch at the top of the chain rather than over the loop.

76

Detached twisted chain stitch This variation can be worked in patterns or scattered over the fabric.

Bring the needle up at A, hold the thread to the left and take it down at B, forming a loop, as shown. Then work a small stitch at the bottom of the loop to hold it in place.

Tête de boeuf These "bull's head" stitches make charming miniature flowers.
1 Work a single detached chain stitch (see p.76).
2 Then work two diagonal straight stitches on either side of the chain.

Fly stitch This stitch can be used realistically to suggest distant birds, or in an abstract way to create a rough-looking texture. Equally, fly stitch can be joined up to form a band or border.

Bring the needle up at A, take it down at B, holding the loop down, and bring it out at C, making a small stitch to anchor the loop.

ROUND MOTIFS

Circular motifs are obviously ideal for stylized flowers and fruit, cartwheels and other round objects. Here are several, both flat and three-dimensional, which can be used for different effects.

To practice these motifs, first draw a circle on the fabric, using a coin or circular piece of cardboard as a pattern. When you become more adept at working the stitches, you may want to dispense with this step and work the motifs more freely.

Another stitch often used for small round shapes is padded satin stitch (see p.78).

Buttonhole wheels First draw a circle on the fabric. Then bring the needle up at some point on the outer edge and work buttonhole stitches (see p.72) all around the circle, working each one into the center.

Semicircles and fan shapes can be made in the same way.

Circular couching For this variation of simple couching (see p.71), first draw a circle, then mark the lines for the couching stitches. Bring up the main thread at the center, then bring up the couching thread and work stitches over the main thread in the chosen pattern.

Whipped spider's web
1 Draw a circle on the fabric. Using a tapestry needle and a thread at least 18in long, cross the circle with four diagonal stitches (A–B, C–D, E–F, G–H). Place point H closer to D than to B in order to leave room for the ninth "spoke" between them. Bring the needle up at I, slide it under all threads where they intersect, and loop the working thread over the needle.

2 Pull the thread through to tie the stitches together at the center.
3 Working from the center outward, slide the needle under two threads, pull the thread through firmly, then take the needle back over the second thread and then under both it and the next one.

Repeat step 3 all around the circle, as often as necessary to cover the threads (or leave them partly uncovered if you prefer), loosening the tension gradually toward the edges.

For a woven spider's web, take the needle under and over the threads alternately, as though weaving.

77

SATIN STITCH

Apparently one of the simplest of all embroidery stitches, satin stitch is also one of the most difficult. You can learn the basics of how to work it in no time at all, but you will need a great deal of practice before you can work it well, so that the stitches lie side by side in perfect parallel lines.

Keeping the edge smooth can also be a problem. To make this easier, first work a line of split stitch (see p.70) along the edges of the area to be filled. This will serve as a guide for your needle and will also give the work a well-defined edge.

Wherever possible, satin stitch should be worked at an angle to the edges of the shape being filled. This makes it easier to work the stitch evenly. The stitches should not be too long. About $5/8$in is the limit on an item that will be handled frequently, otherwise the threads are likely to catch.

For basic satin stitch, bring the needle up on one edge, take it down on the opposite edge, then back up on the first one again.

To fill a shape:
1 Work a line of split stitch around the edges.
2 Work a straight stitch diagonally across the shape, somewhere around the middle, to establish the slant.

3 Work satin stitch to the nearer end, working over the split stitch but very close to it for a smooth edge.
4 Take the thread under the stitches on the wrong side and work in the other direction. To prevent the angle from flattening out, exaggerate it slightly toward the end.

Padded satin stitch
1 Work lines of running stitch (see p.69) across the shape to be filled. For a gently sloped effect, work the stitches more thickly on one side of the shape than on the other.
2 Fill the shape with satin stitch.

Alternate method of padded satin stitch
1 Fill the shape with satin stitch, running the stitches in the opposite direction from that intended for the finished work.
2 Work a second layer over the first, at a right angle to it. More than two layers may be worked, if desired, but take care to keep the edges neat.

Satin stitch tied with backstitch Satin stitches should not be too long or they may become damaged. Anchoring them with a line of backstitch is one way around the problem.
1 Work satin stitch in the usual way.
2 Work one or more lines of backstitch across the satin stitches.

Roumanian stitch This is sometimes called Roumanian couching.
1 Bring the needle up at A, take it down at B, then work a stitch diagonally over the long stitch from C–D.
2 Work another long stitch just below the first, as in step 1, but bring the needle up for the diagonal stitch before pulling the thread through.

Bokhara couching This is similar to Roumanian stitch, but has more tying stitches.
1 Work a long stitch from A–B across the shape.
2 Work short diagonal stitches (C–D, E–F, etc.) at regular intervals over the long stitch.

Repeat steps 1 and 2, arranging the short couching stitches in a diagonal pattern.

Darning This is a simple way of filling an area with smooth lines of stitching while allowing the fabric to show through.

Simply work lines of running stitch (see p.69) to fill the shape. The stitches may be worked evenly, perhaps to form a pattern, or at random.

Encroaching satin stitch This is also known as block shading, since it is often used with thread in graduated shades of a single color.
1 Work a row of vertical satin stitches.
2 Work a row below, bringing the needle up on the lower line and taking it down between the ends of the stitches in the row above.

Brick stitch This stitch is named for the brick-like pattern it produces.
1 Work vertical satin stitches along the top edge, making them alternately long and short.
2 On following rows make all the stitches the same length, as shown. Fill in the gaps in the last row with short stitches.

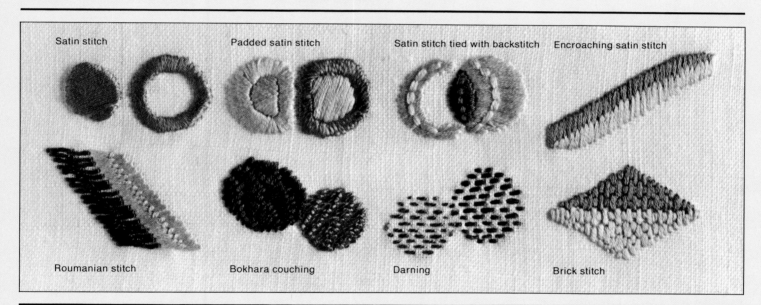

Satin stitch   Padded satin stitch   Satin stitch tied with backstitch   Encroaching satin stitch

Roumanian stitch   Bokhara couching   Darning   Brick stitch

LONG AND SHORT STITCH

This stitch figures prominently in some types of traditional embroidery, such as crewel work, and is used to achieve subtle effects of shading in flower petals, leaves and other motifs. Like satin stitch, it is basically simple but is difficult to execute well. The rows of different colors must seem to flow into each other as in a realistic painting, and the stitches must lie smoothly. This is relatively easy to achieve if the area to be filled is rectangular. But more often it is curved, and angling the stitches correctly involves occasionally working a "wedge" stitch (see p.80), which is not worked into in the next row.

When practicing long and short stitch, begin by working the stitches regularly, as shown. As you become more skilled, you can vary the length of the stitches more freely.

Long and short stitch in straight lines
1 Work a line of split stitch (see p.70) along the upper edge.
2 Work vertical stitches down from this edge, taking the needle over it, and making every alternate stitch about three-quarters the length of its predecessor. The longer stitches should be at least $3/8$in long.

3 Using thread a shade or two lighter or darker than the first, work another row of stitches, all the same length, below the first. Bring the needle up through the corresponding upper stitch, splitting the thread, as shown.

Repeat step 3 as required.

Long and short stitch in a curved shape
1 Mark guidelines within the shape to help you slant the stitches correctly.
2 Outline the shape with split stitch.

3 Starting at the center of the shape, work long and short stitches alternately to one side, then return to the center and work to the other side. Slant the stitches as indicated by the guidelines, working a short "wedge" stitch (see arrow) where necessary.

4 Work subsequent rows in graduated shades, working into the upper stitches as in step 3 of straight long and short stitch. Keep the stitches fairly long for a satiny effect. Some practice is needed to cover the split stitch at the sides without distorting the angle of the long and short stitches.

LAID WORK

If a large area needs to be filled with a flat, solid stitch, laid work can be a good choice. Unlike satin stitch, which it superficially resembles, laid work covers only the right side of the fabric, and thus is more economical of thread, a factor worth considering if the area is large.

Because the laid stitches are usually long, they must be held in place by "holding" stitches. Lines of split stitch, stem stitch, chain stitch or couching (see pp.70–71) are all suitable choices for this. The stitching can simply be worked in lines perpendicular to the laid threads or it can form more elaborate patterns.

Subtle effects of shading can be achieved in laid work by using two colors of stranded floss in the needle and altering their proportions as illustrated on page 50.

For basic laid work, bring the needle up at A and take it across the shape and down at B. Bring it up at C, as close as possible to B, then down at D, and up again at E. Continue filling the shape, working first out to one side and then to the other. Avoid pulling the stitches tightly or they may be distorted by the holding stitches.

To change the direction of the threads, if the shape requires it, work a shorter stitch occasionally, taking the needle down a little before the edge, then bringing it up on the edge, close to the last stitch but one, and continuing as before.

Laid threads tied with crossbars
1 Work a row of long holding stitches diagonally across the laid stitches, as shown, starting at the widest point and spacing them $1/4$in to $3/8$in apart.
2 Work another layer of holding stitches across the first at the opposite angle and the same distance apart.

3 Anchor the diagonal stitches by working a small stitch over each intersection. These stitches, and the long holding stitches, may be worked in a contrasting thread. For a simpler pattern, work only one set of diagonal stitches and couch them down at regular intervals.

Squared filling
1 Work a crossbar pattern directly on the fabric, as in steps 1–3 of Laid threads tied with crossbars.
2 Embellish this trellis with other stitches as desired, worked between or over the original stitches. The basic pattern may be worked horizontally and vertically instead of diagonally.

Wave filling

1 At the upper edge of the area to be filled, work a series of short, evenly spaced stitches.
2 Using a tapestry needle, bring the thread up at A, take it through the first straight stitch, then down again at B. Bring the needle up again at C, close to B, and continue in the same way.

3 Work back as for step 2 but in the opposite direction, taking the needle under each pair of stitches, as shown, and taking care not to pull the thread tightly.

To help keep the stitches even, draw horizontal guidelines on the fabric.

Cloud filling

1 Work straight stitches as in step 1 of Wave filling, but over several rows, staggering them.
2 Using a tapestry needle, take the thread up and down under the straight stitches to form a series of loops. Fasten the thread under the last straight stitch before beginning the next row.

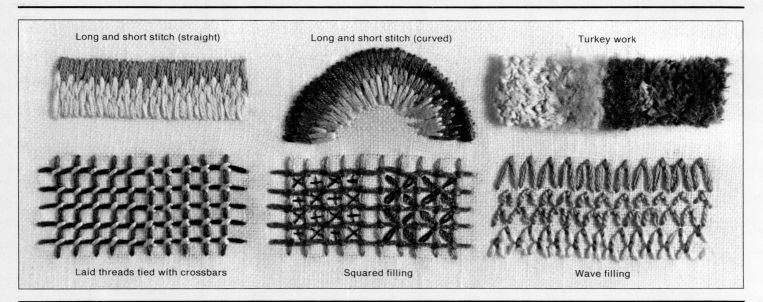

Long and short stitch (straight)

Long and short stitch (curved)

Turkey work

Laid threads tied with crossbars

Squared filling

Wave filling

TURKEY WORK

This stitch can be used to give a raised, velvety texture similar to that of a carpet, which gives it its name. Basically it consists of lines of backstitch (see p.69), in which every alternate stitch is not pulled through but left as a small loop. When the work is completed, the loops can either be trimmed closely and evenly for a pile effect, or left uncut for a looped texture.

Cut Turkey work is best worked closely in straight lines, as shown. (Incidentally, this is one stitch that is best worked with a "sewing" movement, as illustrated, rather than up and down.) If the loops are to be left uncut they can be worked in curved lines – for example, in concentric circles to suggest a flower.

The loops or pile will slant backward slightly, so allow for this by turning the work in the appropriate direction before beginning to stitch.

1 Take the needle down at A and bring it up at B, leaving a short end free.
2 Take the needle down at C and up at A, leaving the working thread below the needle. Pull the thread through, holding the free end in place with the thumb or index finger.

3 Work another backstitch, from D to C, but this time keep the thread above the needle. Pull the thread through, leaving a loop.

Repeat steps 2 and 3, making small stitches and placing the rows close together.

When the work is complete, snip through and trim the loops, or leave them uncut.

81

At its most simple, appliqué consists of stitching one piece of fabric on top of another. One of the most versatile types of needlework, it can take many forms, from a simple monogram or crest machine-stitched on to a jacket to a detailed pattern of tiny leaves and blossoms applied by hand and embellished with surface embroidery. Appliqué can be worked on the underside of a sheer fabric to create a subtle, shadowy effect; it can be padded, stuffed or quilted; it can even be worked in reverse, with the background fabric placed on top and cut away to form the motifs.

Appliqué is best suited to designs featuring strong, relatively large shapes, rather than intricate patterns of line and texture which are better interpreted in surface stitchery, since this is ideal for fine detail. However, if your design was based

on a bowl of fruit, for example, appliqué could be an excellent medium in which to convey the solidity and well-defined shapes of the various fruits and the bowl itself. It would be easy to find fabrics in the appropriate colors, and their textures might even suggest the textures of the fruits too—red satin for an apple, perhaps, and coarse-weave orange linen for the rough surface of an orange. The finished work would make a bold statement about shape and color, with a fresh, spontaneous quality similar to that of a paper cut-out.

In a more sophisticated form, appliqué can benefit from the addition of some stitchery. In some appliqué methods the motifs are attached with embroidery, which can be used to soften or accentuate the edge of a shape, depending on the type of stitch and the color of the thread. Stitchery can be used on the motifs them-

selves, too, to suggest texture. For example, instead of choosing a textured fabric for the orange, you could use a piece of smooth cotton or lightweight wool, then work a few seeding stitches (see p. 76) near the edges to suggest both the texture and the special contours of the fruit.

Embroidery can also be used to provide detail. A picture or panel depicting an urban scene might use appliqué for the buildings themselves, to create a solid look, then embroidery for the windows, doors and other architectural features.

The following pages describe several methods of working appliqué, suitable for different types of project and design as well as for different fabrics.

FABRICS FOR APPLIQUÉ

Virtually any fabric can be used for appliqué, indeed this is much of the craft's appeal. The wide variety of materials available can inspire all sorts of design ideas. Blue moiré taffeta or shot silk might suggest water; gray velvet the fur of a cat; dark brown tweed the bark of a tree. Layers of chiffon could be placed on top of each other to depict the sky at sunset, while leather or suede could be used realistically for a pair of boots; or as abstract shapes to provide textural interest.

However, although the choice is wide in theory, it may be more limited in reality, at least for practical items. In this case, you will have to consider whether the fabrics will stand up to a degree of wear, and whether or not they are washable. Felt, for example, is an easy fabric to appliqué,

since its edges do not fray, but it cannot be washed. For any appliqué that will be washed, such as a child's jacket, all the fabrics, including the background, must be compatible in terms of their care. So do not mix rayon with linen, for example, as they will not only need washing, but also ironing, at different temperatures.

Another consideration is the chosen method of appliqué. If you are using the turned-edge method shown on page 85, you should avoid thick, springy fabrics unless you are an experienced embroiderer. A lightweight, closely woven cotton is ideal, although it should not be so fine that the turnings will show through on the right side. Slippery fabrics, or those that fray badly, can be made easier to handle either by applying iron-on interfacing to the wrong side or by applying them to the background fabric with bonding web, as

shown opposite. Both methods will arrest fraying, and interfacing will give a flimsy fabric the necessary body.

On any item that will receive wear, always appliqué motifs with the fabric grain matching that of the background. Ideally, the warp threads (those parallel to the selvage) should be aligned, but if you are using scraps without a selvage this may be impossible to ascertain. In this case, make sure that the grains cross at right angles. Even if the work is purely decorative, the shapes will be easier to apply if the grains match.

TRANSFERRING THE DESIGN

The shapes to be appliquéed must first be transferred to the appliqué fabrics. This is normally done by means of patterns.

If the design is simple, the motifs can usually be positioned on the background fabric by eye. If centering them is important, mark the background fabric with lines of basting to serve as guides.

Even a fairly complex design can usually be assembled by numbering the shapes on the master design and referring to this as you work.

If you prefer to mark the positions of the shapes on the background fabric, you can do so using dressmaker's carbon paper or basting (see pp. 64–65).

If you have used the cut-paper method of planning your design (see p. 24), you will already have patterns, but otherwise you must make them, unless you are using the interfacing method shown opposite.

Making the patterns
1 To make the patterns, first number each shape in the master design. (If the design is very simple, this step can be omitted.)
2 Trace each motif from the design, using fairly stiff tracing paper. If you intend to use the motifs for a repeating design, you could use the tracing to cut a more durable pattern from thin cardboard.

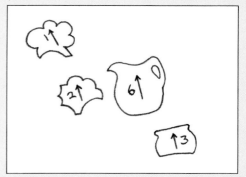

3 Mark each pattern with the number corresponding to that in the design. Mark a small arrow indicating the shape's vertical alignment, so that you cut the motif with the grain running correctly.
4 Cut around the traced lines to make the patterns.

USING IRON-ON INTERFACING

1 Place the interfacing, shiny (adhesive) side up, on the design, and trace the shape, using a pencil or waterproof fabric-marking pen. Cut around the tracing, leaving a small margin (about $\frac{3}{8}$–$\frac{3}{4}$in) all around which will be cut off later. Mark the grain line and the number on the non-adhesive side.

2 Place the interfacing, shiny side down, on the wrong side of the fabric, aligning the grain line with the fabric grain. Using the point of the iron, fix the interfacing to the fabric at one point to hold it in place. Cover the motif with a damp pressing cloth and press with a dry or steam iron.

3 Cut around the shape, on the marked line. The motif is now ready to be applied to the background by machine or by hand, as shown in the following pages.

USING BONDING WEB

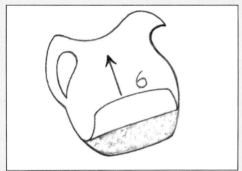

1 Place the pattern, wrong side up, on the non-adhesive (paper) side of the bonding web and draw around it with a pencil. This will produce a mirror image of the original shape. Mark the grain line and the number on the bonding web.
2 Cut around the pencil line, leaving a margin all around.

3 Place the bonding web motif, adhesive side down, on the wrong side of the fabric. Using the point of the iron, fix the bonding at one point to secure it, then cover the work with a damp cloth and press with a hot, dry iron.
4 Allow the fabric to cool, then cut around the outline through both fabric and bonding.

5 When you are ready to apply the motif, simply peel away the paper backing. Position the motif on the background fabric, secure it with the point of the iron and then press, using a damp cloth and a hot iron.
Note When using either iron-on interfacing or bonding web, always test it first on a spare piece of fabric.

PERSIAN APPLIQUÉ

Also called *appliqué perse*, this is one of the simplest ways of decorating fabric. It consists of cutting a whole motif, such as a flower, from a printed fabric and applying it to another (usually plain) one. As the edges are not turned under, it is a good idea to use either the interfacing or the bonding web method.

There is no need to trace the motif onto the interfacing or bonding web; simply cut a piece slightly larger than the motif and iron it on the wrong side of the fabric. Then cut out the motif and apply it to the background fabric either by bonding or by a suitable hand or machine method (see pp. 84–86). If bonding is used, the edges can then be secured with some decorative stitching, such as buttonhole or Cretan stitch, as shown right.

HAND APPLIQUÉ

There are several different methods of hand appliqué. Fabrics that do not fray, such as felt and leather, can be cut to the finished size and applied flat with stab stitch. Woven fabrics that do not fray easily, or fabrics that have been interfaced or backed with bonding web (see p. 83), can also be applied without turnings.

If a fabric is thin or sheer, so that turnings would be visible through the right side, it can be applied using the stitch and cut method shown below. Another way of handling such fabrics is to cut a piece of iron-on interfacing, apply it to the fabric, then cut out and apply the motif using the turned-edge method (see p. 85).

Before basting a motif to the fabric, it is best to mount the background fabric on a frame (see pp. 66–67). This will ensure that the fabrics lie smoothly together.

The fan is hand-appliquéed using the turned-edge method and invisible stitching.

NON-FRAY FABRICS

1 Place the pattern, right side down, on the wrong side of the fabric and draw around it. Cut out the motif on the marked line.

2 Mount the background fabric on a frame, then position the motif and secure it with a few pins. Baste it in place with lines of diagonal basting.

3 Using matching sewing or embroidery thread, stitch the motif in place with stab stitch —tiny running stitches. Work close to the edge.
    Alternatively, work the stab stitches over the edge, as shown on the right.

FRAY-RESISTANT WOVEN FABRICS

1 Mark and cut out the motif as in step 1 above or as described on page 83 for interfaced or bonded motifs. If the fabric is not interfaced or backed with bonding, work small overcasting stitches around the edges with matching thread.

2 Pin and baste the motif to the background fabric.
3 Work buttonhole stitch (see p. 72) around the edges, using matching or contrasting embroidery thread and spacing the stitches as desired. A different stitch, such as Cretan or herringbone (pp. 73 and 74), may be used if preferred.

STITCH AND CUT METHOD

This method is well suited to thin fabrics, including those that fray easily.
1 Place the pattern right side up on the right side of the fabric and mark around it. Cut roughly around the shape, leaving a generous margin.

2 Pin and baste the motif to the background fabric, working the basting over the whole area.
3 Work close buttonhole stitch over the marked line, through both fabrics.

4 Using sharp-pointed embroidery scissors, carefully cut away the excess fabric just outside the stitching line.

TURNED-EDGE METHOD

1 Place the pattern, right side up, on the right side of the fabric and mark around the edge with a fabric-marking pen or tailor's chalk.
2 Mark a turning allowance $1/4$–$3/8$in outside the marked line.
3 Cut out the shape, leaving a generous margin outside the turning allowance.

4 Stay stitch (machine straight stitch) just outside the inner marked line. This step is not strictly essential, but makes it easier to turn the edges under.
5 Cut away the excess fabric, leaving just the turning allowance.

On curved edges Clip or notch the turning allowance up to the stay stitching.
For an inner curve (left), clip the edge so that it will fan out when turned under.
For an outer curve (right), notch the edge to prevent excess bulk when turned.

Mitering corners For an outer corner, miter the turnings as follows. Cut across the corner to eliminate excess bulk, turn down the corner, then turn down the two adjacent sides.
For an inner corner, make one clip into the stay stitching.

6 Turn the seam allowance under and baste it in place. If you are experienced, this step may be omitted, and the allowance turned under as you stitch (see below); but it is recommended for beginners. Make any knots on the right side of the motif for easy removal of basting stitches.

7 Pin and baste the motif to the background fabric using diagonal basting.
8 Using matching sewing thread and slip stitch, sew the motif in place. Make the stitches as nearly invisible as possible and space them about $1/8$–$1/4$in apart.
If the edges have not been basted, turn them under as you stitch. The point of a seam ripper is useful to help turn under the edges.

85

MACHINE APPLIQUÉ

The obvious advantage of machine appliqué is speed, but it has other advantages too. Machine stitching, being stronger than most hand stitching, is ideal for any item that will be subjected to hard wear or frequent laundering.

Some machine appliqué can be done with a straight stitch only, but a machine that will also do zigzag stitch expands the range of possible effects. An open zigzag stitch, perhaps in a contrasting color, will provide a decorative edge, while close zigzag, or satin stitch, will cover raw edges completely. Machine embroidery thread, which is finer and glossier than ordinary thread, will enhance the satiny effect, but for most purposes an ordinary sewing thread is suitable. Cotton-covered polyester thread is ideal, since it is both strong and compatible with all fabrics.

Zigzag machine stitch is used to appliqué this geometric motif.

1 Place the pattern right side up on the right side of the fabric and mark around it with a waterproof fabric-marking pen or pencil.
2 Cut around the motif, leaving a margin of ⅜–¾in.

3 Pin the motif to the background fabric, placing the pins perpendicular to the edge, as shown. Baste it in place using diagonal basting, making sure that both layers lie smoothly against each other.

4 Work straight stitch around the marked outline.
5 Using sharp-pointed embroidery scissors, cut away the excess fabric close to the stitching. Depending on the fabric and the effect desired, the appliqué could be left as it is, but if the edges need to be covered, proceed to step 6.

6 Work zigzag stitch over the edges, covering the first line of stitching. Page 118 includes detailed instructions on working zigzag stitch.

If an open zigzag stitch is to be used, it is better to bond the motif (see p. 83) in place, then work the zigzag, omitting the straight stitch.

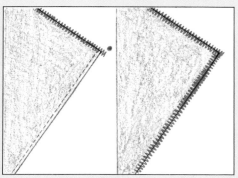

To work a corner Stitch slightly beyond the edge of the first side to the width the new line of stitching will cover. Remove the work and take the threads to the wrong side. Reposition the needle just inside the first line of stitching and continue stitching in the new direction.
To work around tight curves Pivot the work every few stitches: stop the machine with the needle in the fabric on the inside of the curve;

raise the foot, turn the fabric slightly, then lower the foot, and work two or three more stitches. Repeat.
To work sharp points Narrow the stitch width gradually, starting about ¾–1⅛in from the point, until the stitch just covers the edges. Pivot, as described for curves, and resume stitching, gradually widening the zigzag.

SHADOW APPLIQUÉ

In this form of appliqué the motifs are applied to the underside of a sheer fabric such as organdy, organza, fine linen or lawn. The appliqué fabric is usually fairly thin also. It is normally a solid color, which may be the same as the main fabric or contrasting. Any contrasting color will be softened by the top layer.

The motifs are applied using a variation of the stitch and cut method shown on page 85. This lends itself to more intricate designs than are possible with most other appliqué techniques.

A variety of stitches can be used for shadow appliqué. Backstitch produces a thin line and combines well with shadow stitch (see p. 73). Another stitch often used is point de Paris, or pin stitch, a type of pulled thread work (see p. 110) which forms tiny holes along the stitching line.

The sinuous curves of this abstract motif in shadow appliqué are outlined in point de Paris.

1 Place the main fabric right side up over the design (having darkened the lines first if necessary). Hold it in place with weights or tape, making sure that the grain runs straight, and trace the design using tailor's chalk or pencil.

2 Mount the main fabric on a frame (see pp. 66–67).
3 Cut a piece of the appliqué fabric slightly larger than the motif and pin it, right side down, to the wrong side of the main fabric.
4 Baste it in place using diagonal basting.

5 Work backstitch (see p. 69) or another embroidery stitch of your choice over the design outlines. Secure the thread at the beginning by making one or two backstitches in the appliqué fabric. When fastening off or starting a new thread, secure the thread by working it into existing stitches.

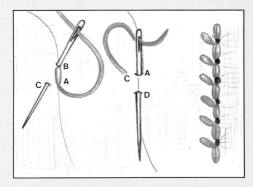

6 Using sharp embroidery scissors, carefully cut away the excess appliqué fabric outside the stitching.

Remove the work from the frame.

Point de Paris Transfer the design, mount the main fabric in a frame, and baste the appliqué fabric in place as described above. Then, using a tapestry needle and ordinary sewing thread in a matching color, work the stitching as follows:
1 Work a backstitch from A to B, bringing the needle up again at A in the same hole.

2 Work another backstitch, bringing the needle up at C, just inside the design outline.
3 Take the needle down again at A and bring it up at D.

Repeat steps 1–3, pulling the thread tightly on each stitch, especially in step 2, to form the holes.

87

REVERSE APPLIQUÉ

In most forms of appliqué, the design is formed by applying motifs to the surface of the main fabric. Reverse appliqué, by contrast, is worked by cutting away one or more layers of superimposed fabric to expose the fabric underneath.

The traditional method of reverse appliqué, sometimes called San Blas appliqué, is a complex procedure in which the design is built up from the bottom layer of fabric.

The simpler version of reverse appliqué, shown here, called cut-through appliqué, involves working from the top downward. The basic method can be varied to create many different effects within the same piece of work, especially if four or five layers of fabric are used.

Choose fabrics that are opaque, lightweight and closely woven, so that the edges will not fray.

Reverse appliqué, showing the permutations using three layers of fabric

1 Cut all the fabric layers to the required size, allowing extra for finishing. (Three layers are used in the illustrations.) Pin them together over the whole surface and baste around the edges.
2 Make patterns (see p. 82) for the outer shapes —those that will be cut from the top fabric. Position these on the top fabric and trace around them lightly with pencil or tailor's chalk.

3 Baste all around, $\frac{1}{2}$ to $\frac{3}{4}$in from the outline, to hold the fabric layers together.
4 Cut away the fabric inside the outline. Leave a margin of a scant $\frac{1}{4}$in and take care to cut only the top layer.

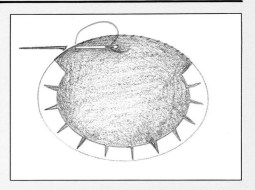

5 Using matching thread and slipstitch, stitch the edges of the cut-out shape to the layer below, turning under the edges as you work. Take an occasional stitch through all layers to hold them in place permanently. Clip the edges where necessary so that they will lie smoothly.

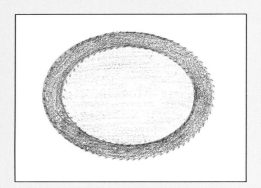

6 Repeat steps 4 and 5 to reveal lower layers of fabric, reducing the size of the cut-out shape as you work downward. It is not usually necessary to draw another outline; simply cut free-hand, remembering to allow a little fabric for turning under.

To miss a layer and reveal the one below it, cut away the top layer as described in step 4, then cut away the next layer, taking it back well under the top fabric. Turn under the edges of the top fabric and stitch them to the third layer.

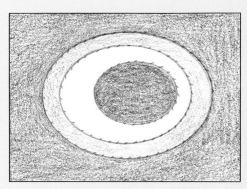

Shapes can be added within the cut-away spaces for additional interest. Simply prepare the shapes and stitch them in place as for turned-edge appliqué (see p. 85), or use another appliqué method if you prefer.

PADDED APPLIQUÉ

Many interesting three-dimensional effects can be achieved with appliqué by padding or raising shapes. A useful padding technique consists of sewing layers of felt to the background fabric to build up a smoothly rounded shape, then applying the motif over them. This technique is used extensively in metal thread work (see p. 99) to enhance the sheen of the metal thread and fabrics. It performs a similar function for shiny fabrics such as satin but can be used with almost any fabric.

A softer effect can be achieved by using layers of lightweight batting instead of felt. For a stiff effect, well suited to architectural forms or hard-edged designs, a motif can be reinforced with cardboard.

Small, freestanding motifs can be made and sewn to the background fabric at one point only so that they project out from it.

Satin fabric accentuates the roundness of the shapes in padded appliqué

1 Using a pattern (see p. 82), trace the motif on felt and cut it out. Then cut one or more smaller shapes (a total of three to six is normally used), making each about $1/4$in smaller all around than the previous one.
2 Cut the appliqué slightly larger than the pattern to allow for the space taken up by the layers of padding.

3 Pin and stitch the felt pieces to the background. Use stab stitch and work upward from the smallest to the largest. For an asymmetrical effect, pad unevenly as shown above, top right.
4 Stitch the appliqué motif to the fabric using one of the methods given on pages 82–83.

Suffolk puffs These small circular motifs can suggest flowers or other round shapes.
1 Cut a circle of fabric twice the desired diameter.
2 Work running stitch close to a folded or turned edge.
3 Pull up the stitches and fasten the thread securely on the underside. The motif is then ready to be sewn into place.

Padding with cardboard
1 Cut a piece of cardboard (or stiff interfacing) the size of the finished motif.
2 Cut the appliqué fabric $1/2$ to $3/4$in larger.
3 Center the cardboard on the wrong side of the motif. Spread fabric glue on the outer edges and stick the fabric edges over it.
4 Apply the shape to the background fabric using invisible or decorative stitches.

Stuffed freestanding motif
1 Trace the motif onto the top fabric.
2 Place the top and bottom fabrics together, with a piece of lightweight batting between them. Baste them together just outside the outline.

3 Machine stitch along the outline using a small straight stitch.
4 Cut out the motif carefully with embroidery scissors. Then work buttonhole stitch around the cut edges by hand.
5 Alternately, work close zigzag stitch over the first line of stitching, then work around the cut edges once more with zigzag stitch to finish them.

The simplest and most familiar kind of quilting, sometimes called padded or English quilting, involves working lines of stitching, either by hand or machine, through two layers of fabric with a layer of padding sandwiched in between. Designs for padded quilting have traditionally been of two main types: repeating patterns, which cover the whole surface, and motifs, which may be used singly or in various combinations. Designs for borders often incorporate elements of both types. Modern designs for quilting, however, can take many other forms, both pictorial and abstract. Quilting can also be used to outline or echo a printed or appliqué motif.

The lines of quilting should be distributed fairly evenly over the area. Dense areas of quilting will flatten the work and cause any adjacent unstitched areas to stand up in relief and assume undue importance.

MATERIALS AND EQUIPMENT
Fabrics for quilting should be soft, light- to medium-weight and closely woven to prevent padding fibers from pushing through to the surface. Those made from natural fibers, such as cotton, wool and silk, are easiest to sew. Solid, light-colored fabrics show off the quilting design to best advantage.

If the underside of the quilting will not be seen, as on a throw pillow, the backing fabric is usually a soft, serviceable cotton such as calico. For a quilt or wallhanging, however, the backing should be of a quality similar to that of the top fabric.

In the past, the padding material, or batting, was usually made of cotton or wool, but today synthetic batting is the usual choice, because it is lightweight, stable and washable. It comes in several thicknesses and widths. Some quilters prefer

cotton batting, which is flatter and denser and thus better suited to traditional, intricate quilting patterns. Pure cotton, however, has a tendency to shift—which may help explain the intricacy of those old designs. A newer type of cotton batting, containing 20 percent polyester, is more stable and is hand-washable.

For hand or machine quilting, use a strong thread. Quilting thread, which is a cotton-wrapped polyester with a lustrous finish, is available from some specialist suppliers. Ordinary poly-cotton thread is also suitable, but should be run over a block of beeswax before use to make it tangle and fray resistant. Use silk twist or pearl cotton to make a special feature of the stitching in hand quilting. Choose a thread one or two shades darker than the fabric.

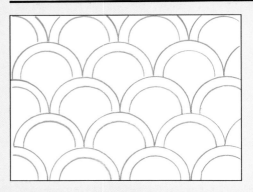

A repeating pattern is the most common type of quilting design. It usually extends over the whole area. Transferring the design is facilitated by using a single pattern.

Traditional motifs are also familiar in padded quilting. They may be used as a single, central motif or repeated around a border. They are usually based on curved lines.

'Echo' quilting around a Hawaiian appliquéed motif takes the form of contour lines following the basic outline of a symmetrical motif based on a cut paper shape.

TRANSFERRING THE DESIGN
The design is normally transferred to the top fabric before the three layers are assembled. Various different methods can be used, including direct tracing, pricking and basting (see pp. 64–65). Transfer pencil and dressmaker's carbon paper are not recommended because they leave a permanent mark which cannot be covered by the stitching.

Two other methods are often used for quilting designs. In one, used mainly for repeating patterns, a pattern is placed on the fabric and its outline traced. Motifs are often transferred by means of a stencil. Both patterns and stencils can be purchased at larger needlework stores. For marking the fabric, use tailor's chalk or a dressmaker's marking pencil, both of which rub off, or a silver-colored pencil especially designed for quilting. This makes an indelible but very faint line.

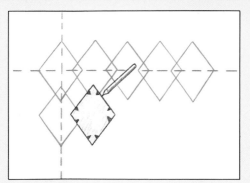

Using a stencil Place the stencil on the fabric and mark through the slits with a quilter's or dressmaker's pencil. The lines of a stencil are necessarily broken; when quilting you simply continue stitching across the breaks where appropriate. The lines of a quilter's pencil are invisible once the quilting is worked.

Using a pattern If you are making your own pattern, cut it from cardboard. Notch the edges as shown if the pattern is composed of overlapping shapes, and use the notches as guides to positioning. Begin tracing at the center of the fabric, which you have first marked with basting, and work outward.

HAND QUILTING

At its best, hand quilting is worked with tiny, even stitches. Like any hand-worked embroidery, it has slight, barely perceptible irregularities that give it a unique charm.

The stitch traditionally used for hand quilting is running stitch. Backstitch can be used instead, if a solid line is preferred, but only in cases where the wrong side of the work will not be visible. Both stitches can be worked either with a vertical, stabbing movement or with a sewing movement. The first method is only possible if the work is mounted on a frame, while the second is easier if the work is not framed.

The use of a frame will help to hold the layers in position. It also enables you to work the very small running stitches even through thick layers. Extra-large quilting frames are available for making quilts.

A quilting design based on the contour lines of a map, worked in backstitch and running stitch

1 Cut the fabrics and batting slightly larger than the finished size, since extra fabric is taken up by the quilting.
2 Transfer the design to the top fabric.
3 Pin the layers together and baste from the center to each corner, leaving long thread ends, as shown, to avoid knots at the center.

4 Now baste concentric straight lines from the center to the edges, placing the lines about 1 in apart. This helps to keep the layers as smooth as possible and prevents excess fabric from bunching up at the center while quilting.

5 Mount the work in the frame if you are using one. If you are using a slate frame, mount the backing fabric first, as shown on page 67, then baste the batting and top fabric to it. If you are using a ring frame, you may need to baste strips of fabric to the edges to allow you to quilt the corners.

6 To begin stitching Knot the thread, bring it up from the wrong side, and tug gently to bring the knot into the batting.

To finish off, knot the thread close to the last stitch, take it into the batting for a short distance, then bring the thread out and cut it; the end will disappear into the batting.

7 Using a single thread, work running stitch along the design lines (ideally 10 per inch). It is important that the stitches are even and that they penetrate all three layers of fabric.
If using a sewing movement, always work toward yourself. Where possible, keep several needles in the work and complete the part of each line that runs toward you before turning the work to stitch in another direction.

Backstitch can be worked for a solid line if preferred (see p. 69). For a thicker line use stem stitch or chain stitch (see p. 70). Other embroidery stitches can be added if appropriate to the design.

91

MACHINE QUILTING

A sewing machine can facilitate padded quilting, especially in simple all-over patterns such as lattice designs. It can also be used effectively, after only a little practice, for working free-hand patterns of wavy lines, which have a spontaneous quality.

The machine produces a solid line similar to backstitch; zigzag stitch is also appropriate for quilting. Some machines can be fitted with a twin needle to produce a double line of stitching. A quilting guide is a useful attachment, since it can ensure that the lines remain parallel.

There are, however, several limitations to machine quilting. The technique is not suitable for complex patterns and motifs which would entail turning the work frequently. Also, the size of the project is limited by the amount of fabric and batting that will fit, rolled up, under the arm

of the machine. And when the center is being quilted, half the work will lie to the right of the needle. So if you wish to work a full-size quilt by machine, you must plan the design in sections that can be quilted separately.

Fabrics suitable for machine quilting are essentially the same as those for hand quilting. For ordinary stitching use quilting or other sewing thread. For a special effect, use embroidery cotton in the bobbin, and work from the wrong side.

It is important to cut the fabric and batting generously to allow for the extra taken up by the quilting. Because the work is not framed, careful and ample basting is particularly important. Always test the stitching on a sample made of the same fabric(s) and batting. You may need to loosen the tension and/or pressure slightly. Use a medium-length stitch (10–12 per in).

A curved lattice pattern can be machine quilted.

1 Transfer the design to the top fabric using a fabric-marking pencil (see p. 65), and a ruler or pattern as appropriate. Only the center lines need be marked if a quilting guide is used.
2 Pin and baste the layers together as for hand quilting (see p. 90), modifying the basting pattern if necessary to avoid the design lines.

3 Begin quilting at the center, since this helps to prevent the batting from slipping to one side or the other. If the design is a grid pattern, work the center line in each direction, as shown.

4 Work following lines from the center out toward one side; use the quilting guide, if you have one, to keep the lines parallel (otherwise, follow the marked lines). Remove the work from the machine and work from the center to the other side. Work the lines in the other direction in the same way.

To start or end a line in the middle of the work, do not reverse to secure the thread as in normal stitching, but leave long thread ends. Make a small knot and take each thread into the batting and out again, then cut it close to the surface.

JOINING BATTING
If you need to join two pieces of batting to make the required width, cut each edge in a notched shape as shown, then fit them together and join them with large running stitches. This prevents excess bulk. Use the same method when hand quilting.

ITALIAN QUILTING

Also known as corded quilting, Italian quilting is a decorative technique in which two layers of fabric are stitched in parallel lines to form channels, which are then filled with yarn or cord. The result is a pattern of raised lines on a flat background.

The top fabric should be a solid color, smooth and closely woven. Unless you are using the shadow technique (see p. 95) it should also be opaque. The bottom layer is a sheer, loosely woven fabric such as muslin or voile, which allows the needle to be brought up and reinserted to take it around curves.

To fill the channels you can use either quilting yarn, a soft, thick yarn made for the purpose, knitting yarn, or piping cord, which gives a firmer effect. (Pre-shrink the cord if the work is to be washed.) Suitable threads are the same as for hand or machine quilting (see pp. 91–92).

The method used to transfer the design depends on whether the stitching is worked from the right or the wrong side. This in turn is determined partly by the choice of stitch. Because the essence of Italian quilting is its linear quality, a solid line of stitching is usually preferred. This can be either hand-worked backstitch or machine straight stitch.

Backstitch must be done from the right side, so the design is transferred to the top fabric. The pricking method (see p. 65) is a good choice if the design is intricate.

If machine stitching is used, the work can be done from either side; transfer the design to the backing fabric by the direct tracing method (see p. 64). The same method can also be used if the design is worked in running stitch.

The intertwined lines of a Celtic motif

1 Transfer the design to the top fabric or the wrong side, as appropriate. Note that where one line goes over another the outline of the lower line must be interrupted.
2 Baste the two fabrics together thoroughly. (If you are working on a frame, two perpendicular lines of basting are adequate.)

3 Work backstitch along the marked lines; or stitch by machine. Where lines are interrupted, end the machine stitching, without reversing, and leave long thread ends for tying later on the wrong side (see opposite).

To work from the wrong side Transfer the design to the backing, then baste the fabrics together. Stitch by machine or by hand, using running stitch. Where one line goes under another, simply take the thread across, as shown.

4 Remove the work from the frame, if used, and remove the basting. Thread the yarn into a large tapestry needle or bodkin and insert the needle into one of the channels from the wrong side, piercing the backing fabric. Slide the needle through the channel, as shown.

On curves, bring the needle up through the backing every inch or so, then reinsert it in the same hole. At corners or sharp curves, leave a small loop of yarn to reduce puckering. Where a line is interrupted, cut the yarn and secure it to the backing with a few stitches.

Work a sample first to determine the best width of channel for the yarn or cord you are using. The yarn should fill the channel well, but not so tightly as to cause puckering around curves.

Running stitch produces a broken line, but if the work is done in a frame, stab stitch can be used for a more solid effect.

When an Italian quilting project is completed, a lining must be added to conceal the wrong side.

TRAPUNTO QUILTING

In essence, trapunto resembles Italian quilting: a design is stitched through two fabrics and sections of the design are then padded. In trapunto quilting, however, shapes rather than lines are filled—usually with stuffing or pieces of batting. The technique is most frequently used for embroidered panels, to give a three-dimensional quality to certain parts of the design. The hard backing of a panel provides a firm support for the padded sections, making them stand out in relief.

Two different fabrics are normally used for trapunto quilting. The top fabric should be soft and closely woven, so that it is pliable but covers the stuffing thoroughly. The backing fabric should be lightweight but firm. If the shapes are small, choose a fabric, such as organdy, the threads of which can be separated for inserting the stuffing. If the backing must be cut, choose a firm, non-fraying cotton.

Polyester stuffing or batting can be used to pad the shapes, and the threads used are the same as for other forms of quilting (see pp. 90–92).

Hand-worked trapunto is best mounted on a frame during both the stitching and stuffing processes. Because the mounted fabric is held taut it is easier to see the effect of the stuffing and thus avoid over-padding the shape. If the backing is stiff, however, you may need to remove the work from the frame before cutting the slits.

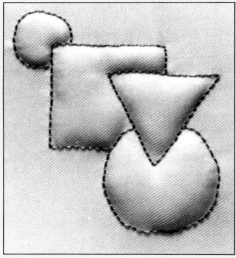

Trapunto shapes are padded with batting.

HAND-WORKED TRAPUNTO

1 Transfer the design to the top fabric by pricking, direct tracing or using a pattern.
2 Baste the top fabric and the backing together as for Italian quilting (see p. 93) and mount the work on a frame.
3 Stitch along the outlines of the motif using backstitch or stab stitch. Backstitch gives the shape a better definition.

4 With the work still framed, turn it wrong side up. Insert the point of a tapestry needle into the backing fabric in the center of the shape and separate the threads. On some fabrics it may be necessary to cut one or more slits in the backing, using sharp embroidery scissors.

5 Insert small pieces of stuffing into the shape, using a knitting needle or large tapestry needle to work them into corners. Take care not to overstuff the shape.
6 If a hole has been made, simply push the threads back together. If a slit has been cut, stitch the edges together. Do not pull the stitches too tightly.

MACHINE-WORKED TRAPUNTO

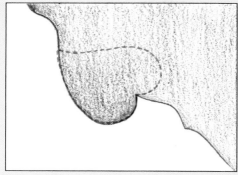

1 Baste the two fabrics together around the edges.
2 Pin the design, which you have first traced on to thin paper, on the top fabric, then baste from the center out to the four corners. If the area is large, a few more lines of basting may be necessary.

3 Machine stitch along the design outlines through all layers, using a short straight stitch. At corners, lift the presser foot, with the needle in the work, turn the fabric, then lower the foot and continue stitching in the new direction.

4 When the stitching is complete, carefully tear away the paper as shown.
5 Open or slit the backing fabric as described in step 4 above.
6 Stuff the motif and close up the hole or slit.

SHADOW QUILTING

Like shadow appliqué (see p. 87), shadow quilting involves the use of two fabrics, the top fabric being sheer. In shadow quilting, however, the design is formed not only by stitching but also by the insertion of other materials between the two fabrics.

Both Italian and trapunto quilting can be adapted to shadow quilting, simply by using colored yarns for the filling. Another shadow quilting technique is to insert a flat motif, usually made of felt, between the two fabrics. The motif is held in place by stitching worked just outside its edges.

For the top fabric choose organdy, organza, voile or a similar sheer fabric. Normally the backing is a firm, closely woven, opaque fabric, either the same color as the top fabric or chosen to match that of the felt or other padding materials.

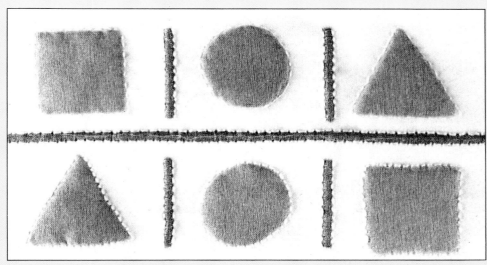

In shadow quilting the flat shapes are stuffed with felt and the lines with lengths of yarn.

TRANSFERRING THE DESIGN

Felt motifs Cut a paper pattern and trace around its edges on to the felt. Cut out the felt shape.
Trapunto and corded motifs Trace the motif(s) on the backing fabric using dressmaker's pencil, dressmaker's carbon or another suitable method (see pp. 64–65).

APPLYING A FELT MOTIF

1 Mount the backing fabric on a frame.
2 Baste the motif to the backing. Make sure that the knot is underneath the backing or you will not be able to remove it later.

3 Place the top fabric over the work and pin it to the backing, aligning the fabric grains. Baste it in place. Two perpendicular lines are usually sufficient, but if the area is large or the top fabric slippery, add lines of diagonal basting.

4 Work around the motif using the chosen stitch. In this example stem stitch is used, but backstitch, stab stitch, chain or another line stitch are alternatives.

If stitching by machine, use the zipper foot, with the foot positioned away from the motif so that you can stitch close to the edge.

Italian and trapunto shadow quilting
Baste the top fabric to the framed backing as in step 3 above. Work the stitching and insert the yarn in one of the ways described on page 93. For trapunto, cut short lengths of yarn rather than one long length and insert them as shown above. Two or more colors of yarn can be combined in a shape for a subtle blend of colors.

In shadow quilting, the yarn must be dark or bright enough to show through the top fabric. For trapunto choose a soft yarn, such as a loosely twisted Icelandic wool.

95

GOLDWORK

Embroidery worked in gold and silver is one of the most highly prized forms of needlework and one of the oldest. There are references to this work in the Bible, and gold threads have been discovered in ancient Egyptian tombs. From early times, metal threads have been used to adorn royal and ecclesiastical vestments, their shimmering, lustrous quality suggesting temporal or divine power.

The costliness, as well as the beauty, of these threads also made them the natural choice for embellishing the court attire of the aristocracy and of other "special occasion" garments for those who could afford such luxury.

Metal thread embroidery is less often seen on modern clothing, except for evening wear, but it is still extensively used on religious vestments, and some of the most valuable examples of twentieth-century metal thread can be seen in churches and synagogues. The subtle effects of the different metal threads are also being imaginatively exploited in panels, wall-hangings and various decorated objects such as boxes, mirror frames and evening bags.

Technically, metal thread embroidery —which is often simply called goldwork since most of it is worked in gold—is a type of surface stitchery, being worked freely on a closely woven fabric. The stitches are, however, almost entirely forms of couching (see p. 71). Most metal threads are either too stiff, too delicate or too expensive to be stitched through the fabric, and thus are couched to the surface with fine silk or other sewing threads. A variety of effects can be created by couching in different patterns, by massing the threads to fill diverse shapes and by padding the work in different ways to accentuate the sheen of the materials.

Gold and silver kidskin may be applied to the fabric to provide smooth areas complementing the lines of couched threads. Small pieces of coiled wire, called purls, can be sewn on to create a range of interesting textures.

THREADS
In the past, gold threads were made of pure gold, which was beaten into paper-thin strips and coiled around a silk thread. The technique was developed in the east, and the thread was known as Japanese gold. Today, real Japanese gold is no longer available, but a good substitute has been developed which, like the original, is smooth, lustrous and non-tarnishing. Substitute Japanese gold comes in several thicknesses. A silver thread is also made.

Many other metal threads can be used for this work. Some contain a small percentage of gold or silver while others, such as lurex threads, are entirely synthetic. The advantage of lurex is that it is non-tarnishing (most real metal thread will tarnish a little in time), but it is less attractive in color and texture than real metal threads.

Most metal threads, both real and synthetic, have a twisted structure, which gives them a "crinkled" appearance, in contrast to the smooth sheen of substitute Japanese gold. In some of the thinner threads, the fineness of the twist produces a matte finish. The finest thread, called tambour, can be stitched through the fabric. At the other extreme are the heavy cords and braids. These are less easy to maneuver than the fine threads, but are useful for bold lines and outlining shapes.

Plate is a bright, flat strip of metal that is usually applied in zigzag patterns.

Purls are coiled metal wires that come in several forms and thicknesses; they are usually cut into short lengths and sewn on like beads. Smooth purl has a shiny finish and rough purl a matte finish. Also available are check purl, which has a crinkly texture, and purl purl, with a beaded appearance.

A limited selection of metal threads, cords and braids can be found in the needlework departments of some of the larger stores, while specialist embroidery stores carry a wider range. Some of these will supply, at a small cost, sample cards of metal threads from which the required varieties can be selected, then ordered by mail.

Although the metal threads currently available are less expensive than pure Japanese gold, they do cost rather more than wool, cotton or even silk threads. Treat them with care; store them in a plastic or fabric-lined sewing box or wrap them in acid-free tissue and keep them in a cardboard box. Avoid overhandling the threads when working. A selection of metal threads is illustrated on page 15.

For couching the metal threads use fine silk sewing thread in gold or silver-gray.

FABRICS AND EQUIPMENT
The only general requirement of the fabric for goldwork is that it should be firmly woven and unpatterned. It can be a lustrous fabric such as Thai silk or satin, or a matte-finish one such as fine linen. Many upholstery fabrics, both natural and synthetic, are well suited to this work, since they tend to be strong and are often available in a good choice of colors. Those with a slubbed texture make an attractive background for goldwork.

Most fabrics need to be backed to prevent them from puckering under the weight of the work. A medium-weight fabric such as calico is generally suitable.

Gold and silver kidskin are often used for appliqué within a design. Woven gold or silver fabrics can also be applied; these are usually backed with iron-on interfacing (see p. 83) and applied in the same way as the kidskin, over padding.

Felt is required for the padding itself. If it will be covered by threads, use yellow felt for goldwork and pale gray for silver. Other materials used for padding are cardboard—a thin variety that can be pierced by a needle—and string, about $1/4$in in diameter, in yellow or white.

The needles you will need for goldwork include crewel needles for working the couching stitches, large chenille needles for taking the metal threads to the wrong side, a leather needle for applying kid and fine beading needles for applying purls and beads. You will also need some straight-bladed nail scissors for cutting purls.

Beeswax is needed for strengthening the couching thread. Other useful pieces of equipment are a pair of tweezers for picking up beads and purls, a stiletto for opening large holes in the fabric to take thick cords, a small pair of pliers for pulling threads through, and a thimble.

FRAMES; TRANSFERRING THE DESIGN
A frame is essential for all metal thread work. The embroidery must be kept absolutely taut so that the threads and other materials can be positioned accurately. Also, because the finished work cannot be blocked with water in the usual way, the tautness is vital to avoid any creases. A scroll frame is ideal, because the work can easily be retautened as necessary; on a stretcher frame this is more difficult. A ring frame is suitable only for small pieces; bind the inner ring as shown on page 116 to grip the fabric securely.

Basting is the best method of transferring the design to the fabric (see p. 65) since it does not permanently mark the fabric and thus allows a measure of flexibility in working the embroidery. For basting use a fine thread the same color as the fabric. This will be concealed by the metal threads.

96

COUCHING TECHNIQUES

The basic couching stitch is shown on page 71. Goldwork, however, involves special techniques, both practical and decorative, which are shown here. Practice these using string or another cheap material.

Metal threads are usually applied in a double strand. A smoother effect is produced in this way, and it is easier to fill a space. The ends are left on the surface and taken to the wrong side later. If the couched thread is fine and pliable it can be bent double at the starting point.

The thread used for the couching stitches must be strengthened by running it over a block of beeswax, otherwise it will be frayed and weakened by the metal threads. Solid areas of couching are best worked in a brick pattern, to distribute the couching stitches evenly and attractively.

Clockwise from first leaf: Japanese, check purl; Japanese; Japanese, gold twist; gold braid stalk

Basic method of couching
1 Secure the fine couching thread with two stitches in the backing fabric and bring it to the right side.
2 Lay the two metal threads on the stitching line, leaving ends of about 1in at the starting point. Work couching stitches over both threads, placing the stitches about $\frac{1}{4}$in apart.

If the thread is sufficiently pliable, bend it double and secure the fold with one stitch. Then couch the double threads in the usual way. Take care to make the stitches the right size: they should be neither so tight as to pinch the threads together nor so loose that they slide about.

To take the ends through (called plunging), either thread each one into a chenille needle and take it through (using pliers to pull the needle, if necessary) or thread the needle with a loop of ordinary sewing thread and use the loop to pull the end through. On the wrong side, secure the ends with overcasting or cellophane tape.

To turn a corner First couch the outer thread at the corner with a diagonal stitch, then couch the inner thread in the same way. Turn the threads in the new direction and continue couching over both threads as before.

To reverse the direction Couch the threads individually at the turning point, as for a corner. Couch them together close to the turning point to prevent a bulge.

When couching next to previously couched threads, bring the needle up on the outside and take it down between the pairs of threads.

To turn an acute corner when filling a shape
1 Take the outer thread around the corner as shown. Cut the inner thread and take it down just inside the point; restart it and continue couching the paired threads.
2 Work inward from opposite sides of the shape, dovetailing the ends, until the shape is filled.

OR NUÉ

Also known as Italian shading, *or nué* is a method of producing a design by working some of the couching stitches close together, using one or more contrasting colors.

1 Begin by drawing the design on the fabric, using colored pencils, or oil paint and a fine brush.

2 Couch the background (unshaded) areas with matching thread, spacing the stitches as usual. For the shaded areas use silk thread in the chosen color (or colors), placing the stitches close together. By varying the spaces between the stitches you can create subtle contrasts between the silk and metal threads.

CORDS, BRAID AND PLATE

Twisted cord Work couching stitches over the cord at an angle, so that the thread slips down between the twists. Place the stitches several twists apart.

Plunge the cord ends by inserting a large chenille needle into the fabric, then threading the ends into the eye and pulling them through.

Russia braid Apply with small stab stitches, working them down the center as shown.

Use a stiletto to make a large hole for plunging the ends, and take them through with a loop of thread as shown on page 97.

Plate Couch one end of the plate, then fold the strip back over the stitch at a slight downward angle. Work another stitch over the plate and fold it back as shown. Continue in the same way for the desired length. Fold under the end and secure it with the last couching stitch.

PURLS AND BEADS

Purls can be used in many ways to create interesting patterns and textures. They are normally cut into short pieces, about $3/8$ in long or less, then threaded on a beading needle and sewn onto the fabric. A rich, ropelike effect can be produced by sewing pieces of purl closely over string, as shown on page 99.

Purl purl is the most versatile type, since it can be applied in longer lines with couching stitches as well as being sewn on with a beading needle.

Beads provide a textural contrast in goldwork, as in other forms of embroidery. They are available in many different colors, shapes and sizes.

When cutting purls, and for holding both purls and beads in readiness, use a box lid lined with felt to stop the purls from springing about.

To couch purl purl Pull the purl gently to separate the coils slightly. (For a "corkscrew" effect, pull the coils farther apart.) Lay the purl on the stitching line and couch it down with matching thread, pulling the thread so that it slips between the coils and the ends remain on the surface.

To sew purls First cut the purls into short lengths with straight-bladed scissors. Sew them to the fabric with a beading needle and fine thread, picking them up with the point of the needle.

Sew on beads in the same way. Sequins can be sewn on with a bead in the center, as shown, to avoid having to make a stitch on the surface of the sequin.

A variety of metal thread embroidery techniques is shown in the photograph on the right. Clockwise from top left: *or nué*; purl purl; couching over cardboard; gold plate; beads and sequins; metal purls; couching over string; gold kidskin.

PADDING

The use of padding enhances the effects of metal threads and other materials by creating contrasts of light and shadow. This is especially noticeable when the embroidery moves, as it would do on a religious vestment, for example, since the work catches the light at different angles.

Felt, string and cardboard are the usual materials for padding. Layers of felt are sewn to the fabric as described on page 89. This rounded surface can either be used as a base for appliqué in the form of gold or silver kidskin or a metallic fabric, or as a base for couched threads or purls.

String is applied to the fabric in lines, and threads are then couched over it at a right angle, covering it completely. The string can be dyed yellow to ensure that it is inconspicuous. Cardboard can also be painted yellow to prevent a white surface from showing through the metal threads.

Applying gold or silver kidskin Baste the piece in place with a few stitches worked over the shape, as shown. Then work stab stitches around the edge, bringing the needle up outside the shape and taking it down into the edge. **Padding with felt** Apply several layers of felt as shown on page 89.

Padding with cardboard Cut pieces of thin cardboard and sew them to the fabric with a few stab stitches.

Fill the area closely with couched threads, working a couching stitch close to each side of the cardboard.

Padding with string

1 Sew the lengths of string to the fabric by working small stitches from alternate sides into the center. Place stitches about $\frac{1}{4}$in apart. Secure the ends with two stitches to prevent unraveling.

2 Couch the threads over the string at right angles to it, working two couching stitches close to each side of the string to hold the couched threads firmly in place.

Sewing purls over string Cut each piece of purl long enough to go over the string at a slight angle. Sew them with fine thread and a beading needle, working diagonally over the string and covering it closely.

99

EYELET AND RICHELIEU CUTWORK

There are two kinds of cutwork: eyelet, which consists of holes cut in the fabric and edged with overcasting, and true cutwork —also called Richelieu work—which consists of embroidered shapes against a background which is cut away.

Cutwork dates from the nineteenth century. The name Richelieu derives from the resemblance of this type of work to a kind of needle-worked lace fashionable in seventeenth-century France and patronized by Cardinal Richelieu. Both types are most frequently used to decorate clothing, especially lingerie, and household linens, and both are traditionally worked on white fabric with white threads. They can, of course, be worked on a colored fabric, but they look most effective worked in a matching thread. In Richelieu work, however, a thread one or two shades darker than the fabric is sometimes used to accentuate the lines of the motifs.

Both eyelet and true cutwork must be worked on a frame in order to prevent any distortion of the fabric during the stitching. Neatness is vital in both these kinds of embroidery; the stitches must not call attention to themselves but must provide a smooth outline for the motifs. Since the underside is visible, the threads must be fastened inconspicuously.

Repeating design for a decorative edge

EYELET EMBROIDERY

Most eyelet designs consist of round or teardrop-shaped holes, often clustered together in stylized floral motifs. If your design is a repeating pattern, the finished, actual-size design need consist only of a single repeat, which you can then move along the fabric when transferring. The direct tracing method (see p.64) is the best choice, since the fine fabric usually allows the design to be seen through it. Shading in the holes on the design helps to make them clear.

The fabric for eyelet should be fairly thin, in keeping with the delicate, lacy effect, and it should be one that does not fray easily. Choose fine threads, such as one or two strands of stranded floss, or a single strand of quilting thread.

Other surface stitches, such as French knots, satin stitch and thin line stitches such as stem, may be used with eyelet.

1 Transfer the design.
2 Mount the fabric in the frame.
3 Fasten the thread on the wrong side with two tiny backstitches, and then work running stitches around the marked outline. Do not fasten off.

4 Cut across the center twice with sharp embroidery scissors, or pierce the fabric with a stiletto.
5 Work overcasting stitches evenly over the running stitches, folding each corner of fabric to the wrong side as you work.
6 Fasten off neatly on the wrong side, then trim off the points of the fabric.

Working a scalloped edging
1 Draw or trace the two lines of the edging on to the fabric. (You can use a coin as a pattern for the scallops.)
2 Work running stitch, first just inside the outlines, and then to fill in the remaining spaces.

3 Work close buttonhole stitch over the running stitches, keeping them vertical throughout.
4 Carefully cut away the fabric just outside the stitching.

RICHELIEU WORK

Designs for Richelieu work must be carefully planned to achieve a pleasing and workable balance between the solid, stitched areas and the cut-out areas. Shade in the areas that will be cut away, in case the design needs to be modified in some way—by enlarging or reducing some of the shapes, or repositioning them slightly so that they link up at one or more points.

Where a space larger than about half a square inch will be left, work one or more buttonhole bars across the space, to unify the work visually and to hold the edges of the motifs in place (see below).

Choose an opaque, medium-weight fabric for Richelieu work; plain-woven linen or cotton is a good choice. Use a slightly thicker thread than for eyelet, such as no. 8 pearl cotton or matte embroidery cotton.

Stylized floral design for cutwork, incorporating branched buttonhole bars and picots

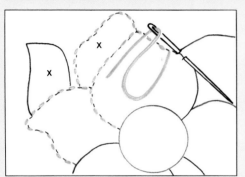

1 Shade the cut-out areas of the final design.
2 Transfer the design to the fabric by pricking or another suitable method (see pp. 64–65). Mark with an X each area that will be cut out.
3 Mount the work in a frame.
4 Work running stitches around the outlines of the areas to be stitched, taking care to work just inside the shapes, not in the marked background areas.

Buttonhole bars When you reach a bar line, take the thread straight across to the opposite edge and make a small stitch. Repeat this twice, so that three strands lie between the shapes.

Work buttonhole stitch over the strands, working back to the first edge.

Branched buttonhole bars These are used to join three edges where necessary. Work as for buttonhole bars until you reach the position for a branch. Then lay three strands across to the edge of the motif as shown and work buttonhole stitch back to the first bar. Continue stitching back to the original edge.

Picots To decorate a bar with a picot, work as above until you reach the center of the bar. Then insert a pin through the fabric as shown. Loop the thread under the pin, over the strands, then under the loop as shown. Remove the pin and pull the thread tight. Continue the buttonhole stitch.

5 Continue working around the design until all outlining and bars are completed.
6 Work buttonhole stitch closely around all the edges, taking care to place the solid edge of the stitching next to the area to be cut away. Where a line crosses a solid area, the stitches can lie either way.

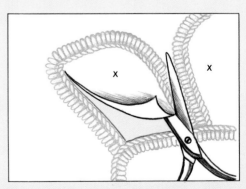

7 When all the stitching is complete, carefully cut out the background areas with sharp embroidery scissors, cutting as close as possible to the stitches. You may find it easier to remove the work from the frame before cutting.

Collectively, cross-stitch embroidery, blackwork, pulled and drawn thread work are known as "counted thread" techniques because each stitch is worked over a definite number of fabric threads. The resulting work is regular and somewhat angular.

Cross stitch is both popular and familiar. The stitch is identical to the one used in needlepoint and is used in the traditional embroideries of many countries. In the nineteenth century it was extensively used in the samplers worked by young girls.

Because of its versatility, cross stitch can be used for both lines and fillings and also lends itself to abstract geometric patterns, especially in border designs. In Assisi work, a limited color range is used. In this, the backgrounds rather than the motifs are stitched, so that the plain areas form the pattern.

FABRICS AND THREADS

The fabric normally used for cross stitch is evenweave, so-called because it contains the same number of warp (lengthwise) and weft (crosswise) threads over a given measurement. Most evenweave is made of cotton or linen, but it comes in a wide range of textures. The coarsest has 12 or 14 threads per inch, the finest 32 or even 34. Since cross stitch is normally worked over two threads, the fabric's fineness determines the stitch size. However, stitches can be worked over one, three or four threads if preferred.

On some evenweave fabrics, groups of threads form the weave, and the embroidery is worked over one or more thread intersections. Hardanger cloth is woven with double threads, while Aida cloth is woven with several groups of threads to form a basketweave pattern.

Evenweave fabric can be bought from specialist stores, but the color range is limited. Some common-weave dress and upholstery fabrics can be used, if the number of warp and weft threads per inch is equal. On closely woven fabrics and those with an irregular weave, cross stitches can be worked over a canvas grid as shown opposite.

Choose a stitching thread of roughly the same thickness as the fabric threads, so that the embroidery covers the fabric well but not solidly. Cotton threads are most often used for cross stitch, but Persian and crewel yarn, linen threads, crochet cottons and silk twists are also suitable.

A tapestry needle is best for cross-stitch embroidery because it does not split the threads. The only exception is in working over canvas, when a crewel or chenille needle may be used.

CHARTS FOR CROSS STITCH

Designs for cross-stitch embroidery are normally presented in the form of a box chart. In this type of chart (which is also used for needlepoint designs worked in cross or tent stitch), each square of the chart corresponds to a single stitch. Instructions for charting an original cross-stitch design are given on page 29. (The other type of chart—a line chart—is explained and illustrated on the same page.)

Most published cross-stitch designs using charts specify the finished size of the work, the weight of the fabric, and the number of threads crossed by each stitch. If any of this information is not included, or if you wish to alter the scale or the size of the finished work, you can easily determine your own specifications as follows.

First count the number of squares on the

chart, vertically and horizontally. Next, decide on the finished size of the work, then divide the number of squares by the chosen measurements in inches. (It is best to use inches for these calculations because of the inch-based classification of fabrics.) This will give you the number of stitches per inch. Finally, multiply by two (the usual number of threads worked over) to determine the weight and weave of fabric you should buy.

For example, if the chart contains 100 squares in each direction and you wish the embroidery to measure 10 inches square, there will be 10 stitches per inch. If the stitches are worked over two threads, a 20-thread fabric should be used. Or you could use a 30-thread fabric and work the stitches over three threads—there would still be 10 stitches to the inch.

When working from a chart, first mark

the center of the fabric with two intersecting lines of basting (see p. 64). Begin working at the center of the design, as shown below, unless the instructions specify another method of positioning the work.

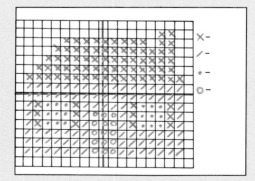

On this box chart the colors are specified by means of symbols, identified in a key. In other types of chart the squares are filled in with the chosen colors as appropriate (see p. 29).

Here the center of the motif is marked with two perpendicular lines.

Begin work at the center of the design (or where instructed), leaving a short length of thread on the right side. After working a few stitches, pull this end to the wrong side, thread it into a needle, and secure it with one or two backstitches in the underside of the stitches worked.

The use of a frame (see pp. 66–67) is recommended for cross-stitch embroidery, since it makes the threads easier to count and helps maintain the work at an even tension.

102

CROSS STITCH

To work a single stitch Work over two intersections, from lower right to upper left, then from lower left to upper right.
To work in rows Work the first "leg" of every stitch, then work back across them. This insures that all stitches slant in the same direction.

To work over canvas Choose a gauge of canvas (see p. 124) that will produce a stitch of the desired size. (Do not use interlock.)
1 Baste the canvas to the right side of the fabric, making sure the grain lies straight.
2 Work the cross stitches through canvas and fabric, using a crewel or chenille needle.

3 Remove the basting. Saturate a towel in hand-hot water and place it over the work for a few minutes to dampen it thoroughly.
4 Pull out the canvas threads one by one. If the embroidered area is large, cut the canvas between motifs to make this task easier.

ASSISI WORK

True to its name, Assisi work originated in the Italian town of Assisi, birthplace of St. Francis. But its antique appearance is deceptive: this type of cross stitch is an early twentieth-century invention.

Assisi work uses both cross stitch and double running, or Holbein, stitch. Double running stitch, used also in blackwork, resembles backstitch but is reversible, that is, the right and wrong sides are identical. In Assisi work it is used to outline the motifs, for borders and for details. Cross stitch is used for the background areas. The motifs themselves contain little, if any, stitching, as the photograph shows.

White or cream evenweave fabric is traditionally used for Assisi work, with bright red or blue for backgrounds and black for the lines. However, any other color scheme can be chosen.

An Assisi design outlined in double running stitch with the motif left blank

Double running stitch
1 Work a line of running stitches (see p. 69), working each over the same number of fabric threads.
2 Work another line of running stitches, filling the spaces left in the first line and taking care to work into the same holes.

To work an Assisi design
1 Begin by stitching the outlines and any details in double running stitch.

2 Work the cross-stitch backgrounds in rows, working in two stages as shown.
3 Add individual cross stitches as required for the design.

103

Probably of Spanish origin—and certainly evocative of the Moorish civilization that flourished in Spain in the Middle Ages—blackwork first became popular in sixteenth-century England. At that time, its intricate patterns of black thread on white linen, sometimes embellished with gold threads, adorned sleeves, bodices, collars, cuffs, nightcaps and bed linen.

Today blackwork is enjoying a revival. It is used as abstract bands or blocks of pattern on table linens, but more often occurs in stylized pictorial work on panels and wallhangings.

The enormous variety of blackwork designs provides considerable scope for choosing a suitable pattern, either to suggest the texture of an object or simply to provide interesting tonal contrast. The patterns shown below provide some idea of the range. Many can be varied even further by subtracting part of the pattern, by adding new elements or by altering the thickness of the thread used.

Several different stitches are used to form blackwork patterns. They include double running, or Holbein, stitch; backstitch; cross stitch and Algerian eye. Although the patterns themselves are angular, they can be—and often are—used to fill curved shapes, which are then outlined with a line stitch. For such lines, double running or backstitch are the usual choices, but stem, chain or couching may be chosen for a thicker, more flowing line. Other surface stitchery is sometimes added to contrast with or complement the blackwork patterns.

Make a sampler of blackwork patterns, including your own adaptations or original designs, and keep the sampler for reference when designing.

FABRICS AND THREADS

Evenweave linen or cotton (see p. 102) in white or cream is the usual choice for blackwork. It may be coarse or fine, but the fabric's weight will usually govern the density of a given pattern. Fabric with 22 to 26 threads per inch is the most suitable.

Make sure your selected fabric is opaque enough that the threads do not show through from the wrong side. With dense patterns this is rarely a problem, but on an open pattern any "shadowing" will spoil the effect of clear areas.

Choose a smooth-textured thread to retain the crisp lines of blackwork patterns. Match the thickness of the sewing thread to the fabric threads, but remember that interesting effects can be created by working the same pattern in two or three threads of different thicknesses.

Use a tapestry needle of a suitable size.

BLACKWORK PATTERNS

Blackwork patterns can successfully depict a pictorial design motif as shown here. A combination of patterns from the opposite page is used to suggest the texture of the different fruit, and the same pattern is sometimes worked in varying densities by adding or removing elements of it. A thicker thread is occasionally used for details such as the ends of the bananas. All the outlines are worked in double running stitch.

BLACKWORK STITCHES

Two of the stitches often used in black-work—double running and cross stitch—are shown on pages 102 and 103. Cross stitch is sometimes varied by working a vertical stitch over it, as for Smyrna stitch in needlepoint (see p. 131).

Backstitch is the most commonly used blackwork stitch. Work it as for surface stitchery (see p. 69) but over a specific number of threads—the number varies with, or within, a pattern. Algerian eye, which forms an eight-pointed star on the fabric, is another stitch used in some blackwork patterns.

As a rule, stitches should be worked over an even, rather than an odd, number of threads, to place one stitch perpendicular to another. The number of threads must be even so that the perpendicular stitch can be centered accurately.

SEQUENCE OF STITCHING

Blackwork patterns are normally presented without specific instructions for working them. It is up to the embroiderer to devise a logical, systematic method of working—one that involves a minimum of back-tracking and avoids taking the thread long distances across the back of the work.

Dense patterns are usually worked in rows, with the outlines or framework completed before the smaller elements. Open patterns may entail starting a new thread and fastening off for each motif, in which case start as for cross-stitch embroidery (see pp. 102–103). Before beginning to work a particular pattern, study it to identify its component parts, then practice it, revising your working if necessary.

Shown right is a pattern composed of backstitch and Algerian eye; it is explained in five stages to demonstrate how a particular pattern is constructed.

Backstitch To work in a straight line, take the needle back over, then forward under, the same number of threads.

To work around corners, simply follow the line of the pattern, working over and under the correct number of threads as indicated by the pattern.

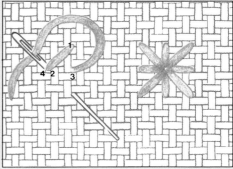

Algerian eye Bring the needle up at one corner of the eyelet (or where convenient, according to the pattern) and take it down in the center. Continue in a clockwise direction, working seven more stitches into the same hole. The stitch is usually worked over four fabric threads, as shown.

1 Work the main shape in backstitch, taking the needle over two threads (or thread intersections) each time.
2 Work an Algerian eye stitch in the center of the shape.
3 Work a vertical cross stitch over four threads to the left of the motif.

Repeat steps 1–3 as often as required to complete the row.
4 Work a vertical cross stitch over four threads below the last motif at left.
5 Work four diagonal stitches clockwise over the four threads between the motifs.
Repeat these two rows to form the pattern.

In this openwork embroidery technique some of the weft or warp threads are withdrawn from the fabric. Stitches are worked over the remaining threads in the drawn area to form lacy, decorative bands or borders. There are two basic kinds of drawn thread work, hemstitching and needleweaving. In hemstitching the stitches are worked along the edges of the drawn area, which holds the remaining threads in place and groups them so that they form patterns. Sometimes additional grouping stitches are worked across the middle of the threads. Frequently, the hemstitching is also worked through the turned edge of a hem, hence the name.

Needleweaving is a method of strengthening the threads that remain in the drawn area by taking a thread around and through them to group them in a pattern. Besides being a traditional form of embroidery, needleweaving also lends itself to free designs, and is used extensively in modern decorative work.

Hemstitching is used mainly for household linen, and in its simplest form is an excellent way of making hems on tablecloths, napkins and place mats. The more elaborate patterns can be used as bands of decoration, either singly or in various combinations. They work especially well on delicate articles of clothing, such as lingerie, blouses and christening gowns, but can also be employed more boldly.

Always remember that withdrawing threads weakens the fabric. A single line of hemstitching is reasonably sturdy, but several bands of lacy hemstitch patterns should not be used on an article that will have much machine washing. Needleweaving is stronger, but all drawn thread work should be handled with care.

FABRICS AND THREADS

In theory, drawn thread work can be carried out on any fabric from which threads can be withdrawn easily, but in practice certain restrictions usually apply. For table or bed linens, evenweave linen or cotton, available in needlework stores, is the best choice. Its smooth texture does not compete with the subtle patterns of the stitches.

Fabrics with a loose weave are the easiest to work on. The finer the weave, the more difficult the work.

For hemstitching, use a thread that matches the fabric in color and weight. A cotton embroidery thread, such as pearl cotton, coton à broder or stranded floss is the usual choice. For needleweaving (see p. 109) the choice is wider.

Always use a tapestry needle for drawn thread work to avoid splitting the threads.

BASIC HEMSTITCH

This simple stitch is the foundation of most hemstitching patterns. To learn it, practice working it as shown here, without turning up a hem.

The first step in drawn thread work is to decide how many of the remaining threads are to be grouped by each stitch. A single line of hemstitch used to turn a hem is usually worked with only one withdrawn thread, while for a more open, decorative effect, more are removed. In this example, three horizontal threads are withdrawn and three vertical threads grouped with each stitch. This means that the number of vertical threads remaining after the horizontal ones are removed must be a multiple of three.

Preparing the fabric
1 Baste along the upper and lower edges of the area to be worked, taking the needle between the horizontal threads as shown.
2 Baste through the vertical center and across both ends to mark the approximate width.

3 Carefully cut the horizontal threads at the center. Using a tapestry needle, ease them out to the ends, counting the vertical threads to make sure you leave the correct number.
4 Darn the thread ends into the wrong side of the work for about 1in, then trim them.

Working the hemstitching
This is done on the wrong side.
1 Leaving an end of about 4in, work two backstitches to the left of the open area.
2 Work a small stitch over the edge, to the left of the first vertical thread.
3 Slip the needle behind the first three vertical threads, from right to left.

4 Pull the working thread gently to draw the fabric threads together, and work a small vertical stitch from back to front to the right of the group.
Repeat steps 3 and 4 to the end.

To fasten off, take the needle back through a few stitches on the wrong side. Undo the backstitches made at the beginning and fasten this thread in the same way.

TURNING A HEM; MITERING CORNERS

When a hem is incorporated in the hem-stitching, the preparation differs from that for a simple band, as shown opposite. The following instructions are for a hem around all sides of the work. Several threads (nine in this case) are withdrawn. This entails mitering the outer corners and strengthening the inner ones with button-hole stitch. For further reinforcement, additional stitching can be worked at the corners (see p. 108). If only one thread is removed, the ends are threaded into the hem folds as shown below.

Evenweave fabric gives the best results for this kind of work.

Begin by cutting the fabric to the desired size, including an allowance for a double hem. The first turning should be slightly less than the second. For example, for a $\frac{3}{8}$in hem, allow $\frac{3}{4}$in extra all around.

1 Measure to slightly less than the finished depth of the hem along one raw edge and withdraw one thread at this point.
2 Measure to the full depth of the hem and withdraw another thread.

Repeat steps 1 and 2 on the other three sides. These spaces mark the hem fold lines.

3 Count the number of threads between the two fold lines and add one to the number. Measure this number of threads from the inner fold line and baste at this point. For example, if there are 10 threads between the fold lines, baste between the 11th and 12th threads. Baste along the inner edge of the border.

4 Cut the horizontal threads between the two lines of basting. Withdraw the threads as far as the corner.
5 Fold the threads back as shown. Using matching sewing thread, backstitch them in place close to the corner edge. Trim the ends close to the stitching. Remove basting.

6 Mark a diagonal line where the inner fold lines meet, as shown, then mark another line parallel to the first, through the outer fold lines. (You can use a ruler to insure straight lines.) Cut along the outer line.

7 Turn in and press the fabric along the remaining fold line. Fold the side edges twice along the two fold lines to form a mitered corner. Baste the hem in place.
8 Join the diagonal edges of the miter with tiny overcasting stitches.

9 Reinforce the corners with buttonhole stitch, using the embroidery thread and working through the folded edge of the hem.

If only one or two threads are withdrawn, this is done after the hem is turned, and the thread ends are simply darned into the hem as shown.

10 Work hemstitching along the outer edge of the drawn threads up to the corners, catching in the hem fold with each stitch.
11 Work hemstitching along the inner edge. At the corners, take the thread around the last and first group of threads on each side before working the vertical stitch.
Hemstitched edges (right), with buttonholing and dove's eye filling in the open corner

107

FILLING A CORNER

To strengthen an open corner, work button-holing and hemstitching as usual, then work a dove's eye filling.

1 Fasten the thread in the lower left-hand corner (right side facing) and take it across to the upper right-hand corner.

2 Overcast the thread back to the lower left-hand corner.

3 Take the needle under the buttonhole stitches to the upper left-hand corner and diagonally down to the lower right.

4 Overcast the thread as far as the point where the two threads cross.

5 Weave the needle under and over the four threads, as shown, to form a circular motif.

6 When the circle is the desired size, overcast the remaining length of the second thread. Fasten off on the wrong side.

HEMSTITCHING VARIATIONS

Serpentine or zigzag hemstitch Work hemstitch along each edge of the open area in turn, grouping an even number of threads with each stitch. Work one side, then turn and work the other, grouping half the number of threads with the first stitch, then half from each of the two adjacent groups.

Double hemstitch Withdraw four threads of the fabric, then leave four and withdraw another four. Work over the center strip of fabric from right to left, as shown, grouping upper and lower threads alternately.

Interlaced hemstitch Withdraw horizontal threads for about $\frac{1}{2}$in and hemstitch both edges. Fasten the thread under the right-hand end. Take the needle under the second group of threads from left to right, then under the first group from right to left, thus twisting them, as shown. Repeat to the end.

Knotted groups Withdraw threads for about $\frac{1}{2}$in and hemstitch both edges. Fasten the thread under the right-hand end, then loop it as shown and take the needle under the first three groups of threads and over the loop. Pull the thread taut, forming a knot around the first three groups. Repeat to the end.

From left to right: knotted, interlaced, double and zigzag hemstitch

108

NEEDLEWEAVING

The two basic stitches or techniques involved in needleweaving are oversewing and darning. In oversewing, the groups of threads are wrapped to form bars, while darning weaves over and under groups of threads, to form a braid effect. They can be combined in various ways, both with each other and with hemstitching—although this is normally done only where the needleweaving is worked over the middle of the threads only.

Needleweaving can be worked either in regular patterns, or freely. Open areas of needleweaving can be worked in a plain fabric which is then placed over another layer of embroidery to suggest, for example, tree trunks and branches in the foreground of a landscape. For such decorative needleweaving you can use all kinds of fabric and threads.

Free needleweaving is often a feature in modern decorative work

Oversewing Lay the end of the working thread along the threads to be grouped (here four are shown). Take the needle under the threads from right to left, then over and under again, holding the end in place. Continue in this way, pushing the threads smoothly together. To fasten off, take the needle through the work.

Zigzag oversewing Work over a multiple of three vertical threads. Oversew a group of three as shown. At the bottom, work twice over six threads to bring the first and second groups together. Then work upward over the second group, joining it to the next group of three at the top. Repeat to the end.

Darning Lay the end of the working thread along the threads to be woven (usually an even number and a minimum of four). Take the needle under the first group of threads (two) from right to left and over the other group and the thread end. Take it under the second group and over the first.

Repeat these two movements, working over and under the threads alternately, and gently pushing the weaving thread into place with the needle until the fabric threads are smoothly covered. Fasten off as for oversewing.

Darning variations are formed by working over adjacent groups in various patterns. The joined groups can be split and oversewn individually. Darning can also be worked over three or more groups. The possible combinations are almost unlimited.

For practicing needleweaving, use a fairly coarse fabric and Persian yarn or matte embroidery cotton.

Although darning is slightly more complicated than oversewing, it is easier to learn, since the thread stays in place more readily. Practice darning, then move on to oversewing and combinations of the two.

109

In pulled work, lacy patterns are formed by pulling the embroidery stitches tightly, thus displacing the fabric threads by drawing some close together and separating others. Unlike drawn thread work, no threads are actually withdrawn, which makes the work stronger by comparison.

Pulled work, also known as pulled thread work and drawn fabric, is like drawn thread work in being a counted thread technique, and is normally worked on evenweave fabric. In both types of embroidery it is the texture and patterns created by the stitches, not the stitches themselves, that are the attraction. They are thus best worked in a thread that matches the fabric. Sometimes you can unravel threads from the edge of the fabric and use them for stitching.

Traditionally, white or cream are used for pulled work. To introduce a contrasting color, and display the patterns to advantage, use a neutral color for the work itself, then line it with a fabric of a medium to dark shade. Deep rose might be used under cream, for example, or violet beneath pale gray.

As in the past, pulled work is used today on household linens. In modern embroidery it is also used on pillow covers, lampshades, window shades, screens and other household accessories. Its potential as a medium for purely decorative work is only beginning to be exploited.

Most examples of pulled work are stitched precisely, over carefully counted threads. However, it is possible to work many of the stitches freely and randomly, creating more modern effects. Pulled work is a counted thread technique that can be enjoyed by those who dislike the laborious business of counting threads.

FABRICS AND THREADS

Any fabric used for pulled work must be of an even weave (see p. 102), and loosely woven. Evenweave fabric in linen or cotton, specially made for counted thread work, can be obtained from embroidery stores. Linen scrim (a coarser, more open form of evenweave) and burlap are suitable for some work. Certain sheer fabrics also lend themselves to pulled work.

Threads used for pulled work must be strong enough to withstand the tension applied to them. As a rule, choose thread of about the same thickness as the fabric threads. Button thread, buttonhole twist, coton à broder, pearl cotton, crochet cottons, and threads used for lace making are all suitable.

Use a tapestry needle for the embroidery, to avoid splitting the fabric threads. A large size needle will facilitate the work.

BASIC METHODS

Always use a frame for pulled work; this will help you count the threads and maintain an even tension.

Some pulled work designs are given as line charts (see p. 29), others in diagram form, with the position of each area of stitching indicated in relation to the edge and/or center. In both cases, mark the center of the fabric with two perpendicular lines of basting and work the embroidery outward from the center. If the design is asymmetrical, scale it up (see p. 21), trace it, and baste the outlines of the stitching through tracing and fabric as shown on page 65. Practice the stitches first on spare fabric.

For the sake of clarity, the stitch diagrams given here show the stitches as they would be if worked untensioned. In most cases, however, the thread is pulled.

To begin stitching Work a few running stitches toward the starting point along the line to be covered. Then either work one backstitch to secure the thread or anchor it with a knot a short distance away and darn the end in later. When ending a thread, darn it into the wrong side of the work.

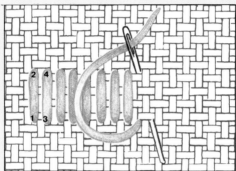

Satin stitch in rows Work vertical stitches over three or more fabric threads, pulling the thread tightly or, for a contrasting texture, leaving the stitches untensioned. Interesting effects can be achieved by random variations in tension within the row.

Chessboard filling This consists of rows of satin stitch arranged in blocks and worked in alternating directions. Each block consists of three rows of 10 stitches each, all worked over three fabric threads. Work the blocks in rows as indicated by the arrows.

Satin stitch blocks This consists of groups of diagonal stitches worked in a square over any number of threads; here it is five. When the stitches are pulled tightly, a diamond shape results. A group of four, worked in alternate directions, forms a star motif, as shown inset.

The pulled thread stitches shown in this sampler include (top to bottom): rows of satin stitch with the tension varied randomly to produce irregular lines; satin stitch blocks going in the same direction; four-block motif in satin stitch (center); freely-worked eyelets.

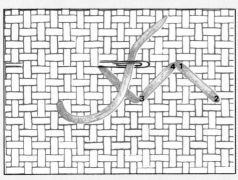

Square eyelets There are several types of eyelet. This type is worked over an even number of threads, with the needle taken down into the center each time. A medium or tight tension can be used, depending on the desired size of the central hole.

Free eyelets The basic method of working a square eyelet can be varied by placing the hole off-center, by working over a rectangular area, by varying the tension, and by working only part of the eyelet, so that it seems to emerge from the background. Groups of such irregular eyelets form an interesting "organic" texture.

Zigzag backstitch This simple stitch makes a subtle pattern for a border. Work backstitch in a zigzag pattern as shown, over the same number of threads each time; here it is three. Pull the stitches tightly.

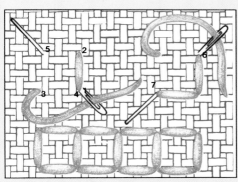

Wave stitch This is essentially zigzag back-stitch, worked to fill a space. Work from top to bottom in rows, back and forth, working over two, three or four vertical and horizontal threads. Pull the stitches tightly.

Triangle stitch This subtle diagonal pattern is created by backstitches worked over two sides of a square. Each stitch is worked over two threads and pulled tightly. Work in diagonal rows from upper left to lower right.

Four-sided stitch This makes an attractive border and can also be worked in rows to fill an area. Each stitch is composed of four back-stitches, worked in the order shown, over any number of threads, and pulled tightly.

111

As practical as it is pretty, smocking is a decorative method of gathering fullness in fabric. In the past it was traditionally used at the necklines and cuffs of men's shirts and women's chemises as well as on the bodices of farm workers' smocks. Clothes for babies and young children are often decorated with smocking, and it can also be used to good effect on lingerie and women's casual clothes.

The appealing textures and stitch patterns of smocking lend themselves to use on home furnishings, such as throw pillows and curtain headings. Modern embroiderers have also been developing the technique in new ways, for use in panels and soft sculpture.

There are two basic methods of smocking. In the traditional "English" method, the fabric is first gathered into even folds, called tubes or reeds, and the embroidery stitches are worked over the folds or pleats. In the direct method, used widely in North America, the smocking stitches are worked on ungathered fabric; the stitches themselves gather up the fabric.

Whether you are using the traditional or the direct method of smocking, you will usually need to mark the fabric with a grid of dots. These will serve as a guide when working the gathering, in the traditional method, or the smocking stitches in the direct method. Smocking pleater machines are now available, which gather the material automatically. They are expensive, however, and probably only worth the investment if you do a lot of smocking.

The finished effect is the same in both methods. A piece of smocking normally includes a variety of stitches, the contrasting patterns of which contribute to the charm of the work. The stitches vary in their elasticity: firm stitches such as cable and outline are often used together with the more elastic ones such as honeycomb, to give the work stability. Some other surface embroidery stitches, including chain, feather and herringbone, can also be used for smocking, while French knots, bullion knots, detached chain and other individual stitches can be added once the main stitching is complete.

To emphasize the stitches, work them in one or more colors contrasting with the fabric. To emphasize the texture of the work, use thread to match the fabric.

FABRICS AND THREADS

The easiest fabrics on which to work smocking are soft, smooth, light- to medium-weight, and woven from natural fibers or from a blend of natural and synthetic. Wholly synthetic fabrics tend to be springy and difficult to gather evenly.

Although smocking is usually worked on solid fabric, interesting effects can be achieved with small prints. When gathered, the print takes on a quite different appearance, so that the gathered area contrasts effectively with the smooth one. Regular patterns such as polka dots, checks and stripes can be exploited in various ways (see p. 47). Small polka dots can serve as a ready-made grid for the gathering. Make sure that the dots follow the grain of the fabric; if not, the gathers will lie incorrectly. Checks and stripes can be gathered in various ways to emphasize different elements of the pattern.

Whatever fabric you select, it is a good idea—especially if you are inexperienced—to buy a small amount first and work a sample or two to see how much fabric will be drawn up by the smocking. As a general rule, you will need three times the finished width of the smocking, but this varies with the fabric, the spacing of the gathers and your own working tension.

Unstranded cotton embroidery threads, such as pearl cotton and matte embroidery cotton are all suitable for smocking. On heavy linen or wool, Persian or tapestry yarn might be used, while silk embroidery or buttonhole thread will give added luster to the work. For the gathering, use cotton-wrapped polyester or pure polyester thread.

A crewel or chenille needle is used for the smocking stitches.

MARKING THE GRID

Transfers of smocking dots which are ironed on the fabric are available in notions departments and needlework stores. These are made with a variety of spacings, both vertical and horizontal. The most useful have the dots spaced between $\frac{1}{4}$in and $\frac{3}{8}$in apart; the rows may be the same distance apart, farther apart or closer. If you cannot find a suitable transfer for a project, you can make your own as shown below.

Before transferring the dots to the fabric you must decide how many you will need. Making a sample will show the overall width required, but the exact number of pleats or dots may depend on the stitches you are using; some stitches must be worked over a specific multiple of pleats and some must be centered (see pp. 114–115).

Applying transfer dots Position the transfer inked side down on the wrong side of the fabric (for the traditional method) or the right side (for the direct method). Make sure that the dots follow the grain. Pin the transfer in place at the corners and run a medium-hot iron smoothly over the surface.

Making your own grid Pierce holes in a piece of graph paper at the chosen intervals, using a large chenille needle. Then position the graph paper smooth side down on the appropriate side of the fabric and mark a dot through each hole with a pencil.

Positioning a grid for a curved area of smocking Slash the transfer (or graph paper grid) between the dots up to the top row. Pin it to the fabric, spreading it evenly to fill the area, and mark the dots as before.

TRADITIONAL SMOCKING

The first stage is to gather the fabric into even folds, or pleats. The gathering threads, which are later removed, have a dual purpose: besides holding the folds in place they serve as a guide for keeping the rows of smocking straight. They should thus be worked in a contrasting thread. For the same reason, the gathers should not be pulled up so tightly that the thread cannot be seen from the right side.

When transferring dots to the fabric, transfer one more dot than the required number of pleats; the extra dot completes the last pleat when the gathering is worked. It is a good idea also to transfer an extra row of dots above and below the lines for the smocking. These, which are gathered but not smocked, help to keep the folds even and facilitate working the top and bottom rows of smocking.

Smocking stitches, from the top: outline, cable, double cable, honeycomb, diamond and trellis (wave stitch worked in opposite directions)

Gathering the fabric
1 Thread the needle with a single strand of sewing thread slightly longer than the width to be gathered. Knot the end, then work even running stitches as shown, picking up a few woven fabric threads at each dot. Do not fasten off.

Gathering checked fabric
1 Use one corner of a check as the point to be picked up for each stitch. Take care to pick up this point consistently and accurately on each row.

2 When all the gathering stitches have been worked, pin the right-hand edge to a padded surface and pull up the threads two at a time until the folds lie closely and evenly together. Tie the threads together in pairs.

Working the smocking Fasten the thread on the wrong side with two backstitches and work across the pleats in the chosen pattern (cable stitch is shown here), picking up only a few fabric threads with each stitch. Fasten off with backstitches at the end. (All the stitches illustrated on pages 114–115 are worked from left to right.)

DIRECT SMOCKING

In this method the smocking stitches are worked directly onto the fabric without first gathering it. Because the time-consuming gathering process is omitted, this method is potentially quicker than the traditional one, although a certain amount of practice is required in order to work the stitches evenly.

For direct smocking the dots must be applied to the right side of the fabric. Each dot counts as one pleat or fold in the traditional method, so you should transfer the exact number of dots required for the stitches, without adding an extra one.

The stitches are worked in the same way as in the traditional method, except that each stitch is worked through a dot rather than through the top of a pleat.

The method of working direct smocking is illustrated on the right with honeycomb stitch.

Honeycomb stitch (direct method)
1 Bring the needle up at dot 1, then take it under dot 2 and up again at dot 1. Pull the dots together.
2 Take the needle down at dot 2 and bring it up at dot 3 on the lower line. Join dots 3–4 as in step 1, taking the needle down at 4 and up at 5. Repeat these steps.

SMOCKING STITCHES

Outline stitch Also called stem stitch, this holds the fabric firmly and can be worked over any number of pleats or dots.
1 Bring the needle up to the left of the first pleat.
2 Take it through the second pleat at a slight upward angle with the thread below the needle. Repeat steps 1 and 2.

Cable stitch This is another firm stitch worked over any number of pleats or dots.
   Work as for outline stitch, but keep the thread above the needle for one stitch and below it for the next, continuing to alternate in sequence.

Double cable stitch This is worked over a multiple of four pleats or dots.
   Work as for cable stitch, but work two rows to touch each other, reversing the sequence of thread-above and thread-below so as to form the pattern shown.

Honeycomb stitch This stitch is worked over two rows of gathering (multiple of two pleats or dots).
   Start on the upper row and join pleats 1 and 2 with two backstitches, then take the thread under the work to join 2 and 3 on the lower row. Continue joining pleats alternately on upper and lower rows.

Diamond stitch This stitch forms a pattern over three rows of gathering (multiple of four pleats or dots plus two).
1 Begin on the middle row. Work a backstitch over pleats 1 and 2 with the thread below the needle, and bring the needle out between the pleats.
2 Work a stitch through pleat 3 with the thread below.

3 Work a stitch over pleats 3 and 4 with the thread above, bringing the needle out between the pleats.
4 Work a stitch through pleat 5 with the thread above. Repeat steps 1-4.
   To complete the diamond pattern, work another row, positioning the stitches as shown, inset.

Wave stitch This is worked over two lines of a grid with rows half as far apart as dots (multiple of eight pleats or dots plus two).
1 Starting on the lower line, join pleats 1-2, 2-3, 3-4 and 4-5 with the thread below the needle. Work upward to the upper line as shown, bringing the needle out between pleats.

2 Join pleats 5-6 with the thread above the needle, then work downward, joining 6-7, 7-8 and 8-9 in the same way. Then join 9-10 with the thread below the needle. Continue working up and down across the row.
Trellis stitch is formed by working lines of wave stitch in opposite directions, as shown inset, to form a diamond pattern.

When working large-scale patterns such as wave or trellis stitch, center the pattern carefully. Mark the point between the two center pleats with a thread as shown, and begin stitching here. Work toward the right-hand side, then turn the work upside down and work toward the other side.

114

EXPERIMENTAL SMOCKING

Like many other forms of embroidery, smocking is now being worked in new and imaginative ways. Some of these new approaches have turned smocking into a new textile art. Panels, wallhangings and soft sculpture exploit the textural possibilities of this work. Such embroidery uses stitches much more freely than is possible on clothing. In some cases the stitches are relegated to the wrong side to allow the folds to "speak for themselves." This page gives several ideas to inspire experiments in smocking. For some of these the fabric is prepared as for traditional smocking by working gathers over a grid of dots (see p. 112), but for the random reverse and honeycomb smocking the stitches are worked on the flat fabric, as shown below, to create a texture of interlaced folds on the right side.

Freely worked smocking stitches

Random reverse smocking

Free surface stitchery can be worked in irregular lines across the work. Gather the fabric on the wrong side as usual, then work the chosen embroidery stitches. The one shown here is Cretan stitch (see p. 74). Do not remove the gathering threads.

Back smocking For more random stitchery, as shown above, or for motifs, provide a firm base by working lines of outline stitch (see p. 114) just above or below the gathers on the wrong side, using strong sewing thread. The stitching, or back smocking, can be worked all the way across each row or along only part of a row as shown. Remove the gathers when all the stitching is completed.

Vertical lines of stitchery can be worked on pleats that have been smocked on the wrong side to hold them in place, as shown left. Open chain stitch is shown here; other possibilities include fern stitch, feather stitch and raised chain band.

Sculptural effects can be achieved by first smocking deep pleats on the wrong side, as shown above, then joining them on the right side with a few backstitches. Use matching or contrasting embroidery thread.

Random honeycomb can be worked on flat fabric to produce an interesting texture. Choose a firm, lustrous fabric for a rich effect. Mark dots at random on the right side, making sure each one is reasonably adjacent to another. Then join pairs of adjacent dots with two backstitches, taking the thread under the fabric between pairs of dots.

Random reverse smocking is worked in basically the same way as random honeycomb, but on the wrong side of the fabric. Using a double strand of sewing thread, join two adjacent dots with several small backstitches for firmness, then take the thread to another dot without pulling it up, and fasten it. Continue joining dots in a random fashion. The result as seen from the right side is shown in the photograph above.

115

Some of the most imaginitive of all modern embroidery is stitched by machine. And although automatic patterns can be used in interesting ways, as shown in the photograph, more inventive designs are being created with straight stitch and zigzag alone. The most original work is produced by a technique called free machining, in which the machine is adjusted so that the fabric can be moved in any direction.

A great variety of different effects can be created with free machining. Delicate linear designs similar to fine pen drawing, corded effects, and loopy textures are just some of the possibilities. Others include pulled work (see p. 48), cutwork and appliqué. The most recent developments are in the area of machine-made lace (see p. 121).

The speed of machine embroidery has an obvious appeal for those who like quick results, but it can also have a liberating effect on the embroiderer whose hand work tends to be over-deliberate and "tight". The machine must, of course, be kept under control, or the result will be a mess, but the act of automatic stitching induces a free, spontaneous approach.

Many decorative effects can be produced with ordinary stitching—that is with the foot on the machine rather than without it, as for free machining. It is a good idea to familiarize yourself with these techniques, especially those that involve adjusting the tension or altering the stitch length, before you try free machining.

In machine embroidery, remember that a mixture of too many techniques may spoil the unity of a design. It is always possible to add texture afterward with hand stitchery, which is slow enough to be applied critically. Mistakes in machine embroidery are notoriously difficult to unpick!

A variety of automatic patterns

SEWING MACHINES

Most modern domestic machines can be used for embroidery. The one essential feature, if you are planning to do free machining, is that it must be possible to lower or cover the feed dog, that is, the jagged teeth that move the fabric along in ordinary stitching. Before you buy a machine, always try it out thoroughly.

Even a machine that does only straight stitch can produce many attractive effects, but the zigzag stitch greatly increases the range of possibilities. A multistitch zigzag and a blind-hemming stitch are useful variations. Fancier automatic stitch patterns are an optional extra. If you are buying a new machine, it is not worth spending extra money on these unless you intend to do a lot of this kind of work.

There are some features that are well worth having and, if necessary, paying extra for. One of these is an easily adjusted lower tension. A few machines have a knob-controlled lower tension, which is a great help in working some embroidery techniques; on most, however, the lower tension is controlled by a screw. When trying out a machine, ask the demonstrator to show you how to do this, and make sure that you can do it yourself easily.

A machine with a flat bed—that is, a large surface around the needle—is best for machine embroidery, since it supports the frame evenly. But if you will also be using the machine for dressmaking it is best to buy a free-arm type (ideal for setting in sleeves and other awkward maneuvers) that will convert to a flat bed with the addition of a metal plate.

A machine on which the teeth can be lowered is generally preferable to one on which they are merely covered, since this allows a framed fabric to lie absolutely flat. It is quite possible to do excellent work on the other kind of machine, but moving the frame with one hand, as is sometimes necessary, requires extra-smooth control.

There are several other features you may find useful: a twin needle, which works parallel lines of stitching; a quilting guide bar (see p. 90); and a speed control, which is often helpful when learning to free machine.

Various kinds of foot are available for sewing machines. A clear plastic presser foot is suitable for general work and makes the area immediately surrounding the needle easily visible. A cording foot facilitates couching; one type will thread several cords at once. A darning foot is sometimes useful when doing free machine work.

Always use needles that are in perfect condition—neither blunt nor bent.

CARING FOR THE MACHINE

Many of the problems experienced by beginners in machine embroidery can be traced to lack of practice, plus inadequate understanding of the machine and failure to keep it in good working order.

Make sure you read the instruction booklet thoroughly and familiarize yourself with the various parts and functions of the machine. Many companies offer courses in using their machines, and such courses certainly help you to avoid problems. They may also reveal other interesting ways of using the machine.

It is especially important to keep the machine clean and oiled. Bits of fluff under the throat plate, in the bobbin case or between the tension discs can easily cause a malfunction.

116

THREADS AND NEEDLES

Many different kinds of thread can be used for machine embroidery, even including knitting yarns. Sewing thread—in cotton, cotton-wrapped polyester or pure polyester—gives good results and comes in a wide color range. Cotton is graded by number; the relatively fine size no. 50 is generally most suitable for machine embroidery, although for whip stitch (see p. 120) the heavier size no. 40 may be preferred.

Fine silk sewing thread has a rich luster, but adds considerably to the cost of a project. The same applies to silk buttonhole twist.

Special machine embroidery threads are becoming more widely available. The cotton variety is softer than ordinary sewing cotton and has an attractive sheen. Size no. 30 machine embroidery cotton is roughly equivalent to a size no. 50 sewing cotton; some embroidery shops sell an extra-fine size no. 50.

Rayon and metallic machine embroidery threads are also available. They can be tricky to handle, but with practice can produce excellent effects.

Hand embroidery threads can be used in the machine in many ways. Some of the finer ones can be used in the needle, but medium-thick ones must be used in the bobbin, with the stitching done from the wrong side. Extra-thick, slubbed, and hairy yarns must be machine-couched to the surface.

A relatively large needle is used for most free-machine embroidery. Sizes no. 90 or 100 are suitable for most purposes; size no. 110 for working on heavy fabrics and using thick thread. For work on delicate fabrics with fine thread, choose a size no. 80.

FABRICS

Virtually any fabric can be used for machine embroidery in which the presser foot is used. However, all thin or slippery fabrics tend to pucker when stitched in a single layer (but see Tip, below).

For free machining the choice is rather more critical. Beginners should select firmly woven fabrics such as calico which are easy to frame up and provide a smooth surface for stitching. Smooth dressmaking fabrics such as poplin, gabardine and cotton-wool blends also work well. With experience you can graduate to sheer, silky and textured fabrics.

Although solid-colored fabrics are usually best for machine embroidery, you can create interesting effects with printed fabrics. Or you can dye or paint your own backgrounds (see pp. 30–33) to provide a "structure" for the stitch pattern.

ADJUSTING THE TENSION

For most machine stitching, including embroidery, the tension of the upper and lower threads should be equal, so that the stitches link exactly in the center of the layer(s) of fabric. Some machine embroidery effects require alterations in tension.

On most machines, the upper tension is easily adjusted by turning a dial. By making this tension tighter or looser than the bobbin tension you can bring the lower or upper thread respectively, to the opposite side.

For some effects, such as feather stitch and cable stitch (see p. 120), the bobbin tension must be loosened. On most machines this entails carefully turning a small screw that controls the tension spring on the bobbin case. For a thick thread it may be possible to remove the tension spring or bypass it altogether.

Equal and unequal tensions of upper and lower threads are shown in cross-section.

A removable bobbin case controls tension by means of a spring held in place by a tiny screw. A very slight turn of the screw will alter the tension. For thick thread, both spring and screw can usually be removed.

TRANSFERRING THE DESIGN

Various methods can be used to transfer designs for machine embroidery. If the work is to be done with the presser foot, it may be easiest to mark the stitching lines directly on the fabric. Use tailor's chalk and a ruler for straight lines or paper templates for curved shapes.

If the design is at all complex, dressmaker's carbon, transfer pencil, or the tracing method may be appropriate.

For free machining, it is best to keep any permanent marking to a minimum. The essence of the work is its spontaneous quality, and most of the stitching should be done freehand. It is useful, however, to transfer the main design lines, which will then serve as a guide for the stitching.

Direct tracing with a sharp pencil can be used on sheer or semi-sheer fabrics. Basting is suitable for thicker fabrics, but use the same thread that will be used for the embroidery so that any bits that cannot be removed will blend into the work.

The pricking and pouncing method can also be used (see p. 65). Small motifs can be transferred to the framed fabric with the powder only and then stitched immediately.

Another useful method is to stitch the main lines through paper. This is practical where the design outlines do not extend beyond the diameter of the frame. First mark the main outlines on tissue or thin tracing paper. Mount the fabric in the frame as usual (see pp. 66–67). Baste the design to the fabric, then work free running stitch in the appropriate color(s) along the lines. (Do not use zigzag, or it will be impossible to remove the paper.) When all the main lines have been stitched, carefully tear away the tracing, then work the remaining embroidery.

Machine embroidery, and particularly free machining, consumes a great deal of thread. Whenever possible, buy machine embroidery thread in large spools, for economy.

Back a fine or slippery fabric with a sheer, closely woven fabric such as organza; apply iron-on interfacing to the wrong side; or place a layer of tissue paper beneath the fabric during stitching.

FRAMING THE WORK

The first step in successful machine embroidery, with or without the presser foot, is to make sure the fabric is properly framed. A ring frame is used for all types of machine embroidery. It can be wood or metal, but must have a screw for adjusting the fit, and should be no more than $3/8$in thick, so that it will slide under the needle and presser foot bar. The metal and plastic spring frames (see p. 66) are suitably slim-line, but can be used only for lightweight fabrics which can be pulled taut without ejecting the inner ring. A ring with a diameter of 8in is most useful; larger ones are awkward to use; smaller ones give an inadequate working area.

Whether the frame is made of wood or metal, always bind the inner ring with woven tape or bias binding to provide an extra-firm grip.

To bind the ring Wrap the end of the tape diagonally around it. Continue wrapping, holding the end in place until it is secure and overlapping the edges slightly. When you reach the starting point, cut off the excess. Using strong thread, sew the second end over the first.
To mount the fabric See p. 66.

The fabric should be as taut as a drum, and the grain should run straight in both directions. Slight adjustments can be made by pulling the edges and tightening the screw with a screwdriver, but if the fabric is not straight it may be better to remove it, tighten the screw, and start again.

EMBROIDERY WITH THE PRESSER FOOT

Designs using either straight or curved lines, or both together, are easily worked with the presser foot on the machine. The most effective work uses several lines together, either in regular patterns or freely flowing designs. Ordinary straight stitch is attractive worked in buttonhole twist or another lustrous thread, using a medium-long stitch length.

To turn a corner, work up to the turning point, stop the machine with the needle in the fabric, raise the presser foot, turn the fabric, lower the presser foot and continue stitching. Fairly sharp curves can be turned once you have gained some practice in manipulating the fabric smoothly.

Zigzag stitch can be used for many different effects, some of which are shown. Always practice the stitching first on a scrap of the same fabric.

For a "beaded" line of straight stitch, tighten the upper tension slightly. This brings the bobbin thread to the surface, forming a tiny loop at each stitch.

A zigzag stitch can be adjusted in width and length to produce many different effects. Practice adjusting the stitch with your right hand while feeding in fabric with your left. In some machines the needle position can be altered to angle the stitch or produce a straight edge to one side.

Satin stitch is very close zigzag. On some fabrics a smoother effect can be produced by working the stitch in two stages, with the stitches slightly open. Work the first line slightly narrower than the effect desired, then work a second to the correct width on top.

Couching can also be worked with zigzag. Position the foot (raised) over the starting point and slip the thread or cord under the foot as shown. Lower the foot and work zigzag over the cord. Vary the effect by changing the stitch length to reveal more or less of the cord.

A "wishbone" effect can be produced by tightening the upper tension. This brings the bobbin thread to the surface. Try using buttonhole twist in the needle and a thin, contrasting thread in the bobbin.

118

FREE MACHINE EMBROIDERY

The technique of free machining is like drawing with a needle and thread. But unlike normal drawing, it involves moving the drawing surface rather than the implement. The movements will seem awkward at first, but with practice they will become more natural. As you gain confidence an amazing variety of effects will be created —and at high speed.

Spend plenty of time "doodling" with the machine before you attempt a project. You may well produce some attractive designs in the early stages, but real mastery of the technique requires much practice.

Always make sure that the fabric is correctly framed before you begin. It must be drum-taut, otherwise the machine may miss stitches, the thread may break and the work will be puckered beyond repair when the frame is removed.

"Drawing" using free machine embroidery

USING THE DARNING FOOT

The darning foot can be used for machine embroidery. The technique is essentially the same as for free machining; the teeth are lowered and covered and the stitch length set to zero so that the fabric can be moved in any direction. However, the foot holds down the material at the moment the stitch is being made and so prevents missed stitches.

The darning foot is useful for beginners or the hesitant, but it obscures part of the stitching. Also, because the frame will not slip under the foot, the frame must be removed and re-attached every time the work is put on or taken off the machine.

Experienced machine embroiderers sometimes use the darning foot without a frame for large projects. This requires considerable skill since the hands must be used to tension the fabric.

The darning foot has a square or circular opening and can be used for straight stitch or zigzag.

BASIC PROCEDURE
To begin stitching:
1 Set the stitch length and width to 0.
2 Lower or cover the feed dog.
3 Remove the presser foot and the holding screw.
4 Thread the needle and insert the bobbin.
5 Place the framed fabric on the machine, lifting the needle to its highest point.
6 Lower the needle into the fabric to bring up the bobbin thread. Pull the thread through. If the bobbin thread is thick, it may be necessary to pierce a small hole in the fabric with a large chenille needle.
7 Lower the presser bar to engage the tension.
8 Lower the needle and, holding both threads with one hand, work two or three stitches. Cut off the thread ends.
9 Practice moving the frame while stitching, holding it as shown right. Move the frame as smoothly as possible.

Hold the frame as shown, resting your fingers on the edge. With practice you may prefer to place your fingers on the taut fabric for greater control, but this position is best for beginners. Make sure that your chair is at a comfortable height and your arms relaxed.

Work in lines, circles and spirals as you progress. To create lines, move the frame back and forth in various directions. Do not stitch quickly in one place or the upper thread may snap. Experiment with all kinds of curves, and try to write your own name or "draw" motifs. Draw some lines on the fabric and try to follow them accurately.

Zigzag lines and curves

Zigzag flower motifs

SPECIAL EFFECTS

A great many different and interesting effects can be created with free machining. The photographs on this page illustrate a small selection. Experiment with your own designs to create patterns with the hallmarks of individuality.

Zigzag lines Set the stitch dial to the desired width and move the frame forward and backward, turning it to form curves. The speed at which the machine is moved determines the stitch length; moving it slowly will produce satin stitch. The stitch width can be adjusted with one hand while you move the frame with the other.

Zigzag used to fill a shape Set the stitch width to maximum (or less, if the shape is small). Move the frame from side to side.

Star and flower motifs are worked with wide satin stitch. Work a few stitches without moving the frame and then, with the needle at the center point, pivot the work and stitch as before.

Whip stitch is a corded line produced by tightening the upper tension and moving the frame slowly, so that the lower thread wraps around the upper one. Use a fine thread in the bobbin (no. 50 machine cotton, if available) and a relatively heavy cotton thread in the needle. Run the machine very fast but move the frame slowly. If the upper thread breaks, loosen the tension slightly, and loosen the lower tension correspondingly (see p. 117). Two-color effects can be achieved by using contrasting colors in needle and bobbin and varying the speed of moving the frame. If the frame is moved quickly, more of the upper thread will show.

Feather stitch This requires a tight upper and loose lower tension. Move the frame quickly in a spiraling motion. The tension of the upper thread pulls long loops to the surface.

Couching can be used to apply a thick thread to the fabric. Use either running stitch or zigzag, holding the thread to be couched with one hand and guiding the frame with the other.

Cable stitch This is produced by using a thick thread in the bobbin and working from the wrong side, so that the decorative thread is on the right side. Frame the fabric in the usual way, but wrong side upward. Wind the bobbin with the chosen thread and use an ordinary sewing or machine embroidery thread in the needle. Loosen the lower tension (see p. 117) so that the bobbin thread can be pulled up easily. The upper tension should be set at "normal". Place the fabric on the machine and bring up the bobbin thread. Work the stitching in the chosen design. Tie the thread ends on the wrong side.

Whip stitch

Feather stitch

Couching

Cable stitch

LACE

Machine embroidery can be used to make delicate lace by working it on a fabric that is later made to disappear. This can be "vanishing muslin", which is ironed away, acetate fabric which dissolves in acetone, or a water-soluble fabric, all available from specialist embroidery stores.

The basic stitching techniques are as for free machine embroidery, except that zigzag can only be used over a line of straight stitch. Remember that all stitching lines must connect, or the lace will collapse once the backing fabric is destroyed. It is advisable to reinforce the principle lines of the design with two or three extra lines of stitching.

Frame the work and use a relatively fine needle to avoid snagging the fabric. A fine thread must be used in the needle, but a thicker one could be used in the bobbin.

Lacy effects worked in circles and spirals, in straight lines and as a motif

USING DISAPPEARING FABRICS

The disappearing fabrics used for lace machine embroidery are fairly tough but still need careful handling. It is vital that they do not become damp or wet when stored or during use, since this will make them disappear prematurely or destroy their "vanishing" properties.

Designs can be transferred to the fabric with a soft pencil. For complex designs it is also sensible to work out a "flow diagram" for the stitching to avoid overstitching delicate areas.

When all stitching is completed, hold the work up to the light to make sure all stitching lines interconnect and that there are no loose ends. Remove the work from the frame and trim away any excess fabric from the edges. Immerse in solvent or hot or cold water, or iron, as appropriate. Leave flat on a towel to cool or dry, then press.

To remove vanishing muslin, place an old towel on the ironing board. Lay on the lace, wrong side up. Cover with a thin, dry cloth. Press with an iron set to the highest possible temperature. Remove the iron from the work as soon as the muslin has vanished or the work may scorch.

The ironed muslin burns to brown or black, then shrivels and becomes brittle as it vanishes. Use an old, clean toothbrush to brush away any fragments adhering to the lace. Always work in a well-ventilated room.

EXTENDING THE RANGE

The advent of vanishing fabrics as backings for machine-worked lace opens up all kinds of possibilities for the inventive embroiderer. As well as ordinary sewing threads, for example, metal and textured threads can be couched into the designs to add impact and interest.

This type of lace work can easily be incorporated into cutwork. Vanishing fabrics soluble in cold water or the iron-away types are best for this kind of work. Lace edgings can be made in a similar way. Another way in which lace designs can be varied is by "suspending" fabric shapes and motifs into the lace.

It is often advisable to outline shapes and emphasize details in the lace with satin stitch (close zigzag worked over a line of straight stitch); these can be indicated on the fabric.

Lace insert incorporated in a cutwork embroidery. To do this, first cut away the desired areas from the fabric and stitch the cut edges with a close zigzag to prevent fraying. Baste on the vanishing fabric, leaving an overlap of 1 or 2 inches. Work the lace, then treat the vanishing fabric to remove it.

Fabric shapes incorporated into machine-worked lace. These should be basted to the vanishing fabric before the lace is worked. Surface embroidery can be added to the shapes as the lace is being constructed.

121

Of all the many forms of embroidery, needlepoint, sometimes also called tapestry or canvaswork, is one of the most popular. The most obvious reason is that it is easy to learn. Many people who doubt their ability to master the subtleties of surface embroidery, or lack the patience for cutwork or drawn thread work, for example, find it reassuring to work over a regular, easily visible mesh of canvas threads. Moreover, the work is soothing. But as well as being a relaxing pastime, needlepoint is a versatile type of embroidery. It can be employed to make a variety of useful and decorative objects, from pillows to chair seats. When appropriate thread and stitches are used, such items can be very hardwearing.

Needlepoint is also appreciated for its aesthetic qualities and its potential for creating works of art. In the sixteenth and seventeenth centuries it was often used to imitate tapestries (woven wallhangings) and other woven textiles such as carpets (hence its misnomer, tapestry).

The basic needlepoint stitch is tent stitch. Because this readily lends itself to depicting fine detail, a great many of the needlepoint kits on the market use only this one stitch. Most are realistically pictorial in character. Enthusiastic practitioners of needlepoint are often unaware that any other stitch exists, which is a pity, since one of the main attractions of needlepoint is the marvelous variety of textures that can be achieved.

There are more than 200 needlepoint stitches, some of the most popular of which are shown on the following pages. Satiny effects can be produced with cushion stitch, for example; kelim stitch can give a smooth "knitted" look, and double straight cross stitch creates a knobbly texture. By using an appropriate stitch it is possible to render the texture of a natural object, such as a pine cone or a weeping willow, much more effectively than through detailed shading with tent stitch alone; indeed, it is possible to create a whole picture or design using only one color but different stitches.

The grid structure of the canvas and the square-based construction of the stitches will always impose some degree of angularity on the design, but there are ways in which this can be minimized. (See Compensating stitches, p. 131.)

As you will discover when you practice the various needlepoint stitches, most of them are easy to work and cover the canvas relatively quickly. Make a sampler of the stitches that appeal to you, and keep it to use as a reference when designing.

MATERIALS AND EQUIPMENT

Canvas There are two basic types of canvas: single thread, or mono, and double thread, or Penelope. Both come in various widths and are sold by the yard. Of the two, mono canvas is the more useful, since any stitch can be worked over it, and the threads are easier to count than the double strands of Penelope. Mono canvas comes in a wide range of gauges. The gauge of canvas (also called its size or mesh) is the number of threads it contains to the inch. Mono canvas is generally available in gauges ranging from 10 to 24 threads to the inch.

A special kind of mono canvas called interlock is also sold in a few medium gauges. The threads of interlock canvas are actually twisted double threads, which are woven through each other in such a way that they cannot be dislocated. This makes interlock canvas especially suitable for work consisting of straight vertical stitches (such as bargello work shown on pages 128–129), which have a tendency to slip under the mesh.

Penelope canvas has the advantage that the strands can be separated, if desired, and worked over individually, thus allowing a change of scale for the purpose of showing fine detail. This type of canvas is used for trammed (or tramé) work (see p. 125). To prevent confusion, the gauge of Penelope canvas is often given as the number of holes, rather than threads, per inch, and sizes range from 7 to 20 holes per inch.

Rug canvas, suitable for large items such as rugs and wallhangings, is also constructed of double threads. Some is of the Penelope type, while in others the warp threads are twisted around pairs of weft threads to form an especially firm mesh. Rug canvas is available in 3, 5 and 7 gauge.

In the past embroidery canvas was traditionally made of linen, but it is now most often made of cotton, and sometimes of acrylic. Plastic canvas is also available. This is a stiff material which is molded, rather than woven. It does not fray, and thus eliminates the need for hems. It is useful for rigid objects such as placemats and boxes.

Woven canvas is most commonly available in white or beige, though it sometimes comes in several other colors —shades of tan, yellow and white. The choice is usually a matter of personal preference. Some people find tan or yellow easier on the eyes, but others prefer white because they find the threads easier to count. Ideally, needlepoint stitches should cover the canvas completely, but certain stitches do leave small areas of the canvas visible. In such a case you may prefer to choose a color that blends unobtrusively with your chosen selection of threads.

When choosing canvas, the main factor to consider is the quality, especially if the item being worked is one that will receive hard wear. Avoid buying canvas that contains knots or other flaws that might cause it to break in use.

Threads Persian, crewel and tapestry yarn are the ones most often used for needlepoint (see p. 13). Of these, crewel is the most versatile, since it is the finest, and can be divided into strands, so that you can adjust the thickness of the working thread to suit the gauge of the canvas (see p. 124). Persian wool comes in a triple strand, and the individual strands, each slightly thicker than a strand of crewel, can be separated, making it almost as versatile as crewel. Both are hardwearing and so are well suited to chair seats, footstools and other such items. Tapestry yarn is much less versatile, since it is usually too thick for canvas finer than 12 or 14 gauge, except for vertical stitches.

For large projects worked on rug canvas, the obvious choice is rug yarn. This is a thick, single strand yarn made in various fibers, including wool and acrylic.

Cotton threads can also be used for needlepoint. The shiny varieties, such as stranded floss and pearl cotton, give the work a definite sheen. These threads can either be used for the entire project or combined with wool threads to highlight parts of the design. Silk thread can be used in similar ways.

For purely decorative items you can be more adventurous in your choice of yarns. Some knitting yarns can be used successfully, as can crochet cottons, metal threads and raffia—in fact, anything you like. Pages 50–53 show some possibilities.

Needles and other equipment The needles used for needlepoint are called tapestry needles and have blunt points to prevent them from splitting the threads (see p. 12). They come in sizes ranging from 13 (the largest) to 24 (the smallest). Choose a needle that slips through the mesh easily, but is not so small that the eye frays your chosen thread.

You will also need a pair of dressmaking scissors for cutting canvas and fine embroidery scissors for cutting threads. A pair of tweezers is useful for unpicking bits of thread when removing a mistake. A waterproof marking pen, specially designed for use on canvas, should be used for tracing the design. A T-square is ideal for checking that the canvas is square, but any right-angled object, such as an album cover, will suffice.

PREPARING THE CANVAS

1 Cut the canvas at least 2in larger than the finished work on all sides. If you are working from a full-size design, the size of the finished work will, of course, be the same as the area of the drawing or tracing. If you are working from a chart, the finished work will probably be larger (or, in some cases, smaller) than the chart, and its size must be calculated. The box on page 128 will help you to make this calculation. Also, the method of preparing the canvas for charted designs is slightly different from that shown here (see p. 128).

When cutting canvas, always cut the vertical edges parallel to the selvage (the firmly woven edges of the canvas), since this makes the work stronger.

1 Mark the top of the canvas with pen or a thread so that you can be sure to place the design correctly.
2 Bind the cut edges with masking tape to prevent fraying. (Omit this step if you are mounting the work on a scroll frame.)

3 Check that the corners of the canvas are square, and if not, pull the canvas gently into shape. Place the canvas on a piece of blotting paper or other tough paper and draw around the edges with a pencil. Save this pattern for use when blocking the finished work (see p. 136).

TRANSFERRING THE DESIGN

Pictorial and free abstract designs are best transferred to the canvas by tracing. The main lines, including the outlines of the design, are first darkened, which makes them visible through the mesh. The design is placed underneath the canvas and its outline then traced on the canvas using a waterproof pen. When working the embroidery, use the outline as a general guide and refer to the detailed plan for the colors and stitch patterns.

If the design is elaborate, with many colors, you may prefer to paint the colors on the canvas. In this case, follow steps 1 and 2 (right), then paint in the colors using oil paint thinned to the right consistency with turpentine.

Some designs, especially the more geometric ones, are worked from charts (see p. 29 and pp. 128–129).

1 Darken the main lines of the design, including the edges, with a black felt-tip pen. You can omit details and incorporate them later as you proceed with the work.
2 Tape the design to a flat surface. (If the design is on tracing paper, place some opaque white paper under it.)

3 Tape or weight the canvas on top of the design, aligning the canvas threads with the edges of the design. Trace the outside edges on the canvas, running the marking pen smoothly along the channel between two threads.
4 Now trace the main lines of the design itself. Trace any curved lines as curves; do not try to square them up to fit the canvas grid.

USING A FRAME

As a general rule it is best to work canvas embroidery on a frame. This can be either a scroll frame or a stretcher frame (see pp. 66–67). A ring frame is not suitable, since it will not accommodate the stiff canvas.

The use of a frame will prevent the canvas threads from becoming distorted. New, unstitched canvas is stiff, because of the stiffener, or sizing, applied to it during manufacture, but when you start to handle and stitch it, it softens and the threads may slip out of alignment. This is particularly true if a strongly diagonal stitch, such as continental tent or slanted Gobelin, is used, or if you work with a firm tension. As a result, the finished piece will be warped, and blocking it to its original shape will be difficult, if not impossible.

However, there are some cases where a frame may not be necessary. For instance

if the piece is small; if the stitches used entail working in different directions, so that a pull in one direction is balanced by a pull in the opposite one; or if you normally work with a relaxed and even tension. (Even in the last case, however, certain stitches will always require a frame.)

To mount canvas in a stretcher frame, use the method shown on page 67, after first preparing the canvas and transferring the design as shown here. If you are using a scroll frame, follow the method shown on page 67, but instead of hemming the side edges and inserting string, bind the edges with wide woven tape. Do this by folding the tape over the raw edge of the canvas and machine stitching or backstitching through all the layers.

MATCHING THREAD TO CANVAS

Before you buy all the thread for a project, make sure that it is suitable for the gauge of your canvas and for the stitches you are using, so that the thread will cover the canvas completely. (If you have decided to use a particular type of thread, you may prefer to match the canvas to the thread rather than vice versa.) The examples here are worked in basketweave tent stitch, each in a thread well suited to working this stitch on the particular canvas. Alternatives are given where appropriate. Bear in mind that a thicker thread—or more strands—may be needed for some stitches, especially vertical ones, and also that different brands of the same type of thread vary slightly in thickness. Work a sample of each stitch you plan to use before making a final decision on thread and canvas.

ESTIMATING THREAD AMOUNTS

It is best to buy all the thread for a project at one time, to avoid variation in dye lots (although this will not matter much if areas of a particular color are separated by other colors). Because some stitches need more thread than others to cover a given area, it is difficult to estimate precisely how much you will need. However, as a rough guide, $1/7$oz of crewel yarn, used in three strands and worked in basketweave tent stitch on 14-gauge canvas, will cover 13 sq in. Less will be required for most other stitches, but it is best to estimate generously; extra thread will always come in useful for a later project.

22 single: stranded floss, 4 strands (shown); French crewel, 2 strands; matte embroidery cotton, 1 strand

18 single: no. 5 pearl cotton, 1 strand (shown); matte embroidery cotton, 2 strands; stranded floss, 6 strands; English crewel, 2 strands; Persian, 1 strand

16 single: English crewel, 2 strands (shown); French crewel, 3 strands; stranded floss, 6–7 strands

14 single: tapestry, 1 strand (shown); English crewel, 3 strands; French crewel, 3–4 strands; Persian, 2 strands

12 single: English crewel, 3 strands (shown); French crewel, 5 strands

10 double: Persian, 3 strands (shown); English crewel, 4 strands

WORKING CANVAS STITCHES

If the needlepoint is being done on a frame, you must work with a stabbing movement, preferably using both hands, as shown on page 68. If you are working without a frame, you can use either the same stabbing method (with one hand) or a sewing movement, in which the needle is used as shown in the stitch illustrations.

Always take the needle up into an empty hole if possible. When the needle and thread are taken down into a partially filled hole, they smooth the fibers down; if brought up into it, the opposite happens. In some cases this is unavoidable, but the fewer threads in one hole, the less likelihood of their being split by the new stitch.

There are no general rules about the order in which to work the needlepoint rows, but there are several alternative approaches, depending on the design. If you start at the top and work down you will

not be touching the stitched areas as you work, so they will receive less handling. On the other hand, if the design has a border, it is a good idea to work the whole border first, as this will help to keep the work square. And if there are several colors, it makes sense to work one whole color area at a time, preferably leaving the paler colors until the end.

Take care not to use so long a thread that it becomes frayed; as a general rule a length of crewel or Persian wool should measure no more than 18in. Move the needle along the thread occasionally to avoid weakening the yarn at the point where it is held in the eye. (For hints on threading the needle, see page 68. Left-handed readers should refer to the note on that page about direction of working.)

Note Throughout this section numbers are used, where necessary, to indicate the order of inserting the needle.

To begin work Knot the thread and take the needle through to the wrong side, a short distance ahead of the starting point. Work over the thread, then cut off the knot.

To end work (or to begin a new thread alongside some stitching) weave the thread through the stitches on the wrong side, as shown on page 68.

TENT STITCH

The basic stitch used in needlepoint is tent stitch. Some people call it petit point and refer to cross stitch or half cross stitch as gros point, but these two terms are properly applied to the size of the stitch (*petit* meaning small, and *gros* large), which is determined, of course, by the canvas gauge. In general petit point describes work containing more than 16 stitches per inch.

The names continental and basketweave refer to the two different ways of working tent stitch. The appearance of the stitch is the same on the right side, but continental tent is worked vertically or horizontally, whereas basketweave tent is worked diagonally. Basketweave tent is preferable, because it does not distort the canvas. But both stitches cover both sides of the canvas completely.

Continental tent, basketweave tent, half cross stitch seen from the front (top) and the back (below)

Continental tent stitch This stitch should be used sparingly, particularly if the work is not on a frame, since it tends to distort the canvas. Work in rows, either horizontally or vertically. On the second and following rows work as shown, so that the needle comes up through an empty hole. At the end of a row, either fasten off (see p. 68) or take the thread through to the wrong side of the work ready for the next row.

Satin stitch This variation of continental tent is worked over two or more threads. It can be combined with ordinary tent to give an interesting shantunglike texture to a background. Or it can be worked in various patterns and slanted in different directions.

Basketweave tent stitch This stitch gets its name from the woven effect produced on the wrong side. It should be used in preference to continental tent wherever possible, since it does not distort the canvas. Begin at the upper right-hand corner (turn the work, if necessary), and work as shown, in diagonal lines alternately up and down.

To turn a 90° corner Begin the next row one stitch up or down from where you would normally begin, at the edge of the worked area.

For a 45° angle, work the next row as if to continue the 90° angle, then on the following row work the last stitch just beside the first stitch of the previous one.

HALF CROSS STITCH OVER TRAMMING

Like tent stitch, half cross stitch covers one intersection on the right side to produce a small diagonal stitch, but on the wrong side the thread crosses only a single canvas thread. This makes half cross considerably weaker than tent stitch (although more economical) and thus unsuitable for any item that will receive hard wear. Also, the stitches have a tendency to slip under the mesh, and thus should only be used on interlock or Penelope canvas.

Half cross is often used over tramming (or tramé). This is a method of laying horizontal threads along paired threads of Penelope canvas and then working over them. The resulting effect has a slightly ridged appearance. (Tramming may be done on mono canvas, see p. 126.)

To tram the canvas Bring the yarn up between a pair of threads and take it down where the color changes.

If the trammed line needs to be longer than 2in, secure the thread by taking it down and bringing it up behind the previous vertical thread as shown.

Using matching thread, work half cross stitch as shown over the tramming, bringing the needle up below the horizontal threads, taking it down diagonally over one intersection and up directly below.

VERTICAL STITCHES

The stitches illustrated on these two pages, though vertical in their structure, form horizontal patterns. The stitches are created by taking the thread vertically over the horizontal threads of the canvas (in two cases they are slanted and taken over one vertical thread also). They are all worked in rows. Despite the basic similarity in their formation, vertical stitches can be used to produce a range of different effects.

The Gobelin stitches are named after the famous Gobelins tapestry works in Paris, whose products they resemble. These stitches are well suited to backgrounds that require a stitch more textured than tent stitch, but do not demand a strong pattern. All of the Gobelin stitches lend themselves well to shaded effects, as does random straight stitch. Start with one color at the top of the work and change gradually to lighter or darker shades in the following rows. One of the best stitches for shading is random straight stitch. This stitch is smooth and flat, making it ideal for backgrounds, yet it has an interesting texture because of the varied lengths of the individual stitches.

Regular patterns of vertical stitches can be created with brick stitch or Parisian stitch, while Hungarian and Hungarian diamond stitches both form diamond patterns.

A special category of vertical stitches, called bargello, or Florentine work, is described on pages 128–129.

Upright Gobelin (also called straight Gobelin) This stitch has a strongly horizontal character and, if worked over only two threads, a ridged texture. Work in rows over two or more horizontal threads. The vertical canvas threads will show slightly between the rows, so use a fairly thick thread to cover them as far as possible.

Upright Gobelin over tramming This method accentuates the ridged effect and prevents the canvas from showing through; it also produces a firmer fabric. Work the tramming (see p. 125) between alternate pairs of threads on single or Penelope canvas, then work the upright Gobelin stitches over them.

Encroaching Gobelin This form of Gobelin makes a smooth texture of interlocking stitches that covers the canvas completely.

Work in rows over three horizontal threads. On the second and following rows, the stitches are taken up into the previous row to the left of each stitch.

Split Gobelin This is essentially the same as encroaching Gobelin, except that the needle is taken down into the center of the upper stitch, rather than to one side of it. Take care to insert the needle into the correct hole of the mesh each time. Split Gobelin is especially good for subtle shading effects.

Encroaching slanted Gobelin This also gives a diagonal effect, and the stitches can slant to the right, as shown, or to the left. It must be worked on a frame. Work the stitch over three or more horizontal threads and one vertical thread. Here it is shown worked over five horizontal threads.

Slanted Gobelin This stitch gives a close fabric with a diagonal effect, and must be worked on a frame, otherwise it will distort the canvas. Work in rows over two or more horizontal threads and one vertical thread.
Variation Work a line of tent stitch between two rows, using contrasting thread.

Clockwise from top left: upright Gobelin, Hungarian, brick (over 2 and 4 threads), split Gobelin, random straight, encroaching slanted Gobelin, Parisian, Hungarian diamond, slanted Gobelin with tent, encroaching upright Gobelin

Random straight stitch Work in rows, varying the length of the stitches as desired, to create texture. Avoid ending two consecutive stitches between the same two horizontal threads. For extra-subtle shading, use two colors, working over a three-row grid: one color for the upper row, and the other for the lower, with a mixture of the two colors in the needle for the intermediate row.

Brick stitch Work over two horizontal threads in a zigzag pattern as shown, working back and forth across the canvas. For a more strongly vertical effect, work the stitches over four threads instead of two. When all the rows have been worked, fill in the gaps at the top and bottom with short vertical stitches.

Parisian stitch Work in rows, making the stitches go over two and four threads alternately. For a two-color effect, work all the long stitches in one color, and the short stitches in another color. Fill in the gaps at top and bottom with appropriate colors to maintain the pattern.

Hungarian stitch Work this stitch in groups of three, one long and two short, across the canvas, leaving one hole between each group. On the second and following rows, work back across the canvas, filling in the gaps as shown. For a two-color effect, work alternate rows in different colors.

Hungarian diamond stitch This is a larger-scale version of Hungarian stitch, and also lends itself to two-color patterns. It is worked in groups of five, with the longest, central stitch crossing six threads. These longer stitches make the work slightly less durable than Hungarian stitch.

127

BARGELLO

The type of needlepoint known as bargello or Florentine, consists of upright stitches arranged in steps to form zigzag or curved repeat patterns. This work was brought to a high degree of refinement in sixteenth-century Florence—hence the name. Its alternative designation is derived from the Bargello Palace in Florence, which contained some particularly fine examples.

Today bargello work retains an enormous popularity. The stitch is simple and covers the canvas quickly, and the number of effects that can be created is virtually infinite. Also, it is easy to design your own embroideries in bargello work once you understand the few simple principles of forming the pattern lines.

There are two main categories of bargello pattern, row designs and motif designs. In a row design all the rows are identical and repeat a regular color sequence. The pattern might consist of zigzags, curves or a combination of the two. All the stitches are the same length —except in the case of Hungarian point designs (see opposite).

In a motif design the basic unit is a medallion shape. This might be a lozenge, an oval, a honeycomb cell or even a stylized flower. Often the upper and lower outlines of the shape form a mirror image.

Either of these two types of design can be adapted to form four-way bargello patterns (see p. 29). In these patterns a square is divided into four triangles and the repeat worked to fill each triangle so that it radiates out from the center.

The finished effect of a piece of bargello work is determined not only by the arrangement of the stitches but also by the choice of colors. Vividly contrasting colors can be used for dramatic impact, or several shades of one color for a restful effect. One of the most striking types of bargello pattern, called flame stitch, uses both shading and sharp contrasts to enhance its dramatic lines.

Bargello work is suitable for many different items, including pillows, glasses cases, chair seats and evening bags. If the item will receive hard wear, it is best to avoid using stitches more than four canvas threads deep, otherwise there is a risk of snagging. A hardwearing yarn, such as crewel or Persian, is a better choice than tapestry yarn. For purely decorative objects, the choice of thread is wider.

WORKING FROM A CHART

Designs made up of repeating patterns, such as bargello work, are not traced onto the canvas, as described on page 123, but worked from a chart. Published designs for needlepoint are generally presented in chart form, since this method saves space (the chart is usually considerably smaller than the finished work) and enables the embroiderer to copy the original exactly.

Where a design consists of a repeating pattern, only the basic repeat will usually be given on the chart. It can easily be duplicated the required number of times both across the canvas and up and down it. Designs consisting of a single symmetrical motif may have only one half (or one quarter) charted; the design is completed by working a mirror image of the chart.

The two basic types of chart, line charts and box charts, are discussed on page 28. Line charts are generally used for bargello work; box charts for designs worked in tent stitch.

PREPARING THE CANVAS

Before you cut the canvas, check the size of the finished work—this is usually given in the instructions. But you may wish to use a canvas with a different gauge to the one recommended, in which case you must count the number of lines across and down the chart and divide the result by the gauge of your canvas. For example, if there are 96 lines both across and down on the chart, and you are using 16-gauge canvas, the finished area will be 6 in square or $96 \div 16$. Use a single thread canvas for bargello.

1 Cut the canvas to the required size (finished size plus at least 2 in all around). Mark the top and bind the edges with masking tape as described on page 123. Mount the canvas on the frame, if you are using one. 2 If the center of the chart is not already marked, find it by drawing two straight lines through the middle. Mark the exact center of the canvas with basting threads or a waterproof marking pen.

For a four-way bargello design Mark the canvas on the diagonal between opposite corners with basting, keeping the stitches fairly small to avoid straying off the true diagonal. Remove the basting as you work.

3 Begin stitching at the center. For a row design you can choose any row, working to the right or left of the center, then to the other side. Refer to the chart frequently to ensure accuracy.

For a bargello motif design Work the upper and lower framework, starting at the center and working outward, then fill in the spaces, referring to the chart frequently.

For a four-way design, choose a dominant line near the center and work it first, then fill in the center and surrounding area.

Basic bargello stitch Zigzags are formed by taking stitches up over three or more threads with "steps" between stitches. The step is the number of threads left between the base of adjacent stitches. Expressed numerically, the first number denotes stitch length, the second step length. The example on the left is 4.2, on the right 6.4.

Hungarian point A distinctive spiky pattern is produced by using two lengths of stitch in a regular sequence, as shown. The short stitches normally cover two threads, the long ones four or six. In every vertical line two long and two short stitches alternate for the entire length.

TYPICAL BARGELLO PATTERNS

  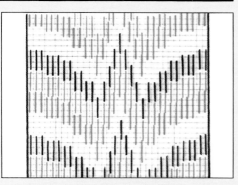

Flame stitch In its simplest form this pattern consists of even zigzag lines worked in a shaded color sequence such as the one shown here. These stitches follow a 3.2 formation.

Oval medallions Like other curved designs, these are formed with blocks of stitches. The "frame" of this oval is made up of stitches four canvas threads deep. Inside and outside the frame, the stitch length varies.

Zigzags and curves The combination of these makes some of the most dramatic bargello designs. Here again, shading is used to heighten the effect. The stitches are all four threads deep.

129

CROSSED STITCHES

There are many different crossed stitches in the needlepoint repertoire. Most of them give the work a knobbly texture and so contrast effectively with flatter or smoother stitches, such as tent (see p. 125) or cushion (see p. 132). Some of them also combine well with each other: for example, large cross stitches worked over four threads can be interspersed with upright cross, as shown in the photograph. The stitches can be worked in two different colors for a lattice effect.

Two colors can also be combined in the same stitch, thus transforming its appearance. If worked in one color, rice stitch, for example, produces a rough-textured fabric with no strong pattern, but if the corner stitches are worked in a contrasting thread, a lattice pattern emerges. Similarly, Smyrna stitch in one color

forms a square, bumpy texture; but if a different color is used for the vertical cross on top, an upright grid pattern is produced.

Some crossed stitches have a horizontal or vertical character (depending on the direction of working); long-armed cross and herringbone fall into this category. Both produce a braided effect. Two colors can also be used effectively in herringbone stitch to bring out its zigzag structure.

Another way of adapting some of these stitches is to use only one color but to work part of the stitch in a matte-finish thread and part in shiny thread. This technique is illustrated in the sample of double straight cross stitch and rice stitch in the photograph. When working a design, you could highlight a small part of an area in this way, leaving most of the stitches

in the matte thread.

You can also vary the scale of some of these stitches. Rhodes stitch, for example, could be worked over six threads in part of the design and over three elsewhere. This is a good way to achieve unity and variety at the same time.

Practice these stitches using different threads and combinations of threads and working them, where possible, in different sizes, to see some of the endless variety of effects you can create.

Cross stitch Work in rows, horizontally or vertically, taking two diagonal stitches over two or more canvas threads in each direction. For an even tension, and to ensure that all the top stitches slant the same way, you can work a whole row in two stages. Cross stitch can also be worked over one mesh on Penelope canvas, as in the inset.

Upright cross stitch This small stitch creates a firm, pebble-textured fabric on its own, or it can be used in conjunction with other cross stitches.

Work in rows as shown, completing each cross before starting the next.

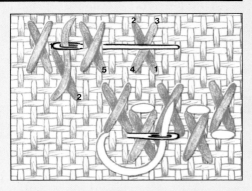

Alternating oblong cross stitch These stitches are formed like ordinary cross stitches, but are twice as tall as they are wide. They do not cover the canvas well if worked in rows, but if staggered, as shown, they make an excellent background. Backstitch may be used in conjunction with these stitches to help cover the canvas threads.

Long-armed cross stitch Also called long-legged cross, this stitch produces a braided effect.

Work in rows, from left to right or right to left, over three horizontal and six vertical threads. For a neat edge, begin and end the rows by shortening the "arm" as shown.

Herringbone stitch This is formed like the same stitch in surface stitchery (see p. 73), but rows are worked close together for an interlaced look.

Work in rows, always in the same direction, taking the short stitch (1–2) over two horizontal threads and the long stitch (3–4) over four. Be careful not to split the stitches in the row above. Fill in any gaps at the top with cross stitches.

Rice stitch Also called crossed corners or William and Mary stitch, this is worked in two stages.

First work ordinary cross stitches, but over four horizontal and four vertical threads. Then work four stitches, in the order shown, over the legs of each cross.

A finer, or contrasting, thread is often used for the small stitches.

Clockwise from top left: cross and upright cross, double leviathan, Rhodes, alternating oblong, Smyrna, rice, double straight, herringbone, long-armed cross

Double straight cross stitch This is a highly textured, firm stitch with a diagonal character. Work an upright cross stitch over four threads (1–2, 3–4). Then work an ordinary cross stitch on top (5–6, 7–8).

Work in rows, fitting each row into the spaces left in the previous row.

Smyrna stitch Also known as leviathan or double cross, this stitch has a square, bumpy texture but does not cover the canvas thoroughly. It is effective worked in two colors, which makes an attractive grid pattern.

Work a cross stitch over four threads (1–2, 3–4), then work an upright cross on top (5–6, 7–8). If desired, the top stitch of the cross can be vertical instead of horizontal.

Double leviathan stitch Similar to Smyrna stitch, this covers the canvas better. Use a relatively thin thread to prevent the center from becoming too bulky.

First work a cross stitch over four threads (1–2, 3–4). Then work two intersecting stitches over each arm of the cross (5–6, 7–8, 9–10, 11–12). Finally, work an upright cross on top (13–14, 15–16).

Rhodes stitch This simple stitch, named after the English embroiderer who invented it, forms small pyramids on the canvas.

Work over a square of three or more threads (six are used here), working counter-clockwise, and moving one vertical thread to the right at the bottom and one thread to the left at the top, for each stitch. Continue until the square is filled; end with a long diagonal stitch.

COMPENSATING STITCHES
The grid structure of canvas and the angularity of canvas stitches can pose a problem when the embroiderer attempts to fill a curved shape. The solution is to fill in awkward corners with ''compensating'' stitches. These are part of, or scaled-down versions of, the stitch being used within a certain area. There are no ''official'' compensating stitches that correspond to the full-size ones; the embroiderer must use her own judgment.

Where possible, work half (or a third, or a quarter, etc.) of the stitch being used. You can sometimes miniaturize the stitch, or use a smaller stitch that resembles it in some way. For example, upright cross stitch might be used to fill in gaps along the edges of Smyrna stitch.

The illustration shows work done in rice stitch and encroaching slanted Gobelin (see p. 126), with tent stitch and various other compensating stitches used to fill in the curves. Tent stitches can always be used to cover any few remaining bare canvas threads.

SQUARE STITCHES

Many, if not most, needlepoint stitches are square, because of the structure of the canvas, but certain stitches have squareness as their dominating characteristic, and the patterns they form make them especially suitable for depicting stonework or tiling.

Scotch stitch, for example, is ideally suited to windows, particularly if the surrounding tent stitches are worked in a darker thread, while weaving stitch realistically suggests basketweave. Cushion stitch (also called flat stitch or satin stitch squares) is perhaps the most versatile of these. It has a pleasing texture and makes an interesting yet unobtrusive background. Brighton stitch, a variation of cushion stitch, softens the gridlike pattern by cutting off the corners and placing an upright cross at the intersections.

Clockwise from top left: cushion, Brighton, Scotch, weaving, small checker, large checker

Cushion stitch Make blocks by working stitches diagonally as shown, over one, two, three and four, then three, two and one intersection(s). Change the direction of working in alternate squares or, to vary the stitch, work all the squares in the same direction.

Brighton stitch Work as for cushion stitch, but omit the first and last stitches over one intersection.

Fill in the resulting spaces with upright cross stitches (see p. 130) in a shiny thread or contrasting color.

Scotch stitch This can be worked over different numbers of threads. Here the center squares are worked over four vertical and horizontal threads.

First work a grid of continental tent stitches (see p. 125), spacing the lines four threads apart. Then fill in the spaces with diagonal stitches as shown.

Large checker stitch In this stitch, squares of satin stitch alternate with those of tent stitch.

Work the satin stitch squares in diagonal rows from upper left to lower right, working the central thread over three canvas threads, as shown, or over four. Then fill in the remaining squares with basketweave tent stitch (see p. 125).

Small checker stitch In this scaled-down version of checker, the squares emerge only if worked in two colors.

Work as for large checker stitch, completing the satin stitch squares first, then filling in with the tent stitches.

Weaving stitch Work groups of three straight stitches over four threads, alternating the direction as shown, and working back and forth in rows across the canvas.

To emphasize the woven effect, use two colors: one for the horizontal and one for the vertical stitches.

DIAGONAL STITCHES

The stitches shown on this page all give a strongly diagonal character to the work. The effect can be subdued, as in small diagonal mosaic, or bold and striking, as in Moorish, Byzantine and jacquard. The steps in Byzantine and jacquard can be emphasized by using contrasting colors for different rows, or they can be softened by the use of graduated shades of the same color. For jagged stripes, try working Milanese stitch in two colors. These large-scale stitches need to be worked over a correspondingly large area for their patterns to emerge.

The diagonal mosaic stitches work well in smaller areas, but can also be used in larger ones. Attractive narrow diagonal stripes can be produced by working small diagonal mosaic in two or more contrasting colors, as shown in the photograph.

Clockwise from top left: Milanese, jacquard, small mosaic, Moorish, large mosaic, Byzantine

Small diagonal mosaic stitch Work up and down diagonally across the canvas, working stitches over one and two intersections alternately.

Large diagonal mosaic stitch This is basically the same as the small version, but worked over a maximum of three intersections (going over one, two, three and then two and one). Worked in a single color, it has a "honeycomb" appearance.

Moorish stitch This stitch consists of diagonal rows of stitches, worked from top left to bottom right and covering two, three, four, five and six intersections, alternating with "steps" of satin stitch (see p. 125) worked over two threads.

Byzantine stitch This consists of regular steps of satin stitch (see p. 125), arranged to form a zigzag pattern. Here each horizontal and each vertical step is four stitches wide (counting the corner stitch twice), but the basic pattern can be varied by increasing the number and depth of the stitches.

Jacquard stitch This is similar to Byzantine, but the satin stitches are separated by rows of continental tent stitch (see p. 125). To maintain the correct method of working the tent stitch, you will need to bring the needle up on alternate sides of the step as shown.

Milanese stitch Diagonal rows of interlocking triangles form this stitch, which creates an intriguing brocaded effect.

Work up and down the canvas alternately, working over one, two, three and four intersections, and fitting each row into the edges of the preceding one.

133

VERTICAL PATTERN STITCHES

With one exception, all the stitches on this page form strongly vertical patterns. They contrast with those given on pages 126–127 which, although vertical in their structure, actually form horizontal patterns. The exception is leaf stitch which, as its name indicates, forms pretty leaf-shaped motifs, perfect for depicting foliage. What it has in common with the others is that it is formed mainly by working diagonal stitches in vertical rows.

Kalem stitch, also called knitted stocking stitch, has the finest "grain" of all these stitches, and makes a smooth, firm fabric. Stem stitch is a wider version of kalem with (usually) a line of back stitch worked between alternate rows. Fishbone and fern stitches form braided effects on the canvas.

Clockwise from top left: kalem, leaf, fern, fishbone, stem

Kalem stitch This stitch is worked over one vertical and two horizontal threads. Begin at the lower right-hand corner and work up and down, changing the slant of the stitches in alternating rows as shown.

The stitch may be worked horizontally if preferred.

Stem stitch This stitch consists of slanting stitches worked in vertical rows.

Begin at the lower right-hand corner and work up and down over two vertical and horizontal threads, as shown. Then work backstitch between alternate rows where the stitches point downward, using a contrasting thread if wished.

Fern stitch Like stem stitch, this stitch gives a pleasing ridged effect. Begin at the top and work each row downward as shown, working each complete stitch over three vertical and two horizontal threads.

A flatter, wider effect can be obtained by working over five vertical threads.

Fishbone stitch This attractive pattern consists of long diagonal stitches worked over three canvas intersections crossed by short stitches.

Start at the upper left-hand corner and work alternately down, then up, slanting the second row of stitches in the opposite direction. Take care to work the short stitches over just one intersection; finding the correct hole can be tricky.

Leaf stitch Begin with the center stitch (1–2), placing it between the third and fourth vertical threads from the edge of the area to be filled. Then work each side. On subsequent rows, take care to place the stitches accurately.

Leaf stitches can be used in blocks or as individual motifs, and lines of backstitch may be added to suggest stems.

TIED STITCHES

The three stitches shown below are each formed by "tying" or "holding" a longer strand or loop in place with a short stitch.

Knotted Gobelin is the simplest of the three, consisting of rows of long diagonal encroaching stitches held in place with half cross stitches. It can be worked in two or more colors, as shown.

Rococo stitch consists of groups of four vertical stitches, each secured in the center with a short horizontal stitch, forming an oval shape.

Velvet stitch is one of several needlepoint stitches that duplicate the pile of a woven carpet. When working velvet stitch, keep the loops even and hold them in place by working them over a knitting needle; hold the needle just below the stitching, as shown below. The loops may be trimmed evenly or left uncut.

Clockwise from top left: square eyelets, diamond eyelets, velvet (uncut), Rococo, knotted Gobelin, velvet (cut), ray, star-shaped eyelets with backstitch

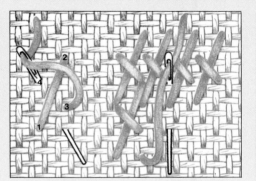

Knotted Gobelin Work in rows from left to right, starting at the top.

Take each stitch up over six horizontal and two vertical threads, then work a half cross stitch over the center of it as shown.

On subsequent rows, begin four threads down and work into the spaces left above.

Rococo stitch Work four vertical stitches from bottom to top over four threads. After pulling each one through (gently), work a backstitch over the center of it. On subsequent rows, skip one thread; this gives the stitch a better shape. If the canvas shows, cover it with backstitches.

Velvet stitch Work a stitch over one intersection (1–2) and bring the needle up again (3) in the first hole. Leaving a loop, take the needle down again (at 4) in the same hole as 2. Bring it up to the right of the loop, one thread down, at 5 and work a diagonal stitch (5–6). Bring the needle up into position for the next stitch at 7 (being the same hole as 5).

Work the next row above, missing one thread.

EYELET STITCHES

The stitches in this group are formed by working a number of individual stitches into the same hole, to produce a radiating effect. One of them, ray stitch, is really one quarter of a square eyelet.

The larger the eyelet, the more difficult it is to place the stitches smoothly so that they do not overlap at the hole. It is often helpful to enlarge the hole first by inserting a point such as a fine knitting needle into it. Always work all the stitches down into the hole, bringing the thread up at the edge. In order to fit all the stitches into the hole, it might be necessary to use a finer thread than normal for needlepoint, which may leave the canvas visible at the edges. In this case, backstitch may be worked between the eyelets if appropriate to the design. A certain amount of experimenting is often necessary to get the right effect.

Square eyelet Start at the top edge and work either clockwise or counter-clockwise around a square of four threads, working into each hole as shown.

When moving to the next row, take the thread under the stitches on the wrong side to avoid crossing the hole.

For a star shape Work into every alternate hole. Add backstitch at the edges if desired.

Ray stitch This is also called fan stitch.

Start with the bottom row and work upward, beginning with a horizontal stitch (1–2).

Work over a square of three threads, taking the needle down into every hole on two adjacent sides. The direction of the stitches can be reversed on alternate rows for a different texture.

135

If you have spent considerable time and care in working a piece of embroidery, it would be shortsighted to give insufficient attention to the finishing stages. Many fine pieces of stitching are spoiled by inept or careless finishing and assembling. Inadequate blocking, wobbly seams and lumpy corners can become obvious, to the detriment of the embroidery itself.

A simple solution to these problems is to take the embroidery to a store that offers a finishing service, although this can be expensive. In the case of a complex project, such as a pair of slippers or a handbag that will be mounted on a frame, it may be well worthwhile paying for a professional finish, but simple articles such as pillows, wallhangings and panels are relatively easy to make yourself.

It is wise to plan the finishing before you begin work on a project, since your design decisions may be influenced by the availability of certain fabrics, trimmings and other items. If you are making a pillow, for example, you should find out whether the required size of pillow form is available. Buy the form at the outset so that you will have it when you need it.

Before mounting embroidery for a panel (see p. 138) discuss the framing with a professional framer. (Do not attempt the framing itself unless you are experienced in this craft.) Decide whether you want the work surrounded by a mount. If no suitable color of cardboard mount is available, you may prefer to double-mount the panel on a fabric-covered board, as shown on page 138.

The finishing of embroidered clothing requires some knowledge and expertise in dressmaking, explanation of which lies beyond the scope of this book. The crucial thing to remember is that the embroidery should usually be worked before the garment section is cut out accurately, unless you are following a pattern that specifies otherwise. To position embroidery, lightly mark the outline and seamline of the piece on the fabric with tailor's chalk. If the work is quilting, you will need to add about 2in all around to allow for the fabric taken up by the quilting itself. The closer and more numerous the lines of quilting stitches, the greater the take-up will be.

If the embroidery has been worked on a frame, leave it on the frame until you are ready to finish it. It will thus remain in good condition and require little, if any, pressing or blocking. (If it has become soiled, either wash it gently in cool soapy water or have it dry cleaned.)

BLOCKING SURFACE STITCHERY

The process of blocking, or stretching, is the technique of smoothing a completed piece of stitchery, removing creases and restoring the fabric's shape. If the work has been done on a slate or stretcher frame it may need only a light pressing, but if it has been worked on a ring frame or looks at all puckered, it should be wet-blocked.

Materials You will need a piece of plywood or masonite at least 2in larger than the embroidery, a sheet of blotting paper slightly larger than the fabric, masking tape, thumb tacks or carpet tacks (for plywood or masonite respectively), a set square, hammer and pliers.

1 Tape the blotting paper to the board.
2 Immerse the embroidery in cold water, then gently squeeze out (do not wring).

3 Place the embroidery right side up on the board on top of the blotting paper. Tack each corner to the board, checking each one with the set square to make sure it is square.
4 Tack the fabric at the center of each side, placing the first two tacks opposite each other. Use pliers, if necessary, to pull the fabric taut.

5 Continue tacking, always placing each tack opposite the last, and checking with a ruler to make sure the edges are straight. The tacks should be about $1/2$in apart.
6 Allow the work to dry thoroughly before removing it from the board.

BLOCKING NEEDLEPOINT

Needlepoint should always be blocked. If the work has been done in the hand, it will almost certainly be distorted, and even work done on a frame will benefit from the freshening effect of the blocking process.

Materials These are basically the same as for blocking surface stitchery, plus a spray bottle and a wet cloth or sponge. First mark an outline of the entire canvas on blotting paper. Measure two adjacent sides of the work and use a ruler and set square to draw the square or rectangle.

1 Tape the blotting paper to the board.
2 Check the canvas to make sure no stitches are missing by holding it up to the light. Trim the thread ends closely on the wrong side.
3 If there is a selvage, slash it at intervals of about $1\frac{1}{2}$in to prevent puckering.

If you have bound the edges of the canvas with masking tape, do not remove it.

4 Place the work right side down on the board if the stitching is fairly flat and right side up if highly textured. Moisten it slightly.
5 Tack it in place within the drawn outline, corners first, pulling it to fit. Tack through the tape, placing the tacks about $1/2$in apart.
6 Wet the work thoroughly and leave it to dry.

PRESSING

Certain kinds of embroidery, such as cutwork, drawn thread, pulled work, appliqué and smocking are never blocked. However, depending on whether or not the work has been done on a frame, such embroidery may need pressing.

A light touch is essential for pressing embroidery. It should always be pressed from the wrong side and placed over a clean, folded, thick towel to cushion the stitches. Use either a steam iron or a dry iron over a damp cloth, set to a temperature suitable for the fabric. Apply the iron gently for a moment, then lift it off and apply it to the adjacent area; do **not** move it back and forth as in ironing. In some cases it is sufficient to hold the iron just above the fabric and let the steam do all the work.

Metal thread embroidery requires no pressing, since it is always worked held perfectly taut on a frame.

WALLHANGINGS

A wallhanging is easy to make. Only basic sewing skills are required, but it is important to make sure that the embroidery fabric and the lining lie smoothly together. For the lining, choose a firmly woven fabric such as an upholstery cotton or rayon, lighter than the embroidery.

Materials Besides the lining fabric, you will need sewing thread to match the embroidery fabric. For hanging the work you can use either two lengths of doweling, one $1\frac{1}{8}$in longer than the upper edge, and some cord, **or** a strip of Velcro to fit across the finished wallhanging, a batten the same length and a length of curtain weights for the lower edge. The size of doweling or batten will depend on the weight and nature of the finished embroidery, but $\frac{3}{8}$in is suitable for most purposes.

For a small or medium-size wallhanging
1 Trim the embroidery to measure $\frac{1}{2}$in more all around than the finished size.
2 Cut the lining to the same size as the embroidery.

3 Place the embroidery and lining with right sides together. Pin and then baste around all four edges.
4 Machine stitch or backstitch by hand $\frac{1}{2}$in from the edge. Leave about 4in open on the lower edge for turning.

If $\frac{3}{8}$in doweling is to be inserted, leave a gap of $\frac{3}{4}$in in the stitching at each corner, as shown.
For needlepoint, stitch just inside the edges of the embroidered area to prevent any canvas threads from showing. A line of tent stitch can be added first, if necessary, to avoid spoiling the design.

5 Trim the seam allowance to $\frac{1}{4}$in, or $\frac{3}{8}$in for needlepoint, tapering the corners as shown. Turn right side out; poke out the corners. Insert curtain weights, if using.
6 Press the edges flat; work on the lining side and push the stitching out to the edge.
7 Close the edges of the gap with slipstitch.

For a large wallhanging
1 Prepare the two fabrics as in steps 1 and 2 above.
2 Press under $\frac{1}{2}$in on all edges of both fabrics, mitering the corners as shown.
3 Place the fabrics wrong sides together. Fold back the lining along the center. Work lock stitch loosely through both fabrics.

4 Baste and slipstitch the fabrics together around the top and side edges, leaving gaps for the doweling, if used.
5 Hang up the work and leave it for a few days to "settle" (it may stretch a little) before finishing the bottom edge.

For hanging with doweling Slip the doweling through the gaps; tie the cord to the upper length.
For hanging with Velcro Separate the Velcro strips and glue the stiffer one to the batten; fix the batten to the wall. Slipstitch the softer Velcro strip to the hanging.

SOME USEFUL STITCHES
Overcasting (top) is used to finish raw edges.
Slipstitch (center) is used for hemming and for joining two folded edges.
Prick stitch (above) is a variation of backstitch used for inconspicuous top stitching.

137

PANELS

An embroidered panel can be framed with or without a mount, or it can be sewn to a fabric-covered board, see below. Ideally, it should not be covered with glass, which detracts from its tactile quality, but if it is likely to become damaged by dirt, as in a city home, it should be glazed.

Before framing, the embroidery is mounted on a board, as shown here. For a smooth effect, cover the board first with flannelette or thin batting. (This is not necessary for needlepoint.)

Materials You will need a piece of stiff cardboard or thin masonite the size of the finished work, plus a small allowance to fit under the frame rebate if you do not want to lose any of the design. To cover the board first, you will also need a piece of flannelette $1\frac{1}{8}$in larger all around than the board, as well as fabric glue and strong thread.

To cover the board

1 Apply thin strips of glue close to the edges on the wrong side of the board.
2 Place the board, glue side up, on the flannelette and fold the fabric edges over it, mitering the corners, as shown. Allow the glue to dry thoroughly.

To lace the embroidery

1 Center the board on the wrong side of the work. Fold the upper edge over the board and fasten with pins inserted through the edge into the fabric or cardboard. (If using masonite, tacks may be needed.) Turn and fasten the lower edge in the same way, making sure that the embroidery lies straight.

2 Leaving the thread on the spool, and starting in the center, work herringbone stitch between the two edges out to one side. Fasten securely.
3 Measure off and cut through enough thread to reach the opposite side and stitch as before, but do not fasten off.

4 Remove the pins or tacks. Starting at the fastened end, pull each thread firmly to tension the fabric evenly. Fasten off the remaining end.
5 Fold over the side edges, pin them in place, and lace them together in the same way.

To double-mount a panel

1 Cover a board with fabric, as for the panel itself, and to the same size.
2 Slipstitch the turned corners.
3 Sew the panel to the mount fabric using a curved upholstery needle.

Fabric-covered or cardboard window mounts are also ideal for panel display.

FINISHING CANVAS EDGES

If the edges of a piece of needlepoint are not to be seamed or laced over a board, they must be turned under and finished in some way. In many cases the edges are simply turned under and pressed, then a lining stitched or glued to the wrong side.

Leather, or the various imitation leathers and suedes, make excellent linings for some articles, such as coasters, belts and bags, since the edges of these materials do not need finishing, thus preventing excess bulk. The lining is simply cut to the finished size and either applied to the wrong side of the embroidery with fabric glue or sewn in place with small overcasting stitches.

Woven fabrics are sewn to the canvas in the same way, with the edges turned under. First trim the canvas edges to $\frac{3}{4}$in and press them firmly to the wrong side, using a steam iron or a dry iron over a damp cloth.

To miter a corner

1 Trim across the corner, leaving two canvas meshes between the cut edge and the work.
2 Fold the cut edge over the corner and press.
3 Turn the edges over the work and sew the diagonal folds together using button thread.

Modified long-armed cross stitch can be worked over the folded canvas edges to prevent any canvas threads from showing.

Begin the stitch with three overcasting stitches, working over two horizontal threads. Then take the needle back through the starting point and work in the order shown.

CORDING AND BINDING

A corded edge gives a professional look to pillows and some garments. For such an edge you will need bias binding and piping cord. You can either buy bias binding or make your own from strips of fabric which are then joined. The fabric for bias strips should be light- to medium-weight and fray-resistant. The amount to buy depends on the number of joins that are acceptable. As a rough guide, 1yd of fabric 36in wide will yield nine strips $1\frac{1}{8}$in wide, the longest measuring about $1\frac{3}{8}$yd, the shortest about $\frac{3}{4}$yd.

Piping cord is available in several thicknesses. Most is preshrunk, but for safety buy 4in extra for each yard you need. Immerse the cord in boiling water for five minutes, then leave to dry flat.

For measuring and marking you will need a metal ruler and tailor's chalk.

To make bias strips
1 Straighten the fabric edges, if necessary, by cutting or pulling along a thread.
2 Fold the fabric diagonally so that two adjacent edges are aligned. Press the fold lightly. Cut along the crease. This cut edge lies on the true bias of the fabric.

3 Measure and mark the bias strips using the cut edge as a guide. The width of each strip should be the circumference of the piping cord plus twice the seam allowance (normally $\frac{1}{2}$in).
4 Cut the strips and join them along the straight grain as shown.

To make and attach cording
1 Fold the bias strip over the piping cord, with right side out and raw edges together. Baste (optional) and then machine close to the cord, but without "crowding" it. Use a zipper foot and a long stitch, and stretch the fabric gently as you go. Alternately, sew by hand, using a small running stitch or backstitch.

2 Pin and baste the cording to the right side of the edge to be piped, with the raw edges of the cording aligned with the raw edges of the article. Stitch the cording in place close to the first line of stitching, inside the seam allowance. Clip any curves.

To join ends of thick cording Cut the cord so that the ends overlap by $\frac{3}{4}$in. Cut two strands from one cord, one from the other, and wind remaining strands together. Bind with thread.

Thin cording can be joined in a similar way, but often it is acceptable simply to abut cut ends of cording. Baste them in place if necessary.

BINDING AN EDGE

3 Place corded fabric and uncorded fabric pieces right sides together. Baste and then stitch very close to the cord, using the zipper foot. Alternately, backstitch by hand.
4 Trim the seam allowance of each of the four layers to different widths (called grading). Make any extra clips in curves as needed.

1 Cut and join bias strips. Fold and press in the edges to meet at the center.
2 Open out the fabric along one creased edge and stitch the binding to the main fabric, along the crease, with right sides together. At corners, end the stitching at the turning point. Fold the strip as shown and continue stitching, beginning at the raw edge.

3 Turn the binding to the right side and press. A pleated miter is formed at the corner.
4 Fold the binding to the wrong side, and slip-stitch the pressed-under edge over the existing stitching. Fold the corner to form a miter, as shown, and secure it with tiny overcasting stitches.

PILLOW COVERS

The simplest kind of pillow cover is made by stitching the front and back, right sides together, with a gap left on one side. The cover is then turned right side out, the pillow form inserted and the edges of the opening slipstitched in place.

This method is perfectly satisfactory, but if the cover will have to be removed for washing or cleaning you will need to insert a fastening of some kind. A zipper is most commonly used, and this is concealed best if the seams of the pillow are corded.

Always buy a pillow form slightly larger than the finished size of the cover. This will make the pillow plump and reduce wrinkling at the corners.

It is easiest to insert a zipper before the front and back of the cover are joined. If the embroidery has a top and bottom, insert the zipper in the lower edge, or in the side seam if you prefer. The zipper should be $3\frac{1}{2}$-4in shorter than the finished length of the seam itself, making it easier to join the seam at the corners.

1 Attach the cording to the front of the pillow cover as shown in step 2, page 139.

2 Turn back the seam allowance on the edge where the zipper is and press to bring the cording to the edge. Press under a corresponding seam allowance on the back pillow piece.
3 Pin and baste the folded edge of the back piece over the closed zipper, overlap it by the same amount at each end; cover the teeth completely.

4 Stitch by hand, using prick stitch (see p. 137), or by machine, using the zipper foot. Stitch $\frac{1}{8}$in from the edge and across both ends.
5 Pin the corded edge over the zipper so that the cording overlaps the folded (back) edge. Baste in place.

6 Work prick stitch invisibly between the front cover fabric and the cording.
7 Open the zipper, then baste and stitch the front and back sections together close to the cording, as shown in step 3, page 139. Use hand stitching if necessary to work close to the zipper ends.

MITERING CORNERS ON A HEM

There are several ways of mitering corners on hems. One method is shown in the Drawn thread work section on page 107. In that method, threads are withdrawn to mark the hem fold lines to insure that the number of threads between fold lines is uniform, but a simpler method, for general use on closely woven fabrics, is simply to press the folds.

On sheer fabric, however, it is better to use the method shown here, which produces a miter that is less noticeable from the right side. When cutting the fabric add twice the depth of the finished hem to all sides.

1 Fold half the hem allowance to the wrong side, overlapping the folds at the corners. Press, then fold again, leaving the corners free as shown. Baste the hem in place.
2 Press each corner first to one side, then to the other, creasing the fabric diagonally.
3 Cut off the corners $\frac{1}{4}$in to $\frac{3}{8}$in from the crease.

4 Slip one cut edge under the other and press the edges flat.
5 Turn under the seam allowance on the top cut edge and slipstitch it in place. Take care to work through the hem only, not through the outer layer of fabric.
6 Complete the hem.

TRIMMINGS

Embroidered home furnishings and articles of clothing are often embellished with trimmings. A decorative braid or cord might be sewn around the edges of a pillow or a fringe could be added to the lower edge of a shoulder bag. A single tassel could provide the finishing touch on a bell-pull; while several tassels could be attached to a wallhanging.

Notione and furnishing-fabric departments of stores usually offer a range of trimmings in various colors, but you may not find exactly the color or type you need, and it is often more effective to make the trimmings from the yarn or thread used for the embroidery.

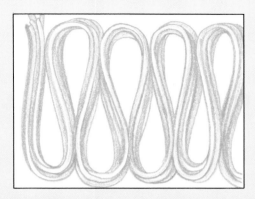

Stitched fringe
1 Take several lengths of yarn and fold them serpentine fashion, as shown, making the loops twice the finished depth of the fringe, plus $3/4$in.
2 Machine stitch twice through the center of the loops, placing the lines of stitching $3/4$in apart.

3 Cut between the lines of stitching.
4 To insert the fringe in a seam, place it as shown, with the stitching along the seamline. Baste it in place.
5 Baste the other fabric piece on top and stitch through all layers.
6 Trim the ends of the fringe.

To make a tassel
1 Wind the thread around a piece of cardboard the depth of the finished tassel.
2 Cut through the ends. Loop a strand of yarn around the folded strands.
3 Bind another strand tightly around the tassel. Slip the end through the loop; pull both ends firmly. Trim ends and push inside.

Bias tubing can be used for shoulder straps or ties, either in single lengths or braided.
1 Cut strips of fabric on the straight grain, four times the finished width of the tubing.
2 Fold each strip in half lengthwise, with right sides together, and stitch down the center and across one end. Trim the seam a little.

3 Turn the tubing right side out by attaching a length of thread to one end and pulling it through the tube, using a bodkin or blunt-ended needle.
4 For a braided tubing, pin three strips together at one end and braid them, then either knot the ends or sew them together, as appropriate to the project.

Twisted cord
1 Estimate the number of strands needed by twisting a few together, then cut them to three times the finished length.
2 Knot the strands together at each end. Slip one end around a doorknob and insert a pencil in the other end. Turn the pencil clockwise until the strands are tightly twisted.

3 Fold the strands in half and hold the knotted ends together. The strands will twist around each other again of their own accord. Shake the cord to even out the twists.
4 Make another knot at each end. Trim the strands evenly.

To sew the cord to a seam Use a single thread and sew through cord and fabric diagonally, working from alternate sides and catching in only a few fabric threads. Leave a small gap in the seam for the ends, then cross them and slip-stitch the fabric edges in place.

141

THE EMBROIDERY DESIGN COLLECTION

The Embroidery Design Collection comprises 46 patterns, each with complete working instructions and photographs of the finished embroidery. Each pattern is a designer original, and the designs have been carefully selected to cover a wide range of techniques, both simple and more challenging. They include many different items, from clothes and household linen to pictures and wallhangings, and cater for different tastes as well as varying levels of embroidery proficiency.

Many patterns also suggest "options" – ideas for altering, adapting or changing the design to suit individual needs, notions or color schemes. Reference to both the Design Your Own and Embroidery Basics sections of the book will be helpful when following the patterns in the Embroidery Design Collection.

CHOOSING THE DESIGN

Having done several embroideries on the theme of teddy bears, the designer turned her attention to a favorite family bear which was showing serious signs of wear. She found it impossible to depict this particular bear's fur in flat surface stitchery, and so hit on the idea of using French knots to give a more textured effect.

She had also been experimenting with different forms of stumpwork, and this led to the solution of padding the bear from behind. The result is a three-dimensional "portrait", which could well outlive the teddy bear itself.

MATERIALS

Fabric
Piece firm, closely-woven fabric for background, enough to mount on a ring frame
Piece dark brown cotton fabric for body, approximately 6in square, or enough to mount on a small ring frame
Red cotton fabric for pillow, $3\frac{1}{2}$in by $4\frac{1}{2}$in
Scraps of dark brown felt for paws
Threads
1 skein stranded floss in each of the following colors: main shade of brown; lighter shade of brown; darker shade of brown; bright red; darker red; black
Tiny amounts of orange and white stranded floss

Medium crewel needle
Small quantity fiber filling for padding
Piece of mounting board the size of required background

Finished size: the teddy measures $3\frac{1}{8}$in long from ear-tip to bottom of pillow; this is slightly smaller than the trace-off design below as the padding reduces the size. The complete picture is 8in by 10in, framed. You could increase or decrease the area of background around the bear.

METHOD OF WORKING

Stretch the background fabric on a frame, and the dark brown fabric on a smaller frame. Trace the design from the Cutting Pattern below onto tissue paper. Place the tracing in the center of the dark fabric and carefully sew around the edges, using small running stitches. Mark the dotted lines also, then remove the tissue paper. Trace and cut around the shapes for the paws in felt.

Following the diagram below, embroider the body in French knots up to the dotted line, using six strands of thread in the main color; use the darker and lighter brown for the highlights. Space the knots out rather more around the edges to facilitate shaping, and leave the eyes, mouth, nose and the area outside the dotted line clear. Appliqué the felt paws as indicated in the Cutting Pattern below, using tiny stab stitches.

Work the red bow in straight stitches, shading with the darker red as shown. Work the mouth in black with small back stitches; use satin stitch in black for the nose; and make a black French knot for the center of each eye. Surround this French knot with a bright orange line and finally a white straight stitch for the highlight.

When the embroidery is complete, cut around it on the marked line, turn the edges under and baste.

Cut out the pillow from the pattern below, making sure the middle is on the straight grain of the fabric. Turn the edges under, pad the pillow with the kapok and attach it to the background fabric using backstitches.

Place the bear on the background fabric so that he sits on the pillow, and sew down one side from the center of the head to the inside of the leg. Stitch firmly through both the bear and the background, using small stitches and making them as invisible as possible. Pad out the body and shape the raised areas as you work, continuing to sew and pad alternately until the bear is completely attached to the background fabric. Remove all basting stitches.

FINISHING

Mount the work by stretching it over a piece of mounting board and either gluing the surplus fabric at the back or fixing it with adhesive tape (see book, p.137).

OPTIONS
A larger version of the teddy could be made as a hot-water-bottle cover or as a child's pyjama case. The body could in this case be left unpadded, or padded lightly for an impression of roundness.

Designed by Jenny Davies

CUTTING PATTERN FOR TEDDY BEAR AND PAWS

CUTTING PATTERN

CHOOSING THE DESIGN

Interest in combining different techniques, in this case tie-dyeing and pulled thread work, was the idea behind this design. The embroiderer has chosen a simple design of diamond shapes against a subtle blue-gray background. Additional color and texture are afforded by the corded embroidery worked in pearl cotton.

MATERIALS

$3/8$yd lightweight white muslin, 45in wide
Pearl cotton no. 2 in white, yellow and pink
Sewing thread and button thread in any color
Sewing needle and fine tapestry needle
1 pack cold-water dye in blue or blue-gray
Tailor's chalk

Finished size: the finished scarf measures approximately 10in by 44in

METHOD OF WORKING

First hem the fabric by rolling it between the fingers to form an even hem, then stitch with small running stitches worked in sewing thread; press.

Tie-dyeing
Following the Pattern Design illustration, mark out the diamonds using tailor's chalk. Then follow the diagram for the steps in tie-dyeing (and see book, pp. 32–3).

First make running stitches around the edge of each diamond. Use button thread, fastening it securely at the start and leaving a long end for wrapping around the shape when drawn up (A). When all the stitching is complete, gather the threads for each diamond, wrap the long end several times around the gathers and fasten off by rethreading the needle and taking it through the bundle (B).

For the border, make running stitches all around about $3/4$in from the hemmed edges, then gather up tightly and fasten off.

Make the dye according to the manufacturer's instructions and immerse the scarf in the dyebath for the length of time recommended.

Leave to dry with the gathering threads still in place. When dry remove all the 'hreads and press (C).

Embroidery

Select the squares to be embroidered, indicated in blue on the Pattern Design diagram below. Either follow the diamond designs illustrated, or design your own. Using the tapestry needle, work rows of straight vertical stitches over three warp (horizontal) threads, pulling the stitches fairly tightly as you go to draw the fabric threads together. This is a pulled work technique called coil filling stitch.

OPTIONS
The scarf could be varied by using diamond shapes in different sizes—for example, a large one in the center surrounded by smaller ones. A variety of other embroidery stitches could also be used. The color scheme could be made brighter by using hot-water dyes, which give much deeper shades.

Designed by Donna Rumble

DIAMOND DESIGNS

TIE-DYEING

a   b   c

PATTERN DESIGN

middle point

middle point

each square = 1cm/³/₈in

CHOOSING THE DESIGN

The bluebell and convolvulus were used as the basis for these cards partly because of their design possibilities and partly because of their symbolic significance. In the ''language of flowers'', the bluebell is said to mean constancy, while the convolvulus symbolizes bonds. The embroiderer has treated the twining stem of the convolvulus in a stylized way so that it forms a heart shape, while the spray of bluebells tied with a simple bow is depicted quite naturalistically.

MATERIALS

$\frac{1}{2}$yd pure silk, 18in wide
1 skein each stranded embroidery floss —for the bluebells: dark blue, light blue, dark green, light green, white and natural. For the convolvulus: pale yellow, darker yellow, 2 silvery greens, cream, blue-gray
Small piece backing fabric such as linen (for convolvulus)
12in cream satin ribbon, about $\frac{1}{8}$in wide
Mounting cards with windows; small amount thin cardboard
Crewel needles, sizes no. 8 and 9
Tracing paper, pencil, pounce powder (see book, p.10)

Finished size: both embroideries measure $3\frac{1}{8}$in by $3\frac{1}{2}$in

METHOD OF WORKING

Bluebell design

Cut a piece of silk 8in long and wide enough to fit in a small ring frame. Trace the design and transfer it to the silk by the pouncing method (see book, p. 65). Mount the silk in the ring frame. Work the embroidery following the colors shown in the photograph.

Using two strands of dark green thread, work the large leaves in satin stitch and the main stems in stem stitch. Work the petals in satin stitch with one strand of blue, using the paler shade for the left side of each one and the darker shade for the right side, to create a light and shadow effect. Before stitching the last top petal, outline the area with a few split stitches or stem stitches and work the satin stitch on top (see book, p. 78). This gives a slightly raised look, and 'lifts' each petal up from the one underneath.

Use one strand of natural for the stamens and one strand of green for the small pieces of stem, varying the shade as desired. The small leaves and wisps can be worked in either satin or stem stitch. Finally, work the forget-me-nots in white satin stitch, with either blue or natural for the centers. Position the ribbon across the stems as shown, secure it with a few stem stitches and then tie a bow, anchoring it unobtrusively with a few stab stitches if necessary.

Convolvulus design

Transfer the design as for the bluebell and mount the silk on top of the backing fabric.

Embroider the leaves first with satin stitch, using two strands of the lighter green thread for one side and the darker for the other. Couch the stems (see book, p. 71), using three strands for the laid threads and two for the couching, varying the shades of green. Satin stitch the flower bases in green, ''lifting'' the raised edge as described for the bluebell. Work each flower in satin stitch using pale yellow thread, adding a few stitches of cream to lighten the centers. Use one strand of the darker yellow for the center spots. Work the butterfly in blue-gray, adding small yellow spots with one strand of thread.

FINISHING

Trim each embroidery to $\frac{3}{8}$in smaller all around than the outer edge of the mounting card. Cut a piece of thin cardboard to the same size and attach the edges of the embroidery to it with fabric glue, then attach the mounted embroidery to the back of the front piece of the mounting card so that it shows through the window. If you are unable to obtain a suitable windowed card, you can make your own from the mounting boards sold in art stores; cut out the window with a sharp knife.

Designed by Caroline Davis

THE BLUEBELL

THE CONVOLVULUS

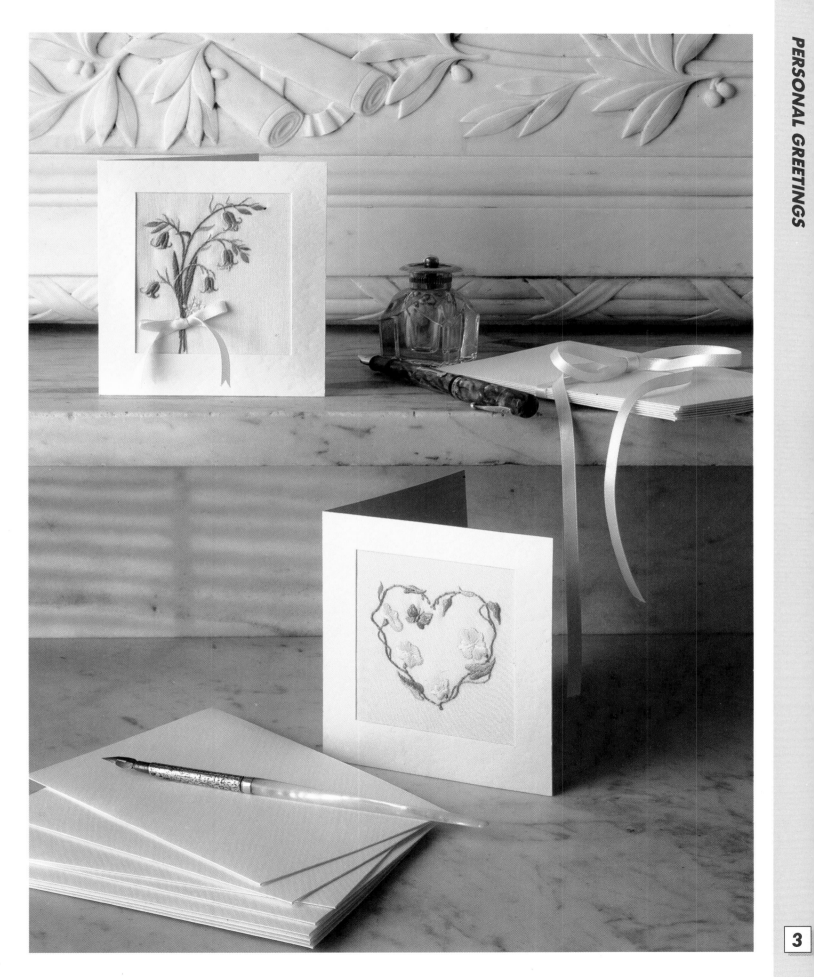

CHOOSING THE DESIGN

The idea for this design came from a photograph. A series of tracings was made, gradually simplifying the intricate details into broader, flatter areas until the right image was achieved. In this case the designer wanted to give a general impression of the goose, emphasizing the wing feathers. The colors of the threads were selected in much the same way as an artist selects paint colors, choosing shades to create an impression, with the freedom to rearrange them as necessary while working.

First the outside edge and then each main area was outlined in running stitch, this being the basic stitch used for the whole picture. Each area was then developed in turn, blending the colors and tones by eye. The gradations of color, in the sky for example, were achieved by using a single thread instead of a double one where one tone or color becomes darker or lighter.

MATERIALS

Linen canvas (available from artists' suppliers) at least 8in by 10in, or large enough to stretch on a slate frame
Note Linen canvas provides a solid background, but any similar close-mesh natural-fiber fabric can be used.
Threads
Stranded floss in a selection of colors. Since this kind of embroidered painting is largely a matter of personal choice, it is not

possible to specify precise colors. However, as a general guide, you will need the following:
8 skeins in shades of gray-blue and blue (for the sky and pond, arranged in different ways)
7 skeins in shades of gray, brown, beige and white (for the goose)
2 skeins pink-beige (for the beak)
2 skeins green (for the pond bank)
1 skein each light beige and donkey brown (for the border)
Scraps of red-brown and black (for the eye)

Crewel needles, 1 medium and 1 fine
Masonite or mounting board, $4\frac{1}{4}$in by 6in
Gummed paper strip or string (See Finishing below)

Finished size: the complete picture, with mount, measures $6\frac{1}{2}$in by 8in. The area of embroidery is $4\frac{1}{4}$in by 6in.

METHOD OF WORKING

Trace the design from the diagram below and transfer it to the canvas (see book, p.64). The diagram is actual size and shows the direction of the stitches. Stretch the canvas on the frame, if you are using one.

Outline the outside edge in running stitch (see book, p.69), then outline each main area in the appropriate color, before filling in the areas of the design with the stitches indicated.

Referring to the diagram and the color photograph as necessary, continue the work in running stitch on each area in turn, except for the wing feathers, using one or two strands of thread as required. The medium needle, with two strands of thread, will cover the large areas best, while the fine needle, with one strand of thread, can be used for any small details, such as the eye and the beak.

Work the wing feathers in fly stitch (see book, p.77), varying the size and direction of the stitches to create texture and detail.

Finally, work the border in satin stitch (see book, p.78).

FINISHING

Using a damp cloth or a steam iron, press the embroidery on the wrong side. If the canvas is distorted, gently pull and stretch it back into shape.
Mounting
Stretch the canvas over the piece of board or masonite. If you are using mounting board, secure the canvas at the back with gummed strip; if masonite, lace the canvas at the back as shown on page 138.

Masonite is the best choice if you are not intending to frame the picture. If you are, then mounting board is adequate, since it will be held by both glass and backing.

Designed by Ljiljana Rylands

KEY

satin stitch

running stitch

fly stitch

CHOOSING THE DESIGN

This abstract geometric design exploits the vibrant effects that can be created by the juxtaposition of blending and contrasting colors. Additional interest and texture have been created by the use of the free and inventive stitchery in colors chosen to contrast with the painted squares and stripes.

MATERIALS

6yds white heavy cotton fabric, 36in wide
Screen frame with three panels, each with an inside measurement of 22in by 60in
Threads
Stranded embroidery floss: 6 skeins turquoise in a light and darker shade; 6 skeins pink in a light and darker shade; 4 skeins pale green; 1 skein pale lilac; 1 skein mid-blue; 4 skeins pink shaded to white; 3 skeins white; 2 skeins red

Fabric paints or printing inks in 10 colors: 4 shades of blue; 2 shades of lilac; 2 shades of green; pink and red (see Note below)
2 large rolls adhesive tape, $3/4$in wide
1 large roll masking tape, 1in wide
1 large and 1 small paintbrush
Yardstick, T-square, pencil
Staple gun and staples
Jars for mixing paint
Note Most fabric paints are available in only a limited color range, so you will have to mix them to obtain the shades used here. To mix the 10 colors you will need red, pink, green, blue, black and white.

Finished size: each panel measures 22in by 60in, without the frame

METHOD OF WORKING

Preparing the fabric

Cut out three rectangles of fabric, each 24in by 64in. Iron one piece and place it on a wipe-clean surface (or place two layers of clean paper underneath before painting). Using masking tape, fix the fabric firmly to the work surface, making sure that the grain is quite straight.

To mark each rectangle, first draw a line 22in long along the bottom, leaving an equal margin below and at each side. Using the T-square, draw a vertical line at a right angle from one corner and extend it to 60in. Mark the other sides in the same way. Measure and draw a margin all around the rectangle the exact depth of the recess in the screen frame. Using yardstick and T-square, and measuring carefully, mark in the squares and stripes from the diagram.

Painting the fabric

Mix the colors so that you have 10 blending but distinct shades. Paint the fabric according to the photograph or your own design. Paint one color at a time, masking all the areas for each color. Paint as evenly as possible, forcing the color through the fabric without leaving any excess lying on top or beneath to form blotches. Leave each area to dry thoroughly before starting on the next. To fix the colors, iron on the back with a hot iron.

Making the screen

Trim the excess fabric outside the design, leaving the small margin, then turn this under so that the fold is on the edge of the design, and press. Staple the fabric to the top recess of the frame, working from left to right and placing the staples about $3/8$in apart, then turn the frame the other way up and staple the other short end, pulling the fabric slightly to stretch it. Staple the sides.

The stitching

The embroidery for the squares, indicated by blue lines in the diagram opposite, consists of long stitches running diagonally across each square or block of squares. The larger areas also have stitches worked vertically and horizontally to outline each square or block. The colors contrast with the painted colors, and are changed for every pair of squares. Use six strands of thread throughout, starting at the inner corner of each square. Knot the thread to secure it at the start, and fasten off by sticking the thread to the side of the frame on the wrong side with masking tape. Sew all the diagonals first, then the outlining stitches, following the diagrams.

The stitching inside the stripes and in the free areas is a series of long and short stitches arranged in a zigzag pattern and running the length of each stripe. Using the diagrams as a guide, vary the size and direction of the stitches, allowing some stitches to extend over the edges.

When complete, trim all the threads on the inside of the screen. Cover the staples in the screen recesses with strips of wood.

Designed by Christine Calow

MAKING UP

SMALL PATTERN SQUARES

LARGE PATTERN SQUARES

one square = 1cm/$3/8$in

5

CHOOSING THE DESIGN

The simple dog-rose motifs, in bright sunny colors, are worked in buttonhole and fly stitch, rather than a more solid filling stitch, to give a feeling of airiness to this design. The French knots in the centers add texture.

MATERIALS

$1\frac{3}{8}$yd white poly/cotton fabric, 45in wide
Stranded embroidery floss: 2 skeins each deep yellow, pale yellow, cream and leaf green
1 spool white sewing thread
Crewel needle, size no. 9/10
Tracing and dressmaker's carbon paper

Finished size: the diameter of the tablecloth is 44in

METHOD OF WORKING

Preparing the cloth

Cut off the selvages. Make an exact square by folding the fabric diagonally and trimming off the excess. Press the fold, then fold in half twice more as shown, so that there are eight thicknesses of fabric; press well. Measure from point A to point B as shown in the Pattern Design diagram below and mark this measurement along the bottom (long) edge. This is point C. Mark several points between B and C exactly the same distance from point A, then join them to form a curve. Cut along the curve through all thicknesses to make a perfect circle. The folds will serve as a guide for placing the motifs.

To prevent fraying, work the hem before starting the embroidery. Turn under $\frac{3}{4}$in, then $1\frac{1}{8}$in to make a double hem and baste well. The cloth illustrated was hemstitched by hand, but a quicker alternative would be to use machine straight stitch. For a more elaborate hem an embroidery stitch could be chosen, such as herringbone, fly stitch or chain stitch, in either white or a contrasting color.

The embroidery

Trace the outlines of the motif and transfer it to the fabric using dressmaker's carbon paper (see book, p. 64), placing each one centrally over one of the creases and $4\frac{1}{2}$in from the hem.

Two strands of thread are used throughout for the embroidery. Start with the whole flower, working the inner petals in buttonhole stitch in deep yellow. The spacing of the stitches is an important part of the effect: they should not be so close together that the fabric does not show, and they must radiate out from the center so that there is more space between stitches at the outer edge than in the middle. You will find it easiest to start at the center of each petal and work first to one side and then out to the other side.

Work the second row of petals into the first row, using the pale yellow thread. To keep the same density of stitches, it will be necessary to increase their number. Work the outer row in cream, again increasing the number of stitches to maintain the density. Finally, work deep yellow French knots in the center. Work the second flower in the same way, filling in the small areas in straight stitch as indicated on the pattern design.

Work the leaves in fly stitch (see book, p. 76), starting at the tip and using the vein of the leaf as the center of the stitch. Space the stitches a little farther apart on the leaves and fill in with straight stitches.

FINISHING

Wash the cloth if it has become at all dirty. Iron it on the wrong side while damp on a pad of felt or a clean blanket. This will stretch the embroidery while retaining its texture.

Designed by Margaret Horton

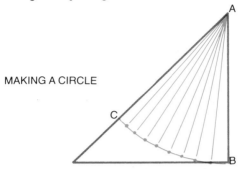

MAKING A CIRCLE

MAKING UP

PATTERN DESIGN

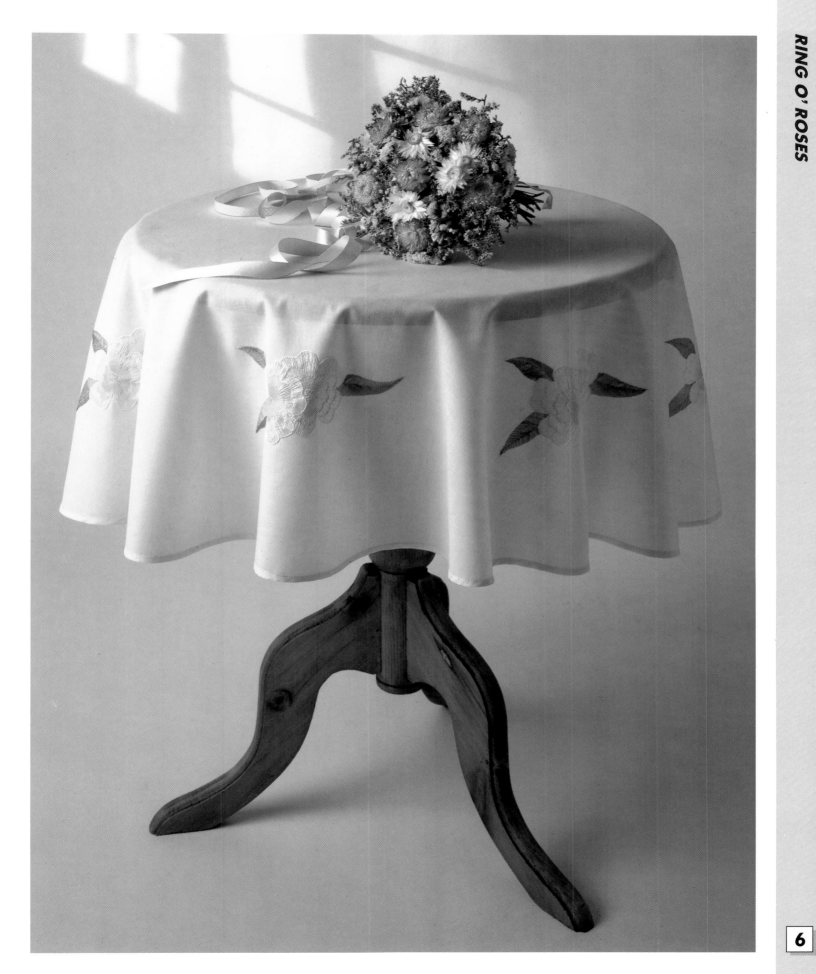

CHOOSING THE DESIGN

For this rag book the designer has chosen as her theme the sequence of night and day, starting with the north star, the herald of night, and ending with the rising sun. The bright colors make the images easily recognizable to a small child, as well as rendering the creatures of night—the bat and the owl—less frightening.

MATERIALS

Fabric
30in lightweight cotton fabric, 36in wide, in black and white
Small piece synthetic batting
Threads
1 spool black machine thread
Stranded embroidery floss: 1 skein black, 1 skein yellow
Coton à broder: 1 skein each in black, yellow, blue, red or pink, white
1 spool gold lurex thread

Fabric paints in black, blue, yellow, red
Artist's paintbrushes, small and large
Dressmaker's carbon paper, pencil

Finished size: each page measures 7in by 9in, the cover 9in by 15in

METHOD OF WORKING

Painting the fabric
Enlarge the designs and transfer them to the white fabric, using carbon paper. Transfer the stitching lines around the sun on page 4 also, since you will need them as a guide for the embroidery. The design for the star on the front cover can be taken from page 1. Cut out the pages and front cover, allowing a margin of ³/₄in all around.

Practice fabric painting on a spare piece of white fabric. When you feel confident, place the batting under the fabric and paint in the outlines of each shape, using the black paint and a small brush. Leave to dry, then press with a hot iron under a damp cloth to fix the paint.

Referring to the photograph, paint in each area in the relevant color, leaving the owl and all the background areas until last. For these areas a color wash technique is used. Dampen the fabric slightly with a brush so that the colors run into one another when applied; paint the paler colors first. Try out the technique on some spare fabric – if too much water is used, the colors will spread too far. When painting the background, take care not to cover the black lines: paint just outside the outline and allow the paint to run up to it. When dry, fix as before.

The embroidery
Page 1. Work the eye of the moon in satin stitch using two strands of black thread.
Page 2. Work seeding stitch (see book, p. 76) for the bat's wings and tail, using gold lurex thread and white coton à broder. Work the eyes in satin stitch.
Page 3. Work the owl's eyes as before,

then work zigzag stitch around them with one strand of yellow thread. Work the body in plush, or knot stitch, shown below, using blue, yellow and pink coton à broder. Page 4. Work the sun's eyes in French knots, using black coton à broder. Place the knots as close together as possible.

ASSEMBLING AND FINISHING

Cut the black fabric to the same size as the painted pages and front cover. Seam around each edge with right sides together, leaving an opening at the bottom edge to turn. Turn right side out and press, pushing the corners out well, then slipstitch to close the opening.

Pin and baste along the edges and then diagonally across as for quilting (see book, p. 91). Press lightly along the edges on the wrong side, using a cloth under the iron.

Using two strands of black embroidery thread and running stitch, embroider on top of all the black outlines through both thicknesses of fabric. Work the sun's rays in yellow coton à broder and running stitch.

To assemble the book, slipstitch each page in turn to the center of the cover, stitching ¼in from the edges on both back and front to secure the pages thoroughly.

Designed by Claire Johnson

KNOT STITCH

PATTERN DESIGNS

PAGE 1

PAGE 2

PAGE 3

PAGE 4

one square = 1cm/³/₈in

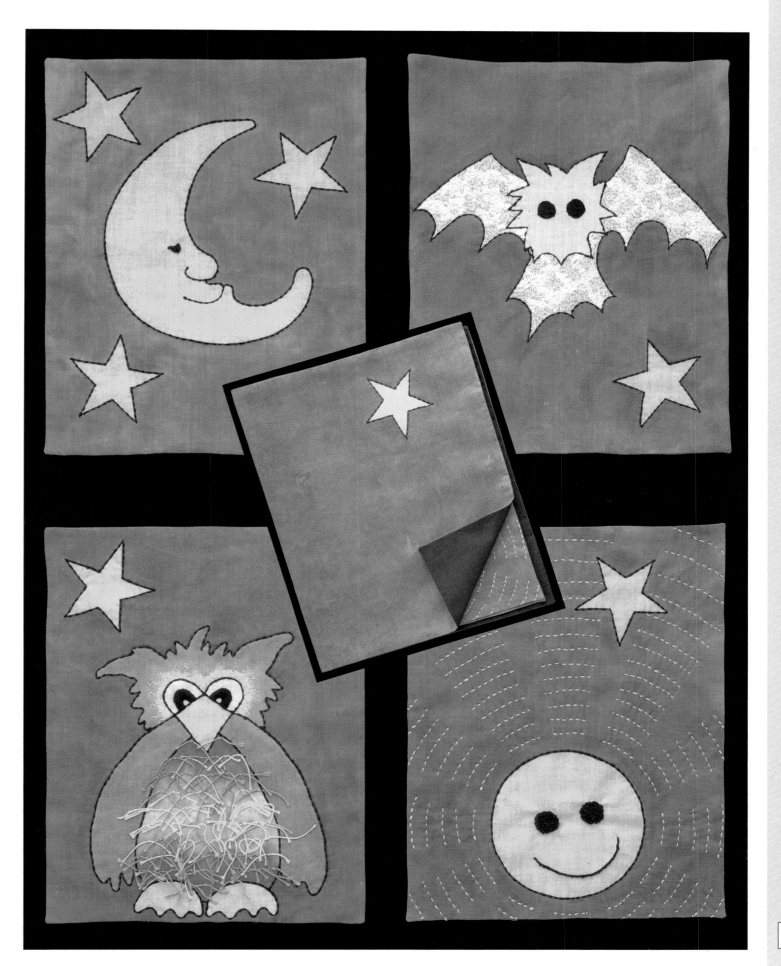

CHOOSING THE DESIGN

The inspiration for this bag was a series of photographs of lobsters in a natural history book. The designer made tracings of these and then combined different elements to form a composite lobster motif, which was then stenciled on the canvas.

MATERIALS

$3/4$yd cotton duck or sailcloth in a natural color, 36in wide
1yd similar fabric in black, 36in wide
1 spool cream polyester machine thread
1 spool black polyester machine thread
Thick black thread, approximately $1/8$in thick, for couching
1 skein black stranded embroidery floss
Sharp, large-eyed needle; crewel needle
12 black glass beads, about 3in long
Red and green fabric paints, printing inks

or acrylic paints; stiff paintbrush
Small sheet heavy stencil paper; craft knife; masking tape
Pencil; tailor's chalk; carbon paper; tracing paper

Finished size: the bag measures about 15in by 19in

METHOD OF WORKING

Stenciling

Two alternative "lobster with seaweed" designs are given here. In Stencil A (used for the bag illustrated), the lobster is a solid color area, while in Stencil B there are gaps between the body sections.

Cut a 7in square of stencil paper. Enlarge your chosen design for the lobster and seaweed and transfer it to the stencil paper using carbon paper. Cut out the stenciled shapes with a sharp knife.

Cut out the front and back pieces of the bag from the natural cotton sailcloth. Mark a $3/8$in seam allowance all around with basting. Then divide the width into three sections of $6^1/4$in each, marking the divisions with tailor's chalk. Cut notches in the corners of the stencil $3/8$in from each edge (these are registration marks) and place the stencil so that the notches are placed on the first marked line of the canvas as shown in the Pattern Design diagram, and $3/8$in from the top. Match the registration marks with basting or marked lines as appropriate. Secure the stencil with masking tape, then mask out the seaweed shape with paper.

Paint in the first lobster. Apply the paint or fabric ink fairly thickly so that it does not run under the stencil. When the first lobster is dry, move the stencil, register and tape it again, and stencil the second and then the third in the same way. When the lobsters are complete, mask out these areas, remove the masking paper from the seaweed motifs, and stencil them in green. Repeat the process for the back of the bag.

Press fabric paint or ink with a hot iron on the wrong side to fix it, but do not press if acrylic paint has been used.

Embroidery

Mark the lines for the couching (indicated in blue on Stencil A and the Pattern Designs) with tailor's chalk. Thread a length of the thick black thread into the large-eyed needle, knot one end and bring the thread through to the right side at the top of a line. Make one long stitch to the end of the line and fasten off by overcasting on the wrong side with the machine thread. Couch the threads (see book, p.71) with the machine thread and crewel needle, working all the downward lines first. Embroider the body markings and antennae with the stranded floss, using either backstitch, stem stitch or chain stitch, then sew on the beads for the eyes.

FINISHING

Cut out the remaining pieces for the bag in the relevant colors, following the Cutting Pattern, then zigzag stitch all the edges to prevent fraying. Using a large stitch on all the straight seams, join front and back pieces to the gussets to make one long strip. Press seams open.

For the handles, press under the seam allowance on both long sides, then fold in half with the hems on the inside. Pin and then top stitch $1/4$in from both edges. Join each pair of top bands to make two strips and press seams open. Fold the strip in half with wrong sides together, then mark the mid-point of each side and baste the handles in place as shown in the diagram opposite. Place the second band on top, with right sides together, and stitch along the seam allowance. Press seam open and fold over with the handles on top.

Pin the right side of the top strip with handles to the wrong side of the bag top. Stitch the seam, then baste under the seam allowance on the other side; fold the band in place and top stitch $\frac{1}{4}$in from the edge. Top stitch along the top to secure.

Join the bottom black bands to make one strip. With right sides together, stitch to the main bag, then fold over and top stitch on the right side. Join the bag side seam, making sure that the top edges meet evenly. Press seam open. Pin the base to the bag with right sides together, matching the bottoms of the gussets to the short sides of the base. Machine stitch the seam. Remove all basting; press. Turn to right side.

Designed by Sue Saunders

CUTTING PATTERN

one square = 1cm/⅜in

PATTERN DESIGN

one square = 1cm/⅜in

STENCIL A

STENCIL B

one square = 1cm/⅜in

ATTACHING THE HANDLES

one square = 1cm/⅜in

CHOOSING THE DESIGN

Each of these three bow ties makes use of a different embroidery technique, but in all of them the embroidery is quite subdued, so that the effect is more that of a printed and textured fabric. The white tie is couched in a diamond pattern, while the larger diamond pattern on the gray tie is machine stitched with a twin needle and then embellished with French knots. The black-and-white tie is simply satin stitched within the pattern of the printed checks.

MATERIALS

The white tie
$1/2$yd white linen-textured polyester, 36in wide
Pearl cotton size no.5 in red and gray
The gray tie
$1/2$yd gray linen-textured polyester, 36in wide
Sewing thread in pale gray and black
The black-and-white tie
$1/2$yd black-and-white checked brushed cotton, 36in wide
Pearl cotton size no.8 in red, dark gray, black and white
Crewel needle, sharps needle
Tailor's chalk, tracing paper

Finished size: each tie is 34in long and measures $2^1/8$in at the widest point

METHOD OF WORKING

For all three ties, make a paper pattern by enlarging the one given. Note that the pieces must be cut on the bias.
The white tie
The couching is best worked on a ring frame, but this is not essential. If using a frame, mark but do not cut the two top pieces on the fabric, leaving enough for the back pieces. Mark the $3/8$in seam allowance and stretch the fabric in the frame.

The laid threads form a diamond grid pattern, and are placed about $3/8$in apart. You may find it helpful to mark the position of the stitches along the seam allowance before starting. Using the red thread and the crewel needle, lay all the threads in one direction first, starting and finishing each one $1/8$in outside the seam line. The last long stitch should be placed about $7^7/8$in from the center seam. Work the laid threads in the opposite direction then, using the gray thread, make small stitches over each intersection.

Remove the work from the frame and cut out the four pieces.
The gray tie
Cut out all four pieces. The grid pattern is stitched on the top two pieces with a twin needle machine, with the rows of stitching approximately $3/8$in apart. Mark along the edges as before, then stitch first in one direction and then in the other using the pale gray thread. When both sides are complete, make a small French knot at each intersection using the black thread.

The black-and-white tie
Cut out the four pieces. Work blocks of satin stitch on the top two as shown, using red, gray, black and white pearl cotton.

FINISHING

Join the center seams of backs and fronts. Trim the seam to within $1/4$in of the stitching and press open. With right sides together, stitch the backs to the fronts, leaving an opening for turning as shown. Trim the seam, clip the corners and turn to the right side, pushing out the edges well. Press, then slipstitch the edges of the opening together.

OPTIONS

Any geometric embroidery stitch could be used for the ties, but the most effective designs will be created with fairly small, regular stitches. Tiny beads could be used instead of the French knots, and the stitching on the check tie could be varied—cross stitch over the checks would create a pleasing texture. Different fabrics could be used also, but they should be crease-resistant.

Designed by Ariella Green

CUTTING PATTERN

one square = 1cm/$3/8$in

MAKING UP

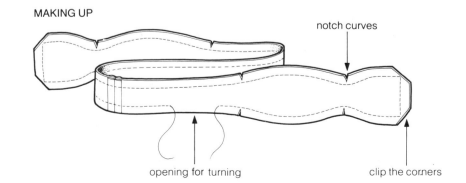

notch curves

opening for turning

clip the corners

CHOOSING THE DESIGN

Nothing gives a more individual look to clothes than hand-made buttons, especially if they are made by the dressmaker to complement a particular garment. All these buttons can be made quite easily from inexpensive materials.

MATERIALS

Dorset buttons
Curtain rings, $\frac{3}{4}$in and 1in in diameter
Threads, such as pearl floss, coton à broder, matte embroidery or crochet floss
Tapestry needle
Toggles
Any embroidery thread sold by the hank
Covered buttons
Self-covering buttons
Evenweave linen or fine, soft canvas
Tapestry needle
Coton à broder or stranded embroidery floss

WORKING THE DORSET BUTTONS

Thread the tapestry needle with a long length of thread (about two and a half arm's length.) Tie the free end to the curtain ring and buttonhole closely around the edge. Catch the short end under the first few stitches to secure it, and cut it off closely. When the ring is covered, slip the needle through the first stitch worked to join the stitches together.

Turn the stitches firmly on the ring so that all the loops are on the inside. Hold the thread to the front of the ring and pass it up over the top of the ring and down the back to the starting position. This forms the first spoke of a wheel. Continue to make spokes in this way, moving around the ring as evenly as possible.

Join the spokes in the center by working a cross stitch over the middle; centralize the stitch by pulling gently but firmly.

Next the spokes are filled in. Backstitch from one spoke to another, beginning in the center and working under spokes 1 and 2, then back under 2 and 3. Continue until the ring is filled with stitches, varying the colors if desired by joining a new thread into the back of the button.

WORKING THE THREAD TOGGLES

Fold a hank of thread until you have the required thickness, then wrap another thread, in a contrasting color if desired, evenly around it. When the hank is well covered, fasten off by pulling the thread back through the hank to the center top and working a small buttonhole loop.

The toggles can be varied by working a row of buttonhole stitch at each end of the wrapped section, or by working detached buttonhole stitch to form a mesh over the wrapping; both are shown in the photograph. Attractive toggles can also be made using random-dyed thread (see book, p.52).

WORKING THE COVERED BUTTONS

Mount the fabric in a ring frame (see book, p.66) and, using the measuring guide on the button card, draw a circle on the fabric. Mark the approximate center, then work the design of your choice from those given below (see book, Blackwork pp.104-105 and Needlepoint pp. 126-127). The needlepoint stitch shown here is diagonal satin stitch; Scotch or mosaic stitch would create a similar pattern. Before removing the embroidery from the frame, run a gathering thread around each circle, 1in from the edge. Cut out and cover the buttons, according to the manufacturer's instructions.

OPTIONS

Buttons of the types shown can be made in almost any threads, colors or combinations of colors, so it is possible to match or blend with any garment.

Designed by Gail Marsh and Jacqueline Blackburn of *Bottom Drawer*

DORSET BUTTONS

THREAD TOGGLES

BLACKWORK BUTTON

CANVAS BUTTON

CHOOSING THE DESIGN

The hat was inspired by Peruvian designs, which make use of bold, stylized shapes and juxtapose bright colors. The motifs on this hat are less ethnic representations.

Felt, which is available in bright, clear colors, is ideal for this kind of bold, simple design. It also has the great advantage of not fraying, so the appliqué shapes can be smaller and more elaborate than is possible with woven fabrics.

MATERIALS

Fabric
10in square pale blue felt
9in squares of felt in red, pink, yellow and gray
Small piece red felt
Threads
$1\frac{1}{8}$yds yellow satin ribbon, $\frac{5}{8}$in wide
$1\frac{1}{2}$yds green satin ribbon, $\frac{1}{4}$in wide
$1\frac{1}{8}$yds green satin bias binding
1 spool cotton sewing thread in red, yellow, green, black and pale blue
1 spool silver lurex thread
1 skein yellow embroidery thread for tassel

Bonding web for appliqué shapes
20 gray mother-of-pearl 4-hole buttons

Finished size: to fit child aged about 2–4

METHOD OF WORKING

Draw the pattern pieces to size from the cutting pattern and make a pattern for each of the appliqué shapes from thin cardboard (cereal boxes are an ideal weight).

Iron bonding web to the backs of the four 9in felt squares, but do not remove the paper backing. Cut out pattern pieces A, B and C from the pale blue felt and D from the small piece of red felt.

Place the patterns on the backing of the felt squares, and draw around them. Cut out the shapes from the appropriate colors.

Using herringbone stitch, either by hand or machine, attach a length of green satin ribbon $1\frac{3}{4}$in from the bottom of piece A.

Remove the backing paper from the backs of the hearts and three of the bears, leaving it on the fourth bear, since this will be attached after the seam is made. Iron shapes in place as indicated in the Making Up diagram, then stitch the hearts in place using backstitch and a double thickness of red sewing thread. Attach the bears using stab stitch and yellow thread, picking out the details—nose, mouth and eyes—with black satin stitch.

Remove the backing paper from all but one of the pink clouds and from all the suns. Iron them on above the green ribbon, placing the suns between alternate clouds so that the clouds overlap them by about $\frac{3}{8}$in. Stitch the clouds using blanket

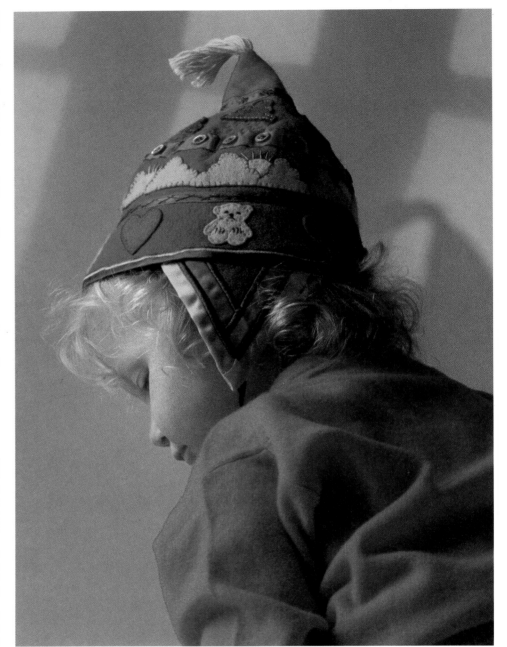

stitch and red thread, and the sun using stab stitch and yellow thread, working long, straight stitches for the sun's rays.

Lay three of the gray clouds in place, remove the backing paper and iron on piece B. Stitch, using backstitch and a single thickness of lurex thread, then use running stitch in a double thickness of lurex thread for the rain.

Stitch piece A to piece B, using close machine zigzag stitch to join them edge to edge. Baste, and then sew, the red ribbon over the seam so that the lower edge of the ribbon just covers it. Sew on the buttons, using green thread for contrast. Join piece C to piece B in the same way, and stitch green satin ribbon over the seam, using a suitable machine embroidery stitch if your machine has one, or by hand if not.

FINISHING

Sew center back seam using a small ladder stitch. Press open. Try the hat on the child if possible, and make any small adjustments at this stage. Appliqué the remaining bear and cloud over the seam and stitch as before.

Fold the yellow ribbon in half over the two lower edges of each earpiece and baste. Place the red ribbon so that its edges butt up to the yellow one; baste in place and then stitch, using green thread and a machine satin stitch about $\frac{1}{4}$in long. Baste green bias binding to the bottom of the hat, baste earpieces in place and secure both earpieces and bias binding with machine satin stitch in yellow.

Sew about 15in of green ribbon to the bottom corners of each flap and knot at the ends to prevent fraying. Make the tassel

(see book, p. 141) from yellow embroidery thread, fit it into the cone at the top of the hat and stitch in place. Finally, steam the work without touching it with the iron to "lift" the fabric and stitching.

OPTIONS

Felt appliqué can be combined with machine stitching for a great variety of different items from outer garments to wallhangings. Felt cannot be washed, however, so it is not suitable for anything that needs frequent laundering. Sequins or beads could be used instead of buttons, and the stitching can be varied to create different effects, color combinations and textures.

Designed by Victoria Brown

CUTTING PATTERN

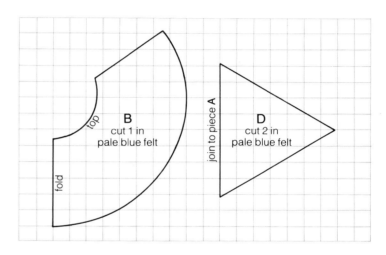

one square = 1.25cm / $\frac{1}{2}$in

APPLIQUÉ SHAPES

MAKING UP

SUN
cut 6 in yellow felt

TEDDY BEAR
cut 4 in yellow felt

HEARTS
cut 4 in red felt

RAIN CLOUDS
cut 4 in grey felt

CLOUDS
cut 4 in pink felt

CHOOSING THE DESIGN

The embroiderer has chosen simple motifs, relying for effect on the way the colored pillowcase shows through the semi-transparent organdy. The stitchery is simple too, in keeping with the delicacy of the design—more elaborate embroidery might look fussy and overdone. An important requirement of shadow work is that the stitching is worked as neatly as possible, since it is visible from both sides.

MATERIALS

$3/4$yd cotton organdy, 36in wide
1 skein white stranded embroidery floss
$2\frac{1}{2}$yd narrow satin ribbon
Baby pillow measuring approximately 13in by 17in or desired size
$\frac{1}{2}$yd colored cotton poplin, 36in wide, to cover pillow
Tracing paper for pattern
Fine crewel needle

Finished size: the pillowcase measures 17in by 22in

METHOD OF WORKING

To cover the pillow, cut two pieces of cotton poplin $3/8$in larger all around than the pillow. With right sides together, seam three sides, then turn right side out, insert pillow and slipstitch the open end to close.

Cut two pieces of organdy $2\frac{1}{2}$in larger all around than the pillow. Make a pattern of the complete pillowcase on tracing paper by enlarging the one given below (if your pillow is a different size, trace the outer lines from the cut organdy). Then transfer the design lines on to the top piece of organdy, including the inner border lines, by basting through the paper and then tearing it away. Alternately, use a water-soluble fabric marking pen.

Cut a piece of organdy large enough to cover the design and position it behind the design, basting it in position. Using one strand of embroidery floss, pin stitch (see book, p. 86) all around the motifs through both layers. When the stitching is complete, carefully cut away the surplus organdy as close to the design edges as possible, using small sharp scissors.

The back opening
Baste the line for the opening on the back piece of organdy, about 3in in from the side inner border line. Then cut a strip of organdy about $1\frac{1}{8}$in wide and place it centrally over the basted line. Stitch down both sides $\frac{1}{8}$in from the line, then cut down the middle to $3/8$in of the marked line for the inner border. Turn the facing to the inside, turn the raw edges under, and machine stitch close to the edges.

FINISHING

Place the back and front of the pillowcase with right sides together and machine stitch all around, about $\frac{1}{4}$in from the outer edges. Trim the seam to $\frac{1}{8}$in, turn the pillowcase right side out and press carefully. Baste, then machine stitch along the inner border line. Cut the ribbon into six 10in lengths and sew three to each side of the back opening at evenly spaced intervals. Insert the pillow.

OPTIONS

The same design could be given a different look by using colored organdy to back the motifs and inserting a plain white pillowcase. The motifs might be enlarged to occupy a greater area, and the border embellished with embroidery at the edges or just outside the inner stitching line.

Designed by Jenny Chippendale

BACK OPENING

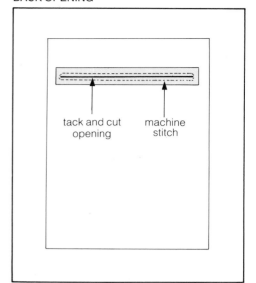

tack and cut opening   machine stitch

PATTERN DESIGN

one square = 2.5cm/1in

CHOOSING THE DESIGN

The starting point for this design was a drawing of a garden made by the embroiderer one hot summer. Because the embroidery is intended to convey the effect of regular flower borders, the design concentrates on the shapes of the yuccas and red-hot pokers against the wall, not on the small details. The motifs are repeated in rows; the sun is also repeated at regular intervals. The warm colors were chosen to accentuate the summer atmosphere.

MATERIALS

Fabric
$1\frac{1}{4}$yds cotton fabric, 36in wide, for backing and lining
1yd blanket or felt, 36in wide
$1\frac{1}{4}$yds gray cotton fabric, 45in wide
$\frac{1}{2}$yd green cotton fabric, 36in wide
$\frac{1}{2}$yd yellow cotton fabric, 36in wide
$\frac{1}{2}$yd each of printed cotton fabrics, 36in wide: yellow-and-white stripe, green stripe, and pattern suitable for a wall

A spool of machine embroidery thread in each of about six colors, to match and blend with appliqué fabrics, plus dark red and dark brown for flowers
$1\frac{1}{4}$yds bonding web, 36in wide
$\frac{1}{2}$yd heavy iron-on interfacing, 36in wide
Machine needle, size no.90

Finished size: the wallhanging measures 25in by 34in

METHOD OF WORKING

The wallhanging is worked in sections, two for the central panel and seven for the borders, as shown, so that each section can be comfortably accommodated under the sewing-machine foot. The appliqué is done first, the pieces being assembled and applied to the background by the bonding web method (see book, p.83). The work is then basted in one piece to the blanket or felt, and the surface machine stitching carried out before all the pieces are joined. You should allow a 1in seam allowance around all sides of the panels, for joining.

Cut the appliqué pieces for panels A and B, outlined in black on the charts; apply the bonding web to the fabrics before cutting, but leave the backing on. Cut patterns for the sun motifs by enlarging those given in panels A and B overleaf, and cut out 21 small suns and one large one. Cut out a piece of the green-striped fabric 8in by 36in and set aside to make binding and loops later.

Cut out 15in-wide strips as follows: two in the pattern chosen for the wall, $1\frac{1}{2}$in and 1in deep; two of yellow-and-white stripe, $4\frac{1}{2}$in and 8in deep; one of gray, $4\frac{1}{2}$in deep, two of green stripe, $1\frac{1}{2}$in deep; and one of yellow cotton, 2in deep.

Cut out two pieces of gray backing fabric: 15in by $17\frac{3}{4}$in for section A and 15in by 16in for section B. Assemble the cut pieces on the gray fabric as shown on the panel charts, remove the backing from the bonding web and iron on, leaving a $\frac{1}{2}$in seam allowance all around. Make sure that those pieces which have to be overlapped by others are ironed on first.

Cut out two pieces of blanket or felt to the same size as the appliqué work and baste both layers together firmly (see book, p.91). The machine embroidery, outlined in blue on the panel charts, is essentially free, and it will be helpful to look at the photograph to get an idea of the stitches and colors used. Try out the stitches on spare pieces of fabric before starting each one; the fabric allowance is sufficient to make test pieces of each.

The stitches used are mainly satin and zigzag, with the widths varied to create different effects. There is a double row of straight stitching inside the satin-stitched border of the large sun; below this are wavy lines of satin stitch in white and gray. The yuccas are dark brown, red and green satin stitch, and the red-hot pokers have satin stitch for the leaves, while the flowers are worked in random zigzag with the foot removed from the machine (this must be done very carefully). On panel B there are rows of gray satin stitch below the first line of suns, and close satin stitch below and beside the yuccas in dark red-brown.

When the central panels are complete, cut the fabric for the borders as shown; use gray fabric as backing for the outer borders and green for the inner ones. Cut 17 suns in yellow-and-white striped fabric for each long outer border and 10 for each short one. Work the appliqué and embroidery as for the central panels.

FINISHING

To join the central panels, cut a strip of interfacing about 2in deep and the width of the panels. Place the panels edge to edge and iron the interfacing onto the back. Cover the join with a wide row of decorative satin stitching. Join the border pieces to each other and to the central panel in the same way, satin stitching over each join.

To make the edging strips, cut two strips of green-striped fabric 2in by 26in and two 2in by 35in. Join one short strip to the top by placing right sides together and working a $\frac{1}{2}$in seam. Turn right side out, turn the raw edge under and hand hem at the back. Repeat for the bottom binding strip and then for each side.

To make the loops for hanging, cut three strips of the same fabric, each 2in by 5in. Fold in half lengthwise, turn in $\frac{1}{2}$in on the long edges and stitch close to the edge. Fold each in half and attach at equal intervals to the wrong side of the hanging so that about $1\frac{1}{2}$in projects above the edge to take the hanging rod.

Finally, cut a piece of lining fabric to the same size as the wallhanging, press under the $\frac{1}{2}$in seam allowances on both, and hand stitch wallhanging to lining around all four sides.

Designed by Chris Crilly

MAKING UP

one square = 2.5cm/1in

PANEL A

one square = 1.25cm/$\frac{1}{2}$in

PANEL B

one square = 1.25cm/$\frac{1}{2}$in

PANEL C

PANEL D

one square = 1.25cm/$\frac{1}{2}$in

CHOOSING THE DESIGN

Quilting is a form of embroidery with a long history that is enjoying a revival. Many modern embroiderers use the technique in new ways, often combining it with other forms such as appliqué, patchwork and machine embroidery. But for this pillow the embroiderer has chosen a traditional design worked on plain fabric, creating a subtly patterned and textured surface.

MATERIALS

Fabric

$\frac{1}{2}$yd pure cotton lawn, 36in wide
$\frac{1}{2}$yd white muslin, 36in wide
$\frac{1}{2}$yd lightweight synthetic batting, 36in wide
1 spool cotton-covered polyester sewing thread to match lawn

2yds bias binding, for piping
2yds preshrunk piping cord, size no.3
2 small pearl buttons
Sharps needles, size no.8
Tracing paper, no.2 pencil, bodkin or tapestry needle

Finished size: the pillow measures 15in by 15in

METHOD OF WORKING

Preparation

Make a complete pattern on the tracing paper by enlarging and repeating the one-quarter shown in the diagram. Cut the lawn into two 18in squares, keeping the long strip left over for finishing. Cut the batting and muslin into two squares the same size.

Lay a square of padding, such as a folded sheet, on a table and iron the first piece of lawn completely smooth. Then place the traced pattern on top and pin in position. Starting from the center, scratch over every line of the design with the bodkin or tapestry needle, thus marking the design onto the fabric. The indentation made will remain long enough to complete the quilting, but the method can only be used on pure cotton fabric. (For other methods of transferring designs, see book, pp.64-65)

Mount the muslin backing on a scroll frame with at least 24in working space (see book, p.67). Leave the muslin slightly loose when assembling the frame, since a little flexibility is needed for hand quilting. Lay the batting and then the marked cotton on top. Pin the top and bottom (the roller sides) through all three layers, then tape the sides, wrapping the tape around the frame and pinning through all layers.

Quilting

Quilt the design with a small running stitch, taking two to four stitches on the needle at a time (see book, p.91). Start working at one corner and work across the pillow to the center, then turn the frame around and work toward you. Aim to have about 10 stitches to the inch, and make sure that all the stitches go through all three layers by pushing the fabric from underneath with your left hand. Fasten off by making two small backstitches and losing the end in the batting.

The back of the pillow can either be left plain or quilted in the diamond grid pattern given here. If you are quilting the back, prepare the design and fabric in the same way, and quilt with running stitches, working from the corner to the center.

FINISHING

Cut a piece of the left-over cotton lawn to the width of the pillow and $3\frac{1}{8}$in deep to make a flap for the top of the pillow front, as on a pillowcase. Turn a $\frac{1}{4}$in hem under twice and stitch, then baste to the top of the pillow front with wrong sides together and raw edges matching.

Fold the bias binding in half lengthwise and insert the piping cord in the fold. Open out the turned-under edges of the binding, then baste close to the cord. Baste, then stitch the piping all around the edges of the pillow front on the right side (see book, p.139). To join the piping, trim the cords so that they abut, then trim the bias binding to a $\frac{3}{8}$in overlap, fold the edge under and wrap around the raw edge. Stitch across the join.

Turn under a 1in hem at the top of the pillow back and hand-hem. Pin the pillow back to the pillow front with right sides together and with bottom and side edges matching. Baste, then stitch, placing the stitching precisely on the previous line, and ironing the top open. Sew the buttons onto the pillow back and embroider corresponding loops on the front, using buttonhole stitch.

OPTIONS

The same design could be worked effectively on satin, which would catch the light and show up the gently curved lines. In this case the design would have to be transferred by one of the methods described on pages 64-65.

Designed by Gail Marsh

FRONT

BACK

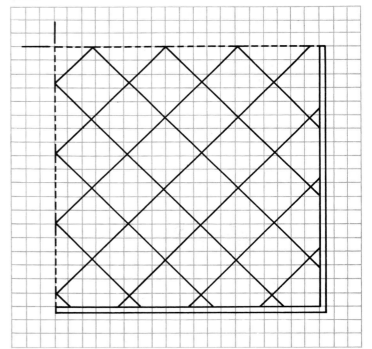

one square = 1 cm/ $\frac{3}{8}$in

14

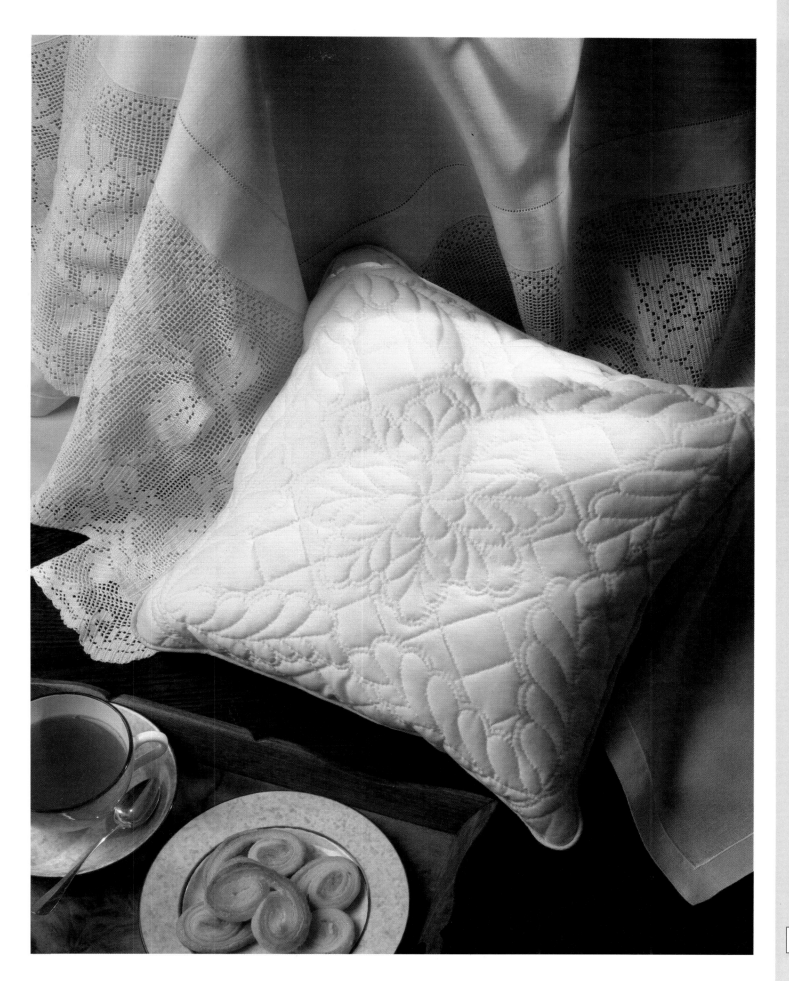

CHOOSING THE DESIGN

The original design idea for this bed-spread sprang from an interest in Japanese architecture. The arrangement of different colors within a square grid was based on floor tiles. The woven ribbon technique is essentially a Victorian one. Here it is given a more modern appearance, and is used to create areas of texture and color which are accentuated by the tassels. A sewing machine with twin needles is essential for the quilting.

MATERIALS

Fabric

$6\frac{1}{2}$yds natural shantung, 36in wide
4yds lightweight batting, 36in wide
$6\frac{1}{2}$yds lawn or lightweight cotton sheeting, 36in wide, for backing

4yds natural or white silk, 36in wide

Ribbons

All $\frac{1}{2}$in wide as follows: $\frac{1}{2}$yd deep pink, $1\frac{1}{2}$yds pale pink, $3\frac{1}{2}$yds pale blue, $2\frac{1}{4}$yds deep green, 1yd pale green, 1yd pale yellow

Threads

3 spools each of machine embroidery thread in green, pink, blue and yellow
3 spools silk thread to match shantung
Stranded embroidery floss in pale pink, pale blue, pale green, yellow for tassels
Machine needles, sizes no.90 and no.70; twin needle
$7\frac{1}{2}$yds satin bias binding, $\frac{1}{4}$in wide in natural color or contrasting for edging (or use strips of the shantung)
Tailor's chalk, yardstick, T-square

Finished size: the bedspread measures approximately 72in by 72in

METHOD OF WORKING

Sixty-four pieces, each 8in square and with a $\frac{3}{4}$in seam allowance all around, compose the bedspread. The Making Up diagram shows the positioning of the squares in the finished bedspread. The design requires each quarter of the quilt to radiate out from the center.

For each square cut out a piece each of shantung, batting and backing measuring $9\frac{1}{2}$in. For the squares marked B and C, and those left plain in the chart, baste the silk, batting and backing together (see book, p.91) before stitching. Squares A, D, E, F and G have the ribbon weaving and decorative stitching worked before the backing is added.

Work the squares C and B first. C consists of a grid of straight stitches placed $\frac{5}{8}$in apart, shown blue in the chart below, and sewn with the natural-colored thread. Mark the grid first with tailor's chalk, yardstick and T-square. B is the same, but with a twin needle used to make tiny pin tucks, giving a raised effect.

For squares A, work as follows. Mark the area for the ribbon weaving and satin stitching with tailor's chalk as shown. Attach the deep pink ribbon to the top and bottom of the ribbon square with a row of straight stitches. Attach the pale pink ribbon to one side only, then weave it in and out of the dark pink and stitch at the other side to secure. Trim the ends, then work satin stitching around the edges with a thread of blending color. Work the yellow, pink and green satin stitching. Make the tassel by cutting six 4in lengths of the yellow and green stranded embroidery floss, folding them in half and then sewing them in place at the fold with a block of wide satin stitch.

For squares D, E and F, work the ribbon weaving and attach ribbons and tassels in the same way, following the colors of ribbons, threads and tassels shown below. Note that squares G have a double tassel. When all the decorative squares are complete, baste them to the batting and backing pieces.

ASSEMBLY

On a flat surface assemble the squares row by row in the order shown. Working from edge to edge, baste and then machine seam with right sides together $\frac{3}{4}$in from the edges. Press seams open as you proceed, then baste and stitch each row together.

For the lining, cut the silk in half, seam down the long edges with right sides together and press seam open. Place the lining wrong side up on a flat surface, lay the quilt right side up on top of it, and pin and then baste through all thicknesses. Using natural-colored thread, machine stitch on the lines marked blue in the diagram. Finish by edging with bias binding. Alternatively, cut $2\frac{1}{4}$in wide strips of shantung on the bias and join them to form a binding strip.

OPTIONS

For a less time-consuming project, the same design, or sections of it, could be used to make a pillow, or matching pillows, each using an enlarged version of one of the decorative squares.

Designed by Chris Crilly

KEY

——— stitching line

 Align arrows shown on charts for individual squares in the direction indicated when making up the bedspread

MAKING UP

SQUARE A

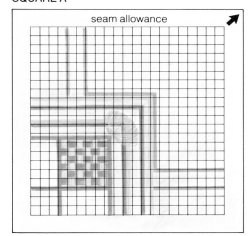
seam allowance

SQUARES B & C

SQUARE D

SQUARE E

one square = 1cm/⅜in

SQUARE F

SQUARE G

CHOOSING THE DESIGN

Kites were chosen as the motifs for this jacket because they appeal to children and because they make simple, bold shapes that can be worked in appliqué relatively quickly. The couched, tasseled tails provide textural interest and give an added touch of individuality to the design.

The jacket, which is cut from straight pieces of fabric, is extremely simple and can be adapted to any size merely by enlarging or reducing the pattern.

MATERIALS

$1\frac{1}{4}$yds each blue and yellow colorfast cotton fabric, 45in wide
$1\frac{1}{4}$yds medium-weight synthetic batting, 36in wide
Small pieces of cotton fabric in chosen colors for kites
Stranded embroidery floss in colors to match kites
Blue and yellow sewing thread
$2\frac{1}{2}$yds yellow bias binding
4 toggles

4 small yellow 2-hole buttons
Tracing paper
Pencil or water-soluble marking pen
Quilting needle

Finished size: the jacket measures 33in around the chest and 17in from shoulder to hem. The sleeve seam measures 14in. To fit a child aged 3–4, approximately.

METHOD OF WORKING

Appliqué and embroidery
The appliqué and couching are worked on the cut pieces before the three layers are joined together for the quilting.

Make a pattern by enlarging the diagram shown. Cut out one back piece, two sleeves and two front pieces from both the yellow and blue fabric. Cut out the same pieces from the batting, but $\frac{3}{8}$in smaller all around.

Cut out the kites, cutting two contrasting-colored pieces for each one, then join each pair together by machine or hand stitching a $\frac{1}{4}$in seam where indicated on the pattern diagram. Fold under a $\frac{1}{4}$in hem all around each and baste. Position the kites on the blue fabric as shown, and attach them either with tiny slipstitches or overcasting. Embroider the tails with couching stitches (see book, p. 71) worked over long laid threads of embroidery floss. Make tassels (see book, p. 141) from embroidery floss and sew them in place.

Quilting
With right sides together, and allowing a $\frac{3}{8}$in seam, join the back and fronts of the blue fabric at the shoulders. Press seams open. Seam the sleeves to the body, matching the central points of the sleeve tops to the shoulder seams. Press seams open. Join the yellow pieces in the same way, then join the batting by butting the edges up together and loosely overcasting on both sides.

Put all three layers together with the batting in the middle. Baste around the outside edges and the shoulders and sleeve seams to align them and hold them together. Run basting thread from top to bottom and from side to side in a grid with lines worked 2in to 3in apart.

Mark the clouds with faint pencil lines or water-soluble pen. Quilt around the clouds using running stitch and three strands of embroidery floss. Quilt around the kites about $\frac{1}{4}$in outside the edges, using running stitch and a double thickness of blue sewing thread.

FINISHING

Remove the basting threads around the sides and sleeve seams. With right sides together, machine stitch the sides and sleeve seams of the blue fabric only, lifting the needle and pivoting the fabric at the

underarm point. Clip at underarm to ease. Join the batting at the sides and sleeve seams as before. Press under the seam allowance on the yellow fabric and pin, then clip at the underarm point and slipstitch the edges together.

Binding and fastenings
To make the loops for the toggles, fold a 12in length of bias binding in half lengthwise and stitch two lines of stitching down the length. Cut it into four pieces, fold each one in half, and attach them to the jacket front, 3in apart, with the top one $\frac{3}{8}$in from the neck opening.

With right sides together, stitch bias binding around the neck, down each side of the jacket front and at the sleeve edges.

Fold the binding over and slipstitch it to the lining. Sew on the toggles, placing buttons on the underside and sewing through them to strengthen the toggles.

OPTIONS
Any motifs could be used for this simple jacket—a design could be based on a child's favorite animal or toy. A simple floral motif could be effective, possibly using the Persian appliqué technique of applying cut-out motifs from a printed fabric (see book, p. 83).

Designed by Penny Rawlings

CUTTING PATTERNS   SLEEVE cut 2

KITES cut 2

one square = 1.25cm/½in

one square = 2.5cm/1in

FRONT cut 1

BACK cut 1

one square = 2.5cm/1in

CHOOSING THE DESIGN

For this bright crib cover, the embroider has chosen the technique of knotted, or tied, quilting—a much quicker method of embroidery than the more traditional stitched quilting. The knots are worked in a pattern that forms a border effect and is enhanced by the striped bias binding.

MATERIALS

Fabric

1yd each blue and yellow broadcloth, 36in wide
$\frac{1}{8}$yd green broadcloth, 36in wide
$\frac{1}{8}$yd red broadcloth, 36in wide
1yd medium-weight synthetic batting, 36in wide

Matte embroidery threads: 1 skein each green, blue, red and yellow
Large-eyed sharps needle
Tailor's chalk or pencil; yardstick

Finished size: the quilt measures approximately 30in by 35in

METHOD OF WORKING

Cut out the blue fabric, the yellow fabric and the batting to 31in by 36in. Following the Making Up diagram, mark the position of the knots on the blue fabric, using yardstick and tailor's chalk or pencil.

Smooth out the yellow fabric, place the batting and the blue fabric on top; baste through all three layers (see book, p. 91).

Work the knots as shown, following the Making Up diagram for the placing of the colors; work from the center outward. Each knot is made twice, the second stitched at a right angle over the first. Leave ends of about 1 inch.

When the knotting is complete, trim the edges of the quilt and trim the ends of the knots to about $\frac{3}{4}$in, making sure that they are neat and even. When the quilt is washed, the ends will spread out a little.

Edging

For the striped bias binding, cut strips of all four colors of fabric 27in long. Make the blue and yellow strips 6in wide, the red and green strips 2in wide. Join the strips down the long sides to form a tube, allowing $\frac{1}{4}$in seams. Press the seams open, turn each tube right side out and flatten it with your hand.

Follow the diagram (right) for folding the edging. Continue rotating and folding until all the fabric is used up, pressing each new fold lightly as you proceed. Press once more, then open the fabric out.

The tube is now cut following a continuous fold line around in a spiral to produce a single piece of diagonally striped fabric. Insert a sharp pair of scissors into the tube and cut carefully through only one thickness of fabric. Press out all the remaining fold lines, then fold the piece in half lengthwise and cut along the fold. Fold each piece in half again and

cut down the fold as before. Join the strips together end to end.

FINISHING

With right sides and raw edges together, stitch the binding all around the edges of the quilt, joining the ends (see book, p. 138). Turn the binding right side out, press the seam, then fold it over. Press under the $\frac{1}{2}$in seam allowance and stitch to the other side of the quilt over the first line of stitching.

Designed by Yvonne Pedretti

MAKING UP

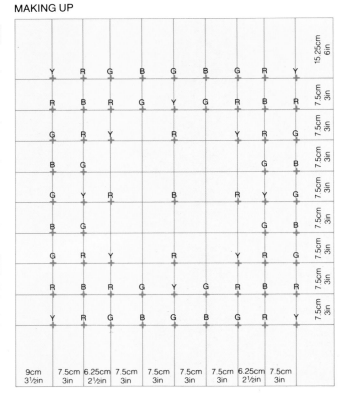

Y = yellow   R = red   G = green   B = blue

MAKING THE KNOTS

FOLDING THE EDGING

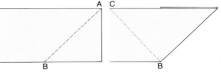

Fold under along the line A-B. Fold over along B-C. Make a third fold C-D, folding over. Fold under along D-E. This completes the first four turns, forming a square of folded triangles.

CUTTING FABRIC TUBE

CUTTING FABRIC STRIPS

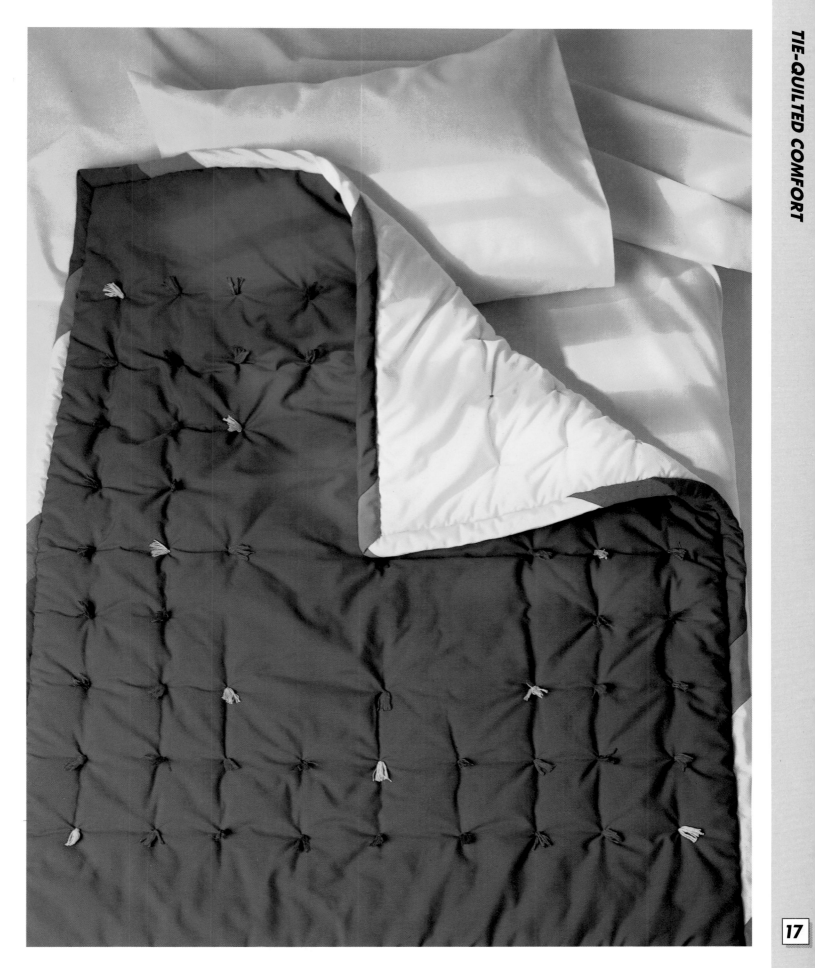

CHOOSING THE DESIGN

This form of quilting combined with appliqué is thought to have developed as a response to the more traditional methods taught to Hawaiians by the missionaries. The motifs represent the shadows cast by the island flowers of Hawaii and bear the names of the plants that inspired them, while the quilted lines echo the waves of the sea. The designs, usually executed in bright primary colors, are cut in one piece by the method children often use for making snowflake patterns in paper—by folding a square of fabric into eight, cutting shapes into it and then opening it out. Intricate designs can be made in this way, which can either have a starting point in nature, like these, or else be quite random and abstract.

Three of the four pillows—breadfruit, carnation and clownflower—are traditional Hawaiian designs, and the fourth was developed in a similar way; it is based roughly on a sunflower shape. Try experimenting with different paper patterns, opening out the paper to assess each one until you arrive at a pleasing design.

MATERIALS

(For each pillow)
Fabric
1yd cotton fabric, 36in wide in background color
$5/8$yd cotton fabric, 36in wide in contrasting color for appliqué
$5/8$yd lightweight batting, 36in wide
Threads
1 spool quilting thread or cotton sewing thread in a color to match appliqué fabric
1 spool sewing thread in background color

Quilting needle, size no. 10 or finest available
16in zipper
Pillow form, 18in by 18in or nearest available size
Beeswax block
Sheet of fairly stiff paper, 17in by 17in

Finished size: Each cushion measures 18in by 18in

METHOD OF WORKING

The pattern
Make the pattern by folding the square of paper into half, then half again, then diagonally to form a triangle one-eighth the size of the original square. Enlarge your chosen design from the charted diagram below, draw it onto the triangle and cut out. Open out the paper to make sure the design is as intended, then cut out one triangle. This forms the pattern. Mark the center point of the design, by referring to the color photograph. Mark the longest side on the pattern also; this must be placed on the bias of the fabric, with the other two sides on the straight grain.

The appliqué
Cut out a square measuring 17in by 17in from the appliqué fabric. Fold the fabric square in the same way as the paper, pressing each fold in turn and taking great care to be accurate. Cut out two squares each measuring 17in by 17in from the background fabric. Fold and press one square of background fabric in the same way, then open it out.

Carefully pin the paper pattern to the folded triangle of appliqué fabric through all eight thicknesses, making sure to match the center points, the bias and the straight grain of fabric. Mark all around the edges of the pattern with a pencil (not a ballpoint or felt-tipped pen), remove the pattern and re-pin the folded layers of the fabric together.

Cut through all thicknesses, using very sharp scissors. Open out and pin onto the background fabric, carefully matching the fold lines. Pin along the fold lines, then baste the appliqué approximately $1/4$in from the edges.

Appliqué the design by hand, using tiny hemming stitches (see book, p. 85) and matching thread. Turn about $1/8$in under as you go. On curves and points, overcast at the outside edges to prevent possible fraying. To make the points look as neat as possible, turn them under at the top first, then down each side.

The quilting
Cut a slightly larger square of batting, 18in by 18in, and lay it on top of the backing fabric. Lay the completed design on top of the batting. Starting from the middle, secure all three layers together with basting stitches in lines spaced about 3in apart.

Wax all quilting thread before use by running it over the beeswax to strengthen it and prevent tangling. Place work in a circular quilting frame and quilt all around the edges of the appliqué (see book, p.91) with small, even stitches. Fill in the background with evenly spaced contoured lines about $3/8$in apart. The motifs themselves can also be quilted, but this is not strictly necessary. (You may find it helpful to mark the lines first with a water-soluble pen; the marks can be washed out when the work is complete.)

The quilting can be done by machine if quick results are desired.

FINISHING

Cut out the pillow back to measure 17in by 18in. Cut this piece of fabric in half down the long side and insert the zipper between the cut edges, turning under $1/2$in on each side to give a square the same size as the front.

Cut two strips of background fabric to measure 2in by 17in, and another two to measure 2in by 18in. With right sides together, baste and then machine stitch the shorter strips of fabric to the sides of the pillow front, stitching $1/2$in from the edge. Turn to right side and press seam open. Join the longer strips of fabric to the top and bottom, as shown in the diagram below, stitching across the side strips. Turn right side out, over the raw edges. Baste, then stitch the pillow back to the strips, leaving one edge open. Turn right side out and hand-hem the opening, turning $1/2$in under.

Designed by Angela Madden

CLOWNFLOWER

straight grain / bias / straight grain / bias

SUNFLOWER

CARNATION

straight grain / bias / bias / straight grain

BREADFRUIT

one square = 2.5cm / 1in

CHOOSING THE DESIGN

Machine quilting is a versatile and quick form of embroidery, which invites experimental, less traditional types of design. It is ideal for work of this size, since any larger pieces are difficult to accommodate under the machine foot.

Designs based on straight lines, rather than curves, work better for machine quilting. This design, although it looks elaborate, is actually quite easy to work.

MATERIALS

Fabric
$5/8$yd lightweight sew-in interfacing or fine cotton, 24in wide

$3/4$yd medium-weight silk (in varying widths)
$1/2$yd batting
$7/8$yd pre-shrunk calico, 36in wide
Threads
Machine embroidery threads in 11 shades as indicated in the Panel Design diagram (sewing thread or twisted silks could also be used)
Silk thread to match silk fabric
Other equipment
Graph paper marked in $1/4$in squares
Black felt-tip pen, No.2 pencil, ruler
Sewing machine and needle, size no. 70
Clear plastic embroidery foot or ring darning foot
Fine sharps sewing needles, fine pins

Fabric-marking pencil or pen
PVA glue and small brush
2 pieces mounting board, $17^{1}/4$in by 19in and $21^{1}/2$in by $22^{1}/2$in

Finished size: the finished panel, when mounted, measures $21^{1}/2$in by $22^{1}/2$in

METHOD OF WORKING

Enlarge the quilted panel design on the graph paper to the actual size it will be worked. Using $1/4$in squared paper, each unit will be $1^{1}/2$in, the size used for this panel, but it can be reduced or enlarged if you wish. On the diagram each line is numbered (1–11) as a guide to the sequence of colors, but these can be ignored for a simpler design using only one or two colors. Trace over the design with a felt-tipped pen to emphasize stitching lines.

Tape the interfacing or cotton fabric over the design and carefully trace the lines, using a well-sharpened pencil, on the wrong side of the fabric. The design is worked on the wrong side throughout.

Cut out a piece of batting to measure $17\frac{1}{4}$in by 19in. Using fine needles (pins will mark the silk), pin together the silk, batting and interfacing or cotton. Make sure the batting is placed within the design lines marked on the backing layer. Using white or cream silk thread and a fine needle, baste the layers together, starting in the center and working outward in parallel rows.

Quilting
Set the machine on straight stitch with the stitch length between 1 and 2. (You may need to experiment with one or two samples to get the stitch and tension right.) Using a needle size no. 70, and a see-through embroidery foot if possible, start working from the central band of the design, then outward to left and right. Use one color at a time and stitch in the directions indicated by the arrows in the Quilted Panel Design diagram, placing the colors as indicated in the key. Leave ends of 3–4in and, when each color is completed, pull them through to the wrong side. Either knot and cut them or sew them into the backing stitches.

The border design and mount
When the machine stitching is complete, lace the work around the smaller piece of mounting board. Cut a top mount $\frac{3}{4}$in deep at the sides and 1in at the top and

bottom from the larger piece of mounting board, then cut a piece of silk $\frac{5}{8}$in larger than the outside edge of the mount and cover the mount with it as follows. Place the mount on the silk, taking great care to keep the fabric grain straight and using pins to hold the fabric along the edges of the board as shown in the diagram for Covering Top Mount (this diagram illustrates the underside). Turn the surplus fabric at the outside edges over and glue it to the board.

Before cutting away the inner area of silk, put slightly watered-down PVA glue on the inner corners (see diagram for Covering Top Mount) and leave it to dry. This will prevent the fabric from fraying. When quite dry, cut away the middle area of silk, leaving $\frac{5}{8}$in all around. Cut diagonally into the corners almost to the mount, turn over and glue.

Cut out a piece of calico 30in by 30in. Stretch the calico on a scroll frame and mark centrally on it the area of the panel and outer frame. Using cut-offs of silk, each about $2\frac{1}{4}$in by $3\frac{1}{8}$in, build up a

border of overlapping mock pleats by folding each piece in half lengthwise. Baste the pleats into place on the calico as indicated in the Making Up diagram. Place the machine-stitched panel centrally on the calico with the silk-covered mount on top so that the edges of the pleats are covered, and complete the panel by hand sewing along the edges of the mounts with tiny up-and-down stab stitches.

Note All measurements given are for the size of panel illustrated. Check your working measurements carefully before cutting mounts, since there may be variations.

FINISHING

Take the embroidery off the frame and re-mount it by stretching the edges of the calico over a piece of masonite, ready for framing. Alternately, make or buy a simple stretcher frame the size of the work and baste the calico to it.

Designed by Irene Ord

KEY
1 = deep red-brown
2 = donkey brown
3 = olive green
4 = forest green
5 = turquoise
6 = bright yellow-green
7 = mustard
8 = light red-brown
9 = brick red
10 = crimson
11 = dark green-brown

COVERING TOP MOUNT

QUILTED PANEL DESIGN

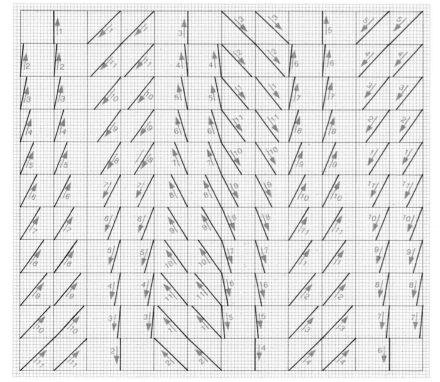

five squares = 2cm/¾in

MAKING UP

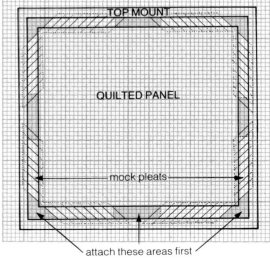

one square = 1cm/⅜in

CHOOSING THE DESIGN

For small items such as these baby bootees, a simple motif is the best choice. The embroiderer has chosen the rabbit motifs both for their associations with childhood and because they can be treated in a simple, stylized way. The central rabbit is cut out from felt and appliquéed, while the others are outline-embroidered with running stitch.

MATERIALS

Fabric
$\frac{1}{4}$yd white brushed cotton, 36in wide
$\frac{1}{4}$yd white cotton, 36in wide
$\frac{1}{4}$yd lightweight synthetic batting, 12in wide
$\frac{1}{4}$yd heavy sew-in interfacing, 6in wide
Scrap of white felt

White sewing thread
White stranded embroidery floss
2 small snaps; 2 small buttons
Tailor's chalk, tracing paper
Small piece thin cardboard for pattern

Finished size: the bootees measure $4\frac{1}{4}$in long and $2\frac{1}{8}$in wide at the widest point

METHOD OF WORKING

Make a paper pattern by enlarging the one given in the diagram. Cut out two of each piece from white cotton and brushed cotton. Cut out two pieces A and B from batting and two of D from interfacing.

To make the soles, trim the $\frac{1}{4}$in seam allowance from the interfacing and mark a trellis pattern as shown, using the tailor's chalk. Place the pieces on the cotton, matching the edges of the interfacing to the seam allowance of the cotton. Baste in position and stitch on the marked lines.

Baste the batting to the wrong sides of pattern pieces A and B, and seam the sides of B, matching notches. Trim the batting close to the seams.

Make a pattern for the rabbit motif by tracing the design given, then cut out two rabbits from felt and pin them in place on the center front of each bootee. Apply by stitching all around the edges with backstitch, using three strands of embroidery thread. Work a cluster of French knots for the tail. Mark the outlines of the other rabbits by drawing around the pattern, positioning them as shown on the pattern. Work the outlines in backstitch, with French knots for the tails as before.

Attach the tops of the bootees to the soles, matching points a and b. Turn to right side. For the straps, stitch the cotton and brushed cotton pieces together, leaving an opening at the center back for turning, as shown. Trim the seams and turn to the right side. Matching points c at center back, and with right sides together, overstitch the straps to the backs of the bootees.

Lining
Stitch together the brushed cotton pieces for the backs, front and soles, allowing $\frac{3}{8}$in seams. Trim seams, then trim $\frac{1}{4}$in from the top edges. Turn over a further $\frac{1}{4}$in at the top edges and press well. Baste the linings into the bootees, pushing them down well into the corners.

Turn over and baste the $\frac{1}{4}$in seam allowance at the top of the outer bootees, then slipstitch the lining to it.

Sew snaps onto the straps and bootees; sew on the buttons as decoration.

Designed by Margaret Horton

CUTTING PATTERNS

SOLE D

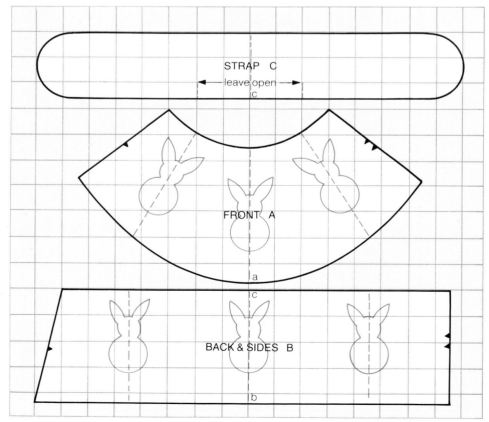

STRAP C
leave open
c

FRONT A
a

BACK & SIDES B
b

one square = 1cm/$\frac{3}{8}$in

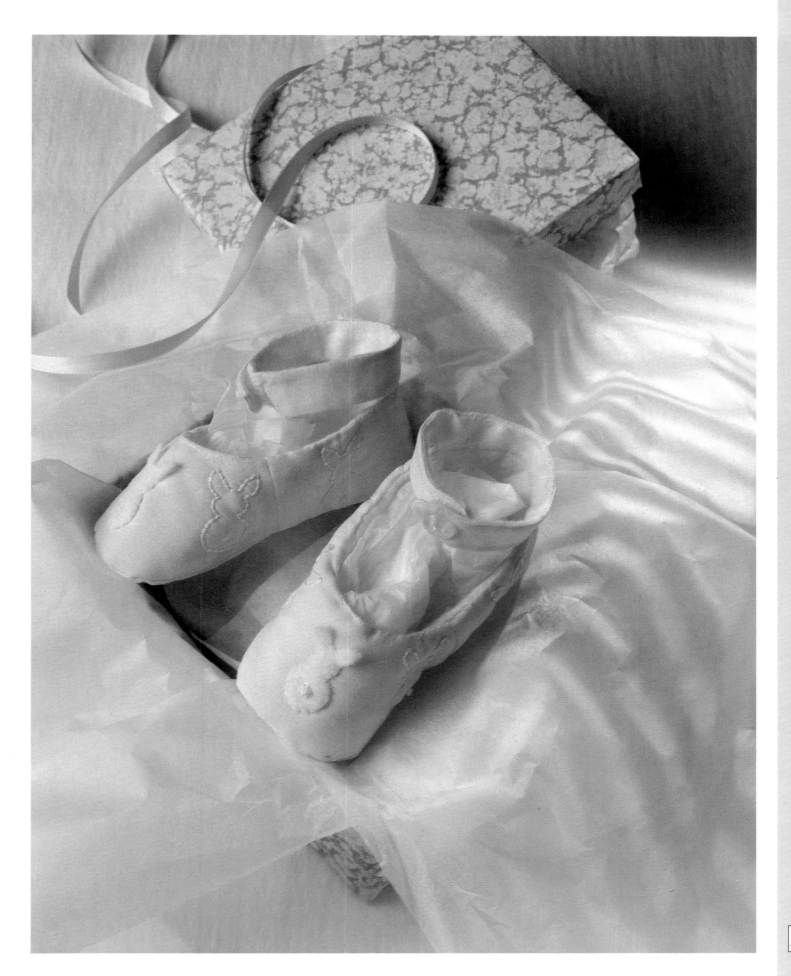

CHOOSING THE DESIGN

In shadow quilting, colored yarn or cord is threaded through channels made in a thin, semi-transparent fabric by double lines of stitching. The colors show through the top fabric in a softened but distinct way. Traditionally, all forms of quilting were worked by hand, with rows of tiny running stitches, but the twin-needle machine is ideal for this type of work, since the stitching itself is less important than the effect created by the threaded yarn.

A geometric design was chosen for this pillow. Although the finished interlaced effect is intricate, it is relatively easy to work. Once the first line is in place, the machine foot acts as a guide for each succesive line. The thickness of the corded lines can be varied by spacing the rows of stitching closer or further apart.

MATERIALS

Fabric
1yd Japan silk, 36in wide
2yds lightweight muslin, 36in wide
Threads
1 skein tapestry yarn in each of the following colors: bright blue, pale blue, deep yellow, bright pink, pale pink, leaf green
1 spool sewing thread, to match silk

Tapestry needles, medium and small
Sewing machine with twin needle
Yardstick, tailor's chalk
12in zipper
Bolster-shaped pillow form 22in by 7in

Finished size: The pillow is 22in long and 7in in diameter

METHOD OF WORKING

Quilting
Cut out a rectangle of Japan silk and two pieces of muslin, each measuring 24in by 30in. These are for the main part of the pillow. They are larger than the finished size, since the quilting process takes up about an extra 2in to 3in of fabric all around.

With the right side of the silk facing you, pin and then baste the three layers of fabric together. Using a yardstick and tailor's chalk, mark out the first lines of the design indicated in red in the pattern diagram overleaf. Stitch on the marked lines, using a twin needle, then stitch the rest of the design in the same way, following each previous line of stitches with the foot of the machine. As the pattern diagram shows, the lines of stitching are placed different distances apart to allow for different

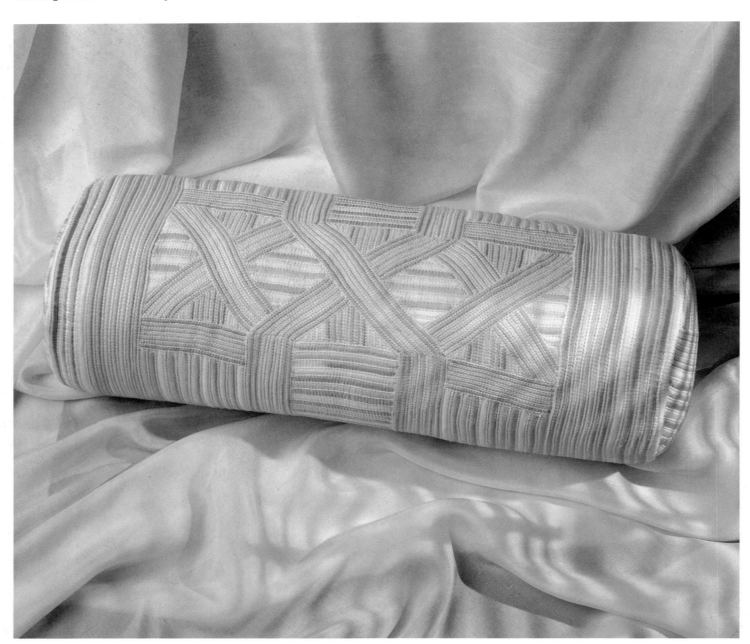

thicknesses of yarn to be threaded. The black lines indicate channels to take one strand of yarn, and the blue lines indicate a double strand.

When all the stitching is completed, turn the work to the inside. Taking each row of stitching in turn, pull through the two top threads made by the twin needle and secure them by tying them to the bobbin threads. Cut off the ends. Do this systematically, row by row, or the threads become tangled.

For the circular ends of the pillow, cut out two 14in squares of Japan silk and four of muslin. Cut a paper circle 7in in diameter as a pattern. Pin the pattern to each of the silk squares in turn, placing it exactly in the center, and mark the outer edges with pins, spacing them evenly to keep the circle in shape. Remove the paper pattern (but do not discard it) and mark a circle $1\frac{1}{2}$in inside the first one using tailor's chalk or basting threads.

Pin together three layers of fabric for each pillow end as before, then mark the first line of the design as shown in red in the diagram with a yardstick and tailor's chalk. Stitch along the line, then, following with the machine foot, continue until all the parallel lines have been worked. Now follow the design in the other direction until all the lines have been stitched. Repeat for the other pillow end.

Threading the yarn

Using a single strand of yarn for the fine lines and a double strand for the wider ones, thread the yarn through the lines of the design, passing the needle between the inner layer of muslin and the silk (see book, p.93). Continue to thread the yarn, using the photograph as a guide to the color changes, until the whole design has been filled in.

FINISHING

Trim the main rectangle to measure 19in by 22in. Use the paper pattern to cut out two circles 7in in diameter for the end pieces. With right sides together pin and baste a seam along the shorter side of the main pillow piece. Machine-stitch about $3\frac{1}{2}$in along from each end, leaving the central part open for the zipper to be inserted. Press seam open and carefully remove basting stitches.

Match the central stitch point of the main pillow piece to that of each end piece. Place right sides together and pin. Pin right around the circles, placing the pins evenly about $\frac{3}{8}$in from the raw edges. Baste and machine stitch. Remove basting, turn the pillow to the right side. Insert zipper in the central seam (see book, p.139). Finally, insert the pillow form.

Designed by Diana Thornton

CENTRAL PATTERN DESIGN

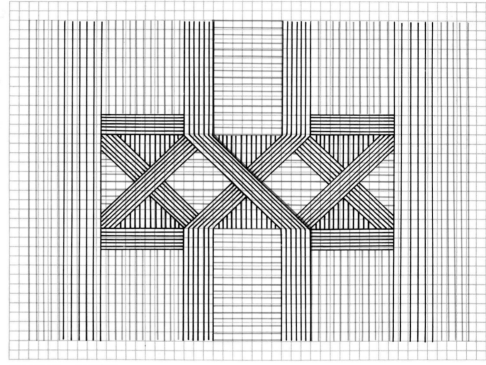

one square = 1cm/$\frac{3}{8}$in

MAKING UP

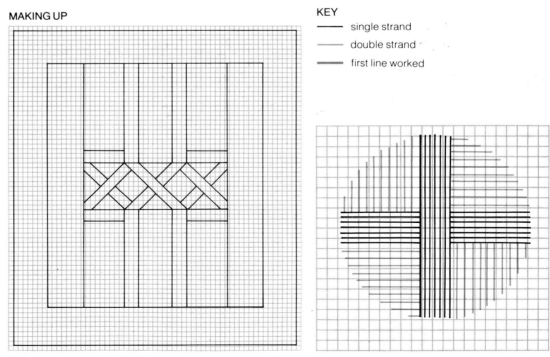

one square = 1cm/$\frac{3}{8}$in

KEY

— single strand
— double strand
— first line worked

one square = 1cm/$\frac{3}{8}$in

CHOOSING THE DESIGN

This design evolved from looking out at a garden and depicting different aspects within it. The outer edges of the panel represent structures such as trellising and fences, while the central squared area reflects the regular paving stones of a path. The stitches, worked in different thicknesses of thread, and with tonal variations, suggest the uneven surface caused by varying degrees of wear on the stones.

The elements of the composition are linked by the large zig-zag cutwork line going from left to right.

Felt was chosen for the background fabric partly for its non-fray properties,

but mainly for its flat surface. It lacks the textural interest of a woven cotton or linen fabric, which would, in this case, detract from the stitches themselves. The designer works with a deliberately restricted number of stitches – in this case only one – in order to exploit the exciting possibilities in using different threads and color grading.

MATERIALS

Black felt 16in by 18in
White felt 16in by 18in
Threads
1 skein black pearl cotton
1 skein white pearl cotton

1 skein black coton à broder
1 skein white stranded floss
1 skein white uneven slub yarn
1 spool white sewing thread
Several strands sewing thread in black and shades of gray

Crewel needles in assorted sizes to match different thicknesses of thread
Piece of masonite $13\frac{3}{4}$in by 15in
String for mounting

Finished size: the wallhanging measures $13\frac{3}{4}$in by 15in

METHOD OF WORKING

Preparation

1 Iron the two pieces of felt on one side; the other side will be the right side. Make sure you get all the creases out, since this will be the only time you iron it.

Never iron the fabric after it has been embroidered.

2 Lay the white felt on top of the black and baste lightly across the centers, first in one direction, then the other. Mark out the size of the actual panel by placing the piece of masonite on top and basting around the felt $\frac{3}{4}$in away from the edge of the board. Also mark points A to J (see diagram below) with a backstitch on the basted line. This will ensure that you stitch beyond the actual edge, and so achieve a neat finish when the fabric is mounted on the board.

Machine work

1 Thread a sewing machine with the same thread top and bottom. Use a straight stitch, with the length set at 2. Before starting on the fabric to be embroidered, check that the machine stitch and tension are correct by experimenting on a spare piece of felt.

2 Following the design chart below, first make a line of stitching from B to F. Place a piece of straight-edged paper between A and F and stitch to the paper edge from the marked points. For the second and following lines (2-8), use the embroidery foot with a guide to ensure straight lines and correct distances between lines. (The distance between lines is $\frac{5}{8}$in.)

Stitch slowly, making sure that the fabric is fed in flat to the machine – felt can stretch very easily. Always stitch lines in the same direction or there will be some pull between the lines. Work from top to bottom and right to left. Do not stitch on top of basting stitches; if they are pulled out later, the felt will become stretched and distorted. The basting can be taken out as soon as some lines of stitching have been worked to hold the fabrics together.

Working steadily without rushing, try to complete all the stitching in one session. If other stitching is done in between, it is difficult to achieve exactly the same tension on a subsequent occasion.

3 To work the first diagonal zig-zag line J-K-L-D, use the straight edge of a piece of paper to stitch between points. At points K and L, turn *on* the machine line.

Then stitch the other diagonal lines, working from left to right. Work down the fabric, parallel to the first line, using the embroidery foot with guide. The last line in this sequence is H-M-N.

The remaining lines on the right-hand side must be worked in the order O-P-Q, R-S-T, U-V-C and, finally, the central-panel last line W-X. Work from left to right, always stitching in the same direction. Turn the embroidery foot with guide over and to the other side to ensure that the lines are spaced correctly.

Note The top left- and bottom right-hand corners of the center panel are not stitched.

4 Take all the machine threads to the back of the work, then tie each pair loosely with a double knot and trim them short.

Hand embroidery

Work up the rows, starting at the top, and following the key to threads given below. Work two rows at a time, not more, or the thread will become worn and tired looking from the continual pulling through the fabric. Start with a knot, and finish with a backstitch. Do not pull the stitches too hard or the fabric may become puckered.

All stitching is Cretan stitch. With a thick thread (such as thread 1), work five Cretan stitches in the square; with a thinner thread (such as thread 2), work six. Work the stitches from left to right.

Cutwork

Cut the layer of white felt away on three rows on the left and three on the right of the center panel. Cut $\frac{1}{8}$in away from the machine line, using fairly small, very sharp scissors. Any fluff that sticks to the black felt as a result of the cutting can be lifted off with masking tape.

MOUNTING

The work must first be stretched to remove any puckers. When dry, it can be mounted by lacing it over the masonite (see book, pp.136–138).

Designed by Anne Morrell

PREPARING THE FABRIC

KEY

1 black pearl cotton
2 black coton à broder
3 sewing thread in shades of grey to black
4 white pearl cotton
5 white stranded cotton (6 strands)
6 white stranded cotton (12 strands)
7 uneven slub yarn
8 white stranded cotton (2 strands)

DESIGN CHART

ten squares = 2.5cm/1in

CHOOSING THE DESIGN

The design for this photograph album cover is derived from print samples which were created in Victorian times to edge advertising and visiting cards. Metal thread techniques are combined with the use of ribbon in this basically floral design. It would be most appropriate for a special album, containing photographs of a wedding, christening or other ceremonial occasion.

MATERIALS

Fabric
16in handwoven Indian silk at least 30in wide, in cream
16in calico, 36in wide for backing
Small piece yellow felt
Piece gold kidskin, $2\frac{3}{4}$in by 4in
Threads
1 spool cream silk thread
$6\frac{1}{2}$yd Japanese gold substitute size 3k
$1\frac{1}{4}$yd imitation Grecian cord
28in purl purl, size 3
30in bright check purl, size 5
16in smooth purl, size 5
16in rough purl, size 1
$1\frac{1}{4}$yd cream ribbon, $\frac{1}{4}$in wide
20in cream ribbon, $\frac{1}{12}$in wide

Crewel needle, size no.9
Chenille needles, sizes no.18 and 20
Piece of lightweight cardboard

Finished size: to fit photograph album, 10in by 11in

METHOD OF WORKING

Cut the silk and calico to measure 16in by 30in, and baste them together. Transfer the design from the Pattern Design chart below onto the silk fabric using the tracing and basting method.

Couch down the imitation Grecian cord (see book, p. 97) on design line 2. Pull out the size 3 purl purl to approximately double its length and stitch into position inside the Grecian cord (1).

Cut out three circles from cardboard approximately 1.3cm in diameter (an old greeting card is suitable). Stitch each one down at four points, by bringing the needle up in the background fabric and then through the cardboard. The cardboard can be prepared by piercing holes before placing in position.

Couch down ten rows of Japanese gold substitute (3) using the bricking method (see book, p. 98). At the top edge stagger the turned ends of the rows. At the bottom edge the ends should be taken down separately and staggered. Take all the ends down when the rest of the work is complete as it is easier to control the purl when it lies on the top rather than underneath. This also applies to the imitation Grecian cord.

Baste the zigzag ribbon into position before finally stitching it along each side with small stitches in a matching sewing thread.

Flowers and leaves
Cut out felt padding for the flowers and leaves (see book, p. 98). Three graduated layers of padding are used for the flowers and two for the leaves. Stitch in position.

Cut the rough, check and smooth purls, on a velvet board, into pieces about twice as long as their width. Purl is most effective if the larger sizes are cut "squarish" and the fine ones long; this works better than using them in a random way.

The top flower has five check purls in the center of the petal; these are stitched on first and the five smooth ones are stitched around, filling the petal, thereby covering the felt. The lower flower is composed of rough purl in the center and check purl around to complete the petal.

Trace the leaf shape on a piece of cardboard. Draw around this shape on the wrong side of the kidskin and cut around it. This will make the kidskin fractionally bigger so that it covers the felt adequately.

Couch down the imitation Grecian cord stem (4). Then stitch purl purl to join leaves to the stem, stitching a small amount as veining on the leaves. It is easier to stitch on kidskin if the needle position is found by putting indentations in the kidskin from the wrong side, checking that the needle position is correct before perforating the kidskin. (A hole where the kidskin has been pierced inadvertently will show.)

Using the fine ribbon, make French knots for the center of each flower, using a size no.20 chenille needle.

Take down all ends using a size no.18 chenille needle. Take the imitation Grecian cord down in three parts, the underneath section of cord first.

FINISHING

Turn under 2in at the top and bottom of the cover. Check that this fits your photograph album, then baste. Fold in $4\frac{7}{8}$in at each end and check against the album; press. It is always difficult to calculate the thickness of fabric when assembling and finishing, so checks should be made at each stage.

Fold under $\frac{3}{4}$in of the $4\frac{7}{8}$in to finish the raw edges and baste. Slipstitch together at the top and bottom and both sides, as shown in the Making Up diagram right. You may have to carry out the final stitching when the album cover is on the album. Remove the basting.

OPTIONS
Cream and gold are used here, but silver yarn could be used with white and silver-gray ribbons. A greater tonal value could be achieved by using golden-brown ribbons, or the gold metal thread retained and a new color scheme devised by changing the background material, the stitching thread (as used for the bricking) and the ribbon, and by using a colored leather instead of gold kidskin.

A photograph could be placed on the front cover as well as the initials of the owner or recipient, or such memorabilia as dried flowers from a wedding bouquet.

Designed by Janice Williams

PATTERN DESIGN

one square = 1.25cm/½in

MAKING UP

CHOOSING THE DESIGN

A sketch of freesia flowers inspired this design for cutwork. The curve of the spray fitted well into the top of the camisole, requiring only a little adjustment to create a pleasing and balanced design. It is essential to ensure that flowers and leaves touch, otherwise the embroidery will fall apart when the open parts of the design are cut away.

Texture on the flowers and leaves is created by twisted chain stitch, bullion knots and trailing, a kind of stem stitch. The outline is worked in buttonhole stitch.

MATERIALS

$1\frac{5}{8}$yd pink satin, 36in wide
Threads
1 spool pink sewing thread
1 spool pink silk twist
2 skeins pink stranded floss

Crewel needle, size no. 10

Finished size: to fit bust 36in (size 12)

METHOD OF WORKING

Use two strands of floss throughout, except for the bullion knots which are worked in silk twist.

You must work all the embroidery before cutting out the garment, so be careful to place the embroidery design on the fabric in a position which allows plenty of room for the rest of the garment to be cut. Trace the design on the cloth with a sharp, hard pencil (see book, p.64), and mark with a cross the areas which are to be cut away.

Work over all the design lines with a small running stitch, to "pad" the embroidery. Then work the main lines of the design in buttonhole stitch, making sure that the knotted edges are against the cut-away areas. Complete all the other embroidery stitches before cutting away the cut-work areas (see book, p.100).

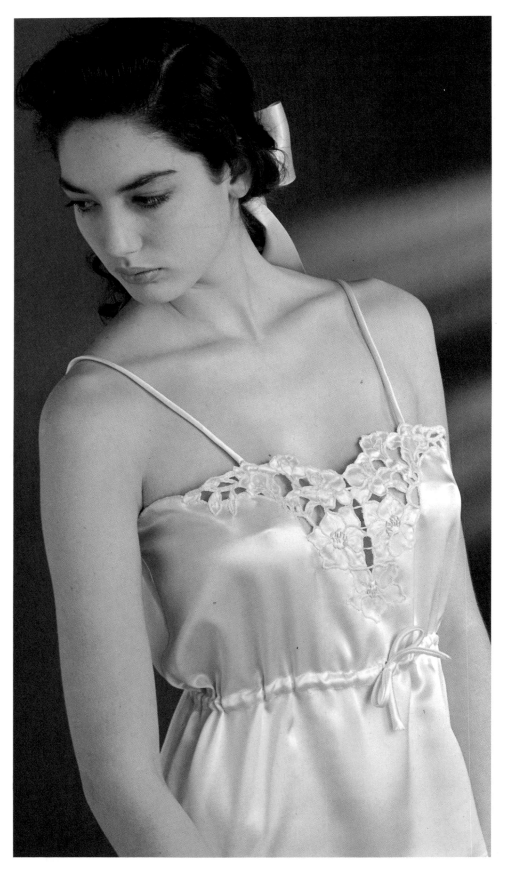

FINISHING

Join the front and back of the camisole with French seams. Hem the lower edge. Make a vertical slit about $3/8$in long in the center front, about 2in below the waistline and work buttonhole stitch around it.

Press small turnings under the long edges of the casing and sew it to the inside of the camisole, about 2in below the waistline. Leave the short ends open until you have inserted the drawstring.

Make the shoulder straps and drawstring from bias tubes. The simplest way to make tubing is to cut strips of bias fabric, then fold them in half lengthwise, right sides together. Stitch, leaving the ends open. To turn the tubing right side out, attach a length of strong thread to one end of the tube at the seam. Pull the thread gently through the tubing, using a large needle or bodkin, eye first.

Fix the shoulder straps neatly inside the front and back of the camisole, at the top, adjusting the length as necessary. Thread the drawstring through the casing, bringing the ends out through the center front hole.

Designed by Angela Dewar

KEY

— bullion knots
— buttonhole stitch
— trailing
— twisted chain stitch

areas to be cut away

CUTWORK DESIGN

one square = $1/2$in/1.25cm

CUTTING PATTERNS

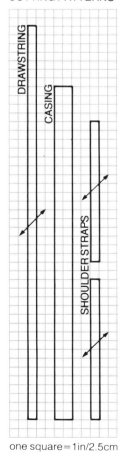

one square = 1in/2.5cm

one square = $1/2$in/1.25cm

CHOOSING THE DESIGN

Elevate a simple store-bought cardigan into the 'designer hand-knit' class with some clever embroidery. The design for the embroidered panels was inspired by, and adapted from, that found on a hand-knitted and embroidered cardigan discovered in a shop selling antique clothes. The original design has been simplified to make the front right and left sides mirror images of each other.

The embroidery is simple cross stitch in sport and fingering yarns and is worked on a plain white cardigan purchased from a chain store. It is important that the background fabric is predominantly woolen (at least 70 percent wool to 30 percent man-made fibers), so that any distortion caused by the embroidery can be corrected by lightly blocking and steaming the garment back into shape. Since knitted and other non-woven fabrics can stretch and 'give', the embroidery is worked through a canvas mesh to give a firmer backing. This is later dismantled.

MATERIALS

1 plain white knitted cardigan (this one is pure wool, size 12)
Tapestry yarn
1 skein in each of the seven colors – light blue, light green, medium green, shell pink (pink I), salmon pink (pink II), yellow, lilac
2 skeins black stranded yarn, used as either 1-strand or 2-strand

Tapestry needle, medium size
½yd rug canvas, 36in wide (5 holes to the inch)

METHOD OF WORKING

Cut a piece of canvas to size for the first embroidered panel: calculate the required dimensions by counting the number of stitches in each direction and adding one or two extra rows to allow for basting the canvas. Loosely baste it into place on the cardigan over the area to be embroidered, matching the center of the canvas to the center of the design.

Work to the color-coded charts below, embroidering one panel at a time. The whole area is worked in cross stitch except for the black outline, which is done in single-strand backstitch at the end.

To start work, make a backstitch on the back of the cardigan – a knot would pull through the knitted fabric. Finish off threads by running them through the back of some embroidered stitches.

When all the cross stitches in one panel are worked, dismantle the canvas by snipping and pulling it away *one thread at a time*. Then work the backstitches in single-strand black yarn to form an outline.

Complete each embroidered panel in this way, then work buttonhole stitch around the neck and front edges of the cardigan, using black sport yarn.

FINISHING

Place the embroidered front on a soft pad (such as a folded towel) to prevent the embroidered area from becoming flattened as you press. Then, using a damp cloth or a steam iron, lightly press the embroidered areas from the back, to smooth away puckering.

OPTIONS

Any cross stitch or needlepoint design could be embroidered on a garment in this way – look at samplers or old needlework books to get ideas.

To scale the embroidery down to a smaller size, for example on a child's cardigan, simply use a smaller gauge canvas, such as 10 holes to the inch.

The technique could also be used on evenweave fabric, using cotton or silk thread.

Designed by Janet Haigh

FRONT OF CARDIGAN
(reverse for right-hand side)

five squares = 1in/2.5cm

KEY

CROSS STITCH

× pink I
○ pale blue
• pale green
● mid green
＼ yellow
∕ pink II
▲ lilac
■ black

BACK STITCH
☐ black

BACK OF CARDIGAN

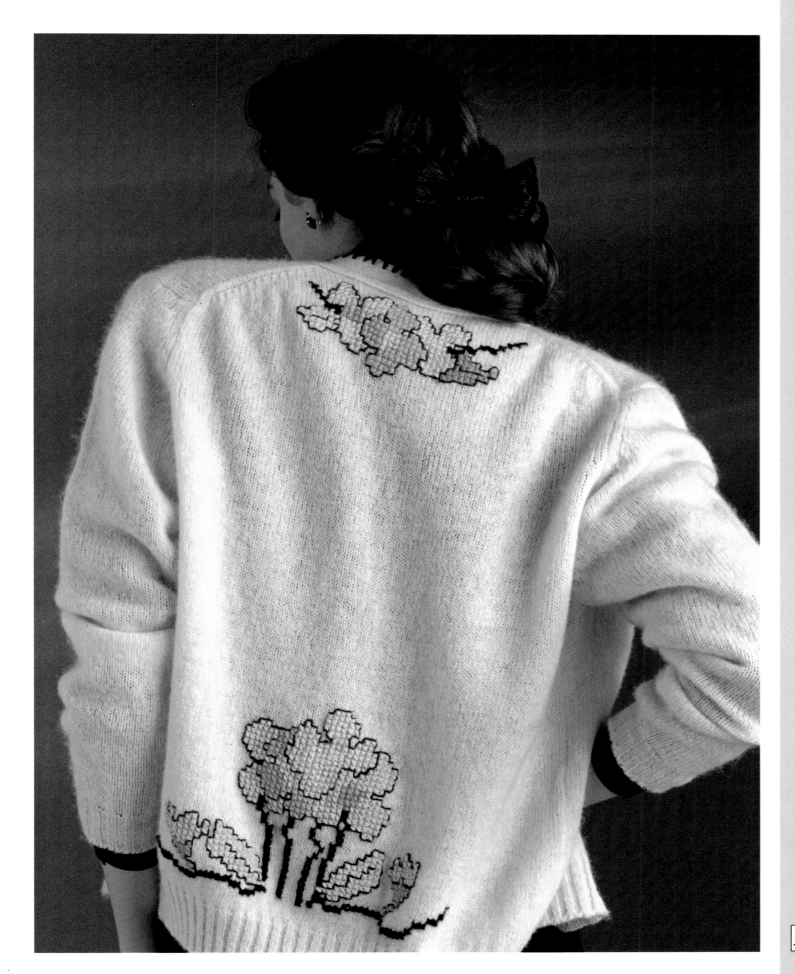

CHOOSING THE DESIGN

Blackwork is a traditional form of embroidery, but its graphic look gives it a modern appeal. The basket of fruit is a perfect motif for blackwork, since it has a well-defined outline and the varied textures of the fruit and the basket are depicted through different patterns and densities.

MATERIALS

1¾yds evenweave linen, 60in wide (20 threads to the inch) for the tablecloth; 20in for each napkin
1 skein stranded embroidery floss, black
1 spool sewing thread, white
Tapestry needle, size no. 22
Fine sharps needle
Tracing paper or graph paper

Finished size: the cloth measures 60in by 64in; the napkins are 19in square

METHOD OF WORKING

The tablecloth

Find the center of the fabric by folding it across the length and the width. Mark the center point, then withdraw three threads 8in from the point on all four sides to form a central square measuring 16in. Weave about 1in of the withdrawn threads back into the fabric to prevent fraying. Work any of the drawn thread patterns shown in the book on pages 106–109, using one strand of black thread.

Hem the edges of the cloth by working three-sided stitch or an edging stitch of your choice.

Trace the motif from the Pattern Design below, either by tracing through the fabric with a water-soluble fabric-marking pen as for needlepoint (see book, p. 122) or by drawing the design on graph paper and counting each stitch onto the fabric. The latter method is more accurate. If you use

1in square graph paper there will be two threads to each small square.

Work the outlines of the design in Holbein (double running) stitch (see book, p.103), using one or two strands of thread depending on the desired effect. Complete the design with filling stitches, either those indicated in the design or any of those shown in the book on page 104.

The napkins

Cut out a square of fabric 20in by 20in for each napkin. Double-hem the edges invisibly using one strand of white thread and tiny hemming stitches. Mark out a triangular area in one corner as shown by withdrawing three threads for 5in on each side; work over them using the same stitch as for the tablecloth. Position the design within the triangle as indicated and work it as for the tablecloth.

Designed by Caroline Davis

PATTERN DESIGN

each square = one thread

CHOOSING THE DESIGN

This form of embroidery, known as needlepoint lace, derives from cutwork and drawn thread work. The design is based on a grid formation, using the warp and weft threads of the fabric. The open areas are filled with detached buttonhole and picot bars.

MATERIALS

Fabric

10in evenweave linen, 36in wide, 30 threads to the inch, in a natural color
10in satin, 36in wide, contrasting color
Small quantity synthetic batting
Small piece plastic cloth, 3in square

1 spool linen lace thread (see end of book)
Sharps needle, size no.6; tapestry needle, size no.22
Thimble, sharp embroidery scissors, pins
Sewing thread for basting

Finished size: the pincushion measures $4\frac{1}{2}$in square, the sachet $7\frac{1}{2}$in high

WORKING THE PINCUSHION

Cut out two 5in squares of linen along a thread of the fabric, checking that each is absolutely square by folding diagonally.

Work the front. For the hem, mark two threads $\frac{3}{4}$in from all edges with pins. Snip these threads at the center of each side and withdraw them (see book, p.107) until they meet at the corners, but do not completely remove them or cut them off. Turn under $\frac{1}{4}$in at the outside edge, then fold hem back to meet the withdrawn threads, turning the opposite sides first. The corners are worked square, with any surplus bulk trimmed inside the hem. Pin, baste and then slipstitch the hem invisibly, using the sharps needle and linen thread, and secure the corners.

Following the diagram, which is shown

actual size, and working toward the middle of the square, leave four threads and withdraw two on all sides. Finish the work by basting the withdrawn threads to the corner of the hem; then, using the tapestry needle, work double four-sided stitch (see book, p.108) over four threads, making the stitch smaller as necessary as you reach the corner.

To mark the inner square, withdraw two threads as shown, leaving ten, then leave four and withdraw two. Finish the work as before, then work four-sided stitch around this square, using the tapestry needle. Now leave four threads and remove one to meet at the corners. To make the cross, count the threads, find the middle three in each direction and remove the outer two threads of the three, both ways.

Padded roll

Mount the linen on the plastic square, first pinning it and then backstitching around the inner four-sided stitch square, making sure the center three threads cross at right angles. To work the padded roll inside the four-sided stitch, first overcast the four-thread area outside the stitching with small slanting stitches, as shown, then cut a length of linen thread three times the length of the whole square to form the padding.

Knot the thread at one end, cut any loops at the other, lay it over the overcast stitches, and work a close satin stitch over both, cutting away the surplus linen just before stitching. Take care not to cut the central three threads of the cross, which will form the foundation for the cutwork lace. Make the stitches even and smooth and catch in any loose ends as you sew. Try to stitch into the threads of the fabric, not between them, and regulate the tension on the square by pulling gently on the padding threads as you go. Work a tight stitch at each corner to hold the padding firm. Finish at the last corner by trimming the padding threads flush and working a final stitch to cover the ends. If you run out of thread during the work, run off the old thread into the overcast stitching and run in the new one in the same place.

Cutwork central square

Cut away any surplus linen from the center, again taking care not to cut the center cross. Begin to work the lace filling.

For the center three bar, lay a reinforcing thread across, going through the roll on both sides and oversewing the bar closely (see book, p.108). Repeat this vertically, making sure the cross is exactly in the middle. For the spokes, lay three threads diagonally and oversew them, stitching through the cross to hold the bars secure each time you cross the center.

At the center, work a bullion knot star as follows. Lay a single-thread ring $\frac{1}{4}$in from the center by passing through the spokes three times. Work three buttonhole stitches, then one picot and another three buttonhole stitches between each spoke, and one buttonhole stitch on the spoke. To work the picot, make a buttonhole stitch on the bar, then another into the top of it. Make a tiny bullion knot (see book, p.78) into the top of the second stitch and come back through the top of the first one.

Lay another ring outside the first and $\frac{1}{2}$in from the center by passing through the spokes three times. Work a petal between each spoke by working nine buttonhole stitches on the inside edge, then returning to the starting point with backward buttonhole stitches. Work a second row of eight stitches and a third of six, then work one buttonhole stitch on the spoke ready to start the next petal.

For the corner bars, lay three threads across the corner, going through the roll and the diagonal bar each time. Work three buttonhole stitches, one picot and three buttonholes in each space as before, with one buttonhole stitch on the bar. This completes the lace.

FINISHING

Finish the withdrawn fabric threads at the corners by folding them back over the hem and making a line of small running stitches to hold them flat. Trim the threads to 1in, then make a backward buttonhole stitch back to the beginning as shown; work buttonhole stitch to cover the cut ends. Repeat for the corners of the four-sided stitch surrounding the cutwork square.

Make the hem for the back of the pincushion as for the front, then press both pieces under a damp cloth; allow to dry.

Stitch three sides together with bullion knots spaced about $\frac{1}{4}$in apart; work two at each corner. On the fourth side work the bullion knots on the front only. Make a small pad of satin, 4in square, fill it with batting and place inside the linen. Slip-stitch the fourth side to close.

WORKING THE SACHET BAG

Cut out a piece of linen 5in by 15in and remove the threads as shown in the diagram. Note that the hems on the short edge have a finished depth of 1in. Count 10 threads in from the bottom and sides and mark the square from these points. Embroider as described for the pincushion.

Press, then make four woven bars in the 12-thread space to take the cord. Baste in the lining and sew up both sides to the deep hem, using bullion knots spaced about $\frac{1}{4}$in apart. Continue around the opening.

Make a twisted cord (see book, p.141) from the linen thread, slot it through the woven bars and knot. Make a small sachet bag from the remaining lining fabric.

Designed by Gail Marsh and Jacqueline Blackburn of *Bottom Drawer*

PINCUSHION

NEATENING THE CORNERS

KEY

------ running stitch

buttonhole stitch

CUTWORK CENTRAL SQUARE

LAVENDER BAG

CHOOSING THE DESIGN

Pulled work is one of the counted thread methods of embroidery, which the designer finds restful and therapeutic. The stitches were chosen not only for their inherent suitability, but because they can be finished on the back satisfactorily, an important consideration in table linen.

MATERIALS

For four mats
$\frac{1}{2}$ yd evenweave linen
5 skeins stranded embroidery thread (white, pink, green, lilac, blue)
1 spool silver lurex embroidery thread
Tapestry needle, size no. 22

Finished size: each mat measures 16 in by 10 in

METHOD OF WORKING

Cut a piece of fabric for each mat measuring 18 in by 12 in (the finished size plus $\frac{3}{4}$ in for the hem). Lightly overcast the edges to prevent fraying while working. Baste the vertical and horizontal center lines as a guide to positioning the central eyelet stitches.

Working from the chart below, mark the position of each eyelet stitch. Each one is worked over six threads, and is separated from its neighbor by two threads. Work the eyelet stitches (see book, p. 111) using three strands of the main color, taking each stitch into the same central hole.

Next work the four sided stitch (see book, p. 111), using a single strand of the main color. Note that this is separated from the eyelets by four threads, and the outside rows of border stitches are separated from each other by two threads.

Work the satin stitch over two threads, using three strands of the main color. Then work four sided stitch over two threads, using one strand of white thread.

This completes the border rows. Now work cross stitches (see book, p. 103), between the eyelets, using two strands of white thread.

Picot edge and hem
Work the picot edge as follows. Approximately 17 threads from the edge, and on the wrong side, work stem stitch (see book, p. 70) twice over three threads, using three strands of the main color. Turn to right side and fold the fabric on the stitch line. Using the silver thread, work two satin stitches between each picot, pulling the satin stitches tight to accentuate the scalloped effect.

Miter the corners (see book, p. 107), turn $\frac{1}{4}$ in under, and secure hem by pin stitching (see book, p. 87) to edge of outer border row.

OPTIONS

The basic design can be varied in many ways. For instance, the eyelets could be worked in a different color to provide contrast with the borders, the cross stitches could be omitted altogether, or a whole central area worked in cross stitch, with the borders made more dramatic by working the stitches over four threads instead of two.

Designed by Margaret Darby

KEY

each line = one thread

- picot stem stitch
- satin stitch
- hem-pin stitch
- four sided stitch (single strand)
- satin stitch
- four sided stitch (single strand)
- four sided stitch (double strand)
- cross stitch
- eyelet

CHOOSING THE DESIGN

This sailor collar was designed to be soft, delicate and feminine, and the materials and technique were chosen accordingly. The fabric is a fine cotton lawn, the embroidery is drawn thread work. To enhance the impression of softness, the collar was made double, with a small, lighter collar lying on top of the larger one.

MATERIALS

$\frac{1}{2}$yd fine white cotton voile, 36in wide
White stranded embroidery floss or machine embroidery thread
White pearl cotton no. 8
Very fine crewel needle

Finished size: the outer collar measures $14\frac{1}{4}$in wide, 16in from front to back and $5\frac{1}{2}$in deep from the facing to the edge. The inner collar measures $10\frac{3}{4}$in wide, $12\frac{1}{2}$in from front to back and $3\frac{3}{4}$in deep.

METHOD OF WORKING

Outer collar

Cut a rectangle of voile measuring $17\frac{3}{4}$in by $19\frac{3}{4}$in for the main collar piece. Withdraw one thread along all four sides $\frac{3}{4}$in from the cut edge. Withdraw a band of threads $\frac{1}{4}$in wide $2\frac{1}{4}$in from all edges, as shown in the Pattern Design diagram. Leave a band of 10 threads, then withdraw another band $\frac{1}{4}$in wide, to join with the first one. Again leaving 10 threads in between, withdraw a third band the same width as the first and to join the first band.

Fold the fabric along the single, outer withdrawn thread, then fold again so that the fold aligns with the outside edge of the first withdrawn band. Baste with a soft, fine thread.

Using a single strand of embroidery thread, work herringbone stitch over the two bands of threads remaining, gathering the loose threads into bundles of four. Using pearl cotton, and working in coral stitch as shown in the Outer Collar diagram, tie bars in the center strips into clusters of three.

Using one strand of embroidery thread, work hemstitch on both inner and outer edges of border, mitering all corners (see book, p. 107).

Inner collar

For the inner collar piece, which forms a layer on top of the one already worked, cut a piece of voile $13\frac{3}{4}$in by $15\frac{3}{4}$in and withdraw one thread for the hem as before. Withdraw a single band of threads, $\frac{1}{4}$in wide and $2\frac{1}{4}$in from the edges. This forms the border. Work the hem as before, but hemstitch only on the outer edge of the withdrawn band. Using pearl cotton, work cross stitch over about four threads on the inner edge. This will divide the bars in half, creating a zigzag effect.

FINISHING

Place the two rectangles together so that the edges of the small one lie just inside the inner edge of the border of the larger one.

Cut the neck and back openings in the collar as shown in the Pattern Design diagram. Cut out the facings from a left-over piece of the voile, using an enlarged version of the Cutting Pattern.

Cut a rectangle of voile the length of the back opening and $1\frac{1}{4}$in wide. With right sides together, stitch to back opening $\frac{3}{8}$in from the edge as shown in the diagram for binding the back opening. Turn to right side, fold under $\frac{1}{4}$in on the raw edge and hand hem on the first stitching line.

Join back and front facings with a $\frac{3}{8}$in seam. With right sides together, join facings to collar, then clip curves carefully to seam and turn to right side. Finish edges with hand hemstitch or machine stitch.

Designed by Gisela Banbury

CUTTING PATTERN

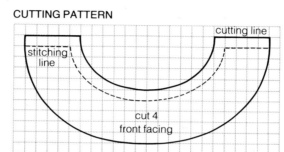

one square = 1cm/$\frac{3}{8}$in

BINDING BACK OPENING

PATTERN DESIGN

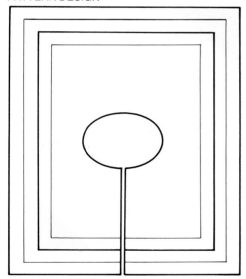

KEY

- ⌒ coral stitch
- 𝟠𝟠𝟠 herringbone stitch
- ⁄⁄⁄⁄⁄⁄ hem stitch
- xxxxx cross stitch
- ☐ voile

OUTER COLLAR

INNER COLLAR

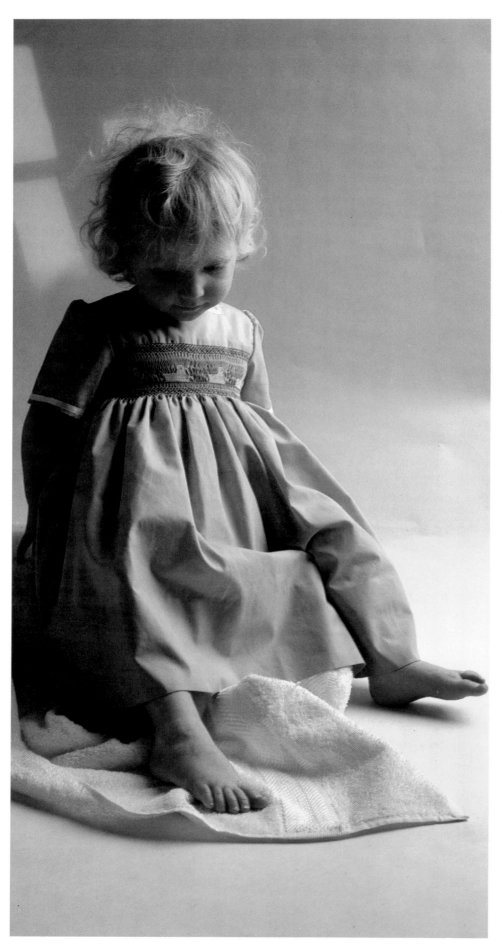

CHOOSING THE DESIGN

Your choice of smocking motif is determined by the limitations of the technique itself, in that smocking is carried out in straight lines, not curves. A completely round motif, for example, will not be successful, and any animal or picture motif has to be simplified and stylized to take these limitations into consideration. Bear in mind that such a motif also has to be supported by lines of back smocking.

MATERIALS

2yds cotton lawn or cotton blend, 36in wide
Threads
4 skeins stranded embroidery floss, one in each of the main colors used: yellow, dark blue, light blue, white
Small amount of brown and black stranded embroidery floss
1 spool light blue sewing thread

3 small yellow buttons
$1\frac{1}{4}$yds narrow yellow ribbon
2 pairs snap fasteners

Finished size: to fit chest 22in, approximate age $1\frac{1}{2}$–$2\frac{1}{2}$ years

METHOD OF WORKING

First make a paper pattern by enlarging the outlines given opposite; pin this on your fabric and cut out the pieces.
    Work all the smocking before starting to assemble the dress.

The smocking

Refer to the section on Smocking in the book (pp. 112–115) before embarking on this. Gather the front skirt into eight rows of closely worked gathering stitches, $\frac{3}{8}$in apart, starting $\frac{5}{8}$in down from the top. Leave $\frac{3}{8}$in at each side for a seam allowance.

Work the smocking stitches as shown in the key below, using three strands of thread. Remove the gathering stitches.

FINISHING

With right sides together, join front yoke to back yokes at shoulder seams. Join front facing to back facings at shoulder seams. Join front and back yoke to front and back facings at neck edge and center back. Clip corners, turn right side out and press. With right sides together, attach front yoke to skirt front at top of smocking, taking a seam of $\frac{3}{8}$in. Turn under $\frac{3}{8}$in on front facing and slipstitch in place.

Attach the back skirt placket as follows. Turn under one long edge of strip by $\frac{1}{4}$in and press. Mark position of placket, in the center of the skirt back and $4\frac{1}{4}$in from the top edge; stitch, as shown, to reinforce seam, then slash to top of stitching. Pin right side of placket to wrong side of skirt and stitch all the way around on the previous stitching line, lifting the machine foot and pivoting the fabric to enable you to stitch down the other side. (The diagram

below gives a simplified view of this step.) Press seam toward placket, turn placket to outside along fold line, and stitch pressed edge over seam. Bring folded edges of placket together, as shown, and stitch across diagonally, then turn front to inside and baste across upper edge.

Gather back skirt, but do not take gathering across placket, and attach to back yoke pieces as for the skirt front. Join front and back side seams from hem to bottom of armholes with a $\frac{3}{8}$in plain or French seam. Finish seams if necessary.

Turn a $\frac{1}{4}$in hem on the bottom of each sleeve piece twice and hem, then attach ribbon $\frac{1}{4}$in from the edges. Join each sleeve with a $\frac{3}{8}$in plain or French seam, and finish if necessary. Gather sleeve tops, adjust gathering to fit armhole. Baste in place and then sew. Finish seam.

Sew ribbon in place around neck $\frac{1}{4}$in from edge, turning it over by about $\frac{3}{8}$in to $\frac{3}{4}$in at the back. Make three evenly spaced buttonholes $\frac{1}{4}$in from edge of right back yoke; sew on buttons in corresponding position on left back yoke. Sew snap fasteners above the top and below the bottom button. Turn up hem to desired length and slipstitch in place.

OPTIONS

To make a dress for a bigger child, either increase the dimensions of this pattern all over, or buy a simple child's dress pattern for the right age and size and enlarge the skirt front to accommodate the smocking. As a rough guide, allow three times the eventual width for the smocked part of the garment.

Designed by Penny Rawlings

TOP OF BACK SKIRT

PLACKET (wrong side)

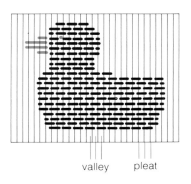

DUCK MOTIF KEY

— cable stitch (yellow)

• French knot (blue)

— oversewn beak (orange)

SMOCKING KEY

cable stitch (yellow)

back smocking (cable stitch)

diamond stitch (blue)

• back stitch (white)

stem stitch (blue)

CUTTING PATTERN

one square = 2.5cm/1in

CHOOSING THE DESIGN

The design of this pillow relies on the use of random-dyed silk thread to create the delicate feathery effect. Threads can be especially dyed in one color or in a range of colors, in this case different tones varying from white to black. The pillow combines machine and hand embroidery, both worked over a geometric grid.

MATERIALS

Fabric
$2\frac{1}{4}$yds medium-weight natural-color silk
$\frac{1}{2}$yd medium-weight black silk
Medium-weight iron-on interfacing 18in square

Threads
7 100yd spools white sewing silk
1 100yd spool black sewing silk
Design equipment
No. 2 pencil or water-soluble fabric marker
Ruler, graph paper ($\frac{1}{4}$in squares), sharp craft knife and metal ruler

Black fabric dye or fabric paint
Small sable or squirrel paintbrush
$2\frac{1}{4}$yd no. 2 preshrunk piping cord
Finest sharps needles for pinning silk
Sewing machine with no. 70 needle
Pillow form 18in square
15in zipper to match silk

Finished size: The pillow measures 18in by 18in

METHOD OF WORKING

Dyeing or painting the threads
For the dyeing method take three spools of white silk and wind each evenly around a straight-sided jar or something that will withstand the heat of a pressure cooker. Paint the dye on as shown opposite. You need three different shades to achieve the effect on the pillow illustrated. Leave the thread on the jars until dry, then place each in turn on the trivet of a pressure cooker with about $1\frac{1}{2}$ cups of water beneath. Arrange a piece of foil over the jar like an umbrella, to prevent water splashed from the lid from marking the silk. Bring to full pressure and steam for 45 minutes.

For the painting method, wind the

thread over a piece of stiff cardboard, then paint on both sides (see book, p. 52).

Machine embroidery

Cut two squares, each 20in by 20in, from the natural-color silk. Using pencil or marking pen, mark a series of lines on the matte side of the interfacing $\frac{1}{4}$in apart. Position the interfacing centrally on the pillow front, with wrong sides together, and baste them together with diagonal lines of basting. The design is worked on the wrong side, following the marked lines. Thread three spools with one of each of the dyed threads and set the straight stitch length to about $1\frac{1}{2}$. Using one of the dyed threads in the bobbin and white silk in the needle, test the stitch first on a spare piece of silk backed with interfacing. Then stitch first along the lines marked red in the diagram below, at 1in intervals. Remove the basting once the interfacing is held in place, and continue stitching, alternating the bobbin colors at regular intervals. Bring threads through to the wrong side of the work at the end of each row, tie and clip them close to the fabric.

A series of closer-spaced lines is worked in the central area between those completed. Mark this area, leaving a $4\frac{1}{8}$in border and machine-stitch as before, then press the fabric lightly on the reverse side, using a dry iron on silk setting.

Hand embroidery

Prepare a pattern by cutting a piece of graph paper into a 10in square. Using the sharp craft knife and a metal ruler, cut out alternate squares to form a grid network. (A quarter of the grid pattern is shown, actual size.) Lay the pillow front right side up and mark with fine sharps needles (*not* dressmaker's pins) the center points of the left side, top and bottom of the central machined square (points A, B and C on the diagram). Lay the paper grid on top so that the top left corner is on point A and the bottom left corner is 1in from the bottom edge. Baste in place and remove needles. (Mount the fabric in a stretcher frame before marking if you feel the stitches may pucker the fabric.)

Stitch through the spaces in the pattern, using the palest shade of dyed silk and an open satin stitch with approximately five stitches within each small square. Work from right to left, row by row, starting at the bottom. Fold the fabric as you work if not using a frame. When the embroidery is complete, remove the basting and pattern, taking care not to tear it. Repeat the process for the second and third grids, placing the pattern as shown.

FINISHING

Cut the black silk on the bias into $1\frac{1}{2}$in wide strips, then join to make one long strip (see book, p. 138). Baste this over the piping cord, then baste the piping to the pillow front all around the edges, joining the silk where the two ends meet, and slightly overlapping the edge of the machine-stitched lines. Using the zipper

foot and black silk thread, machine close to the cord, clipping the bias strip at the corners to ease.

Lay the pillow pieces with right sides together and mark the position of the zipper in the center of the top edge. Using white silk, stitch the seam on each side of the zipper opening, then press the seam open. Insert the zipper, placing the center of the teeth level with the top of the piping,

and stitching the front first.

Pin and then baste around the edges of the pillow, then stitch with the interfacing side uppermost, taking care to overstitch the black machine line. Finish seams by edge stitching with a zigzag stitch, then trim. Clip corners diagonally. Turn right side out. Press, then insert the pillow form.

Designed by Irene Ord

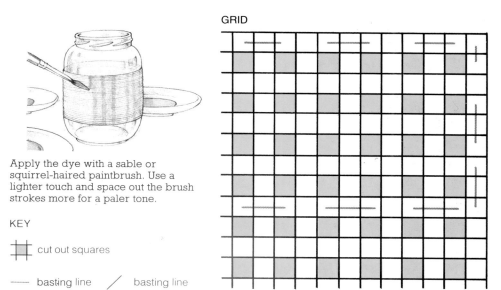

Apply the dye with a sable or squirrel-haired paintbrush. Use a lighter touch and space out the brush strokes more for a paler tone.

KEY

▨ cut out squares

—— basting line ╱ basting line

GRID

STITCH LINES AND GRID POSITIONS

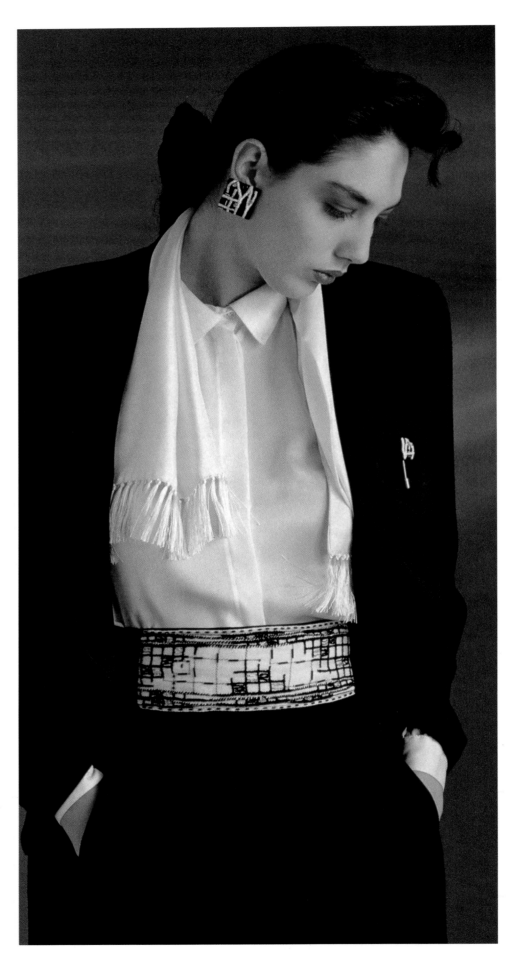

CHOOSING THE DESIGN

The original inspiration for this embroidery came from drawings of seaweeds, shells and fish, which were cut into squares and composed as a collage. Based on this collage, free machine embroidery samples were produced. These were then refined into the design used here.

The black and white color scheme was chosen partly because the stark contrast emphasizes the design and partly because the black and white combination is a fashion classic that can be worn with many different colors and outfits.

MATERIALS FOR CUMMERBUND

Fabric
$3/8$yd white muslin, 36in wide
$1/2$yd black silk rayon, 45in wide
6in heavy sew-in interfacing, 36in wide
Threads
1 large spool black 100% spun polyester thread
1 spool white cotton machine embroidery thread
1 skein black pearl cotton no.5

3 self-covering buttons, $3/8$in diameter
Sharps needle, size no.7; machine needle, size no.80
Beads: 1oz each of black seed beads; clear cut-glass beads; black bugle beads (medium and small); silver bugle beads.

MATERIALS FOR EARRINGS AND PIN

Fabrics, threads and beads from allowance for cummerbund
4in square styrofoam sheet, $3/8$in thick
Small quantity cardboard, $1/16$-$1/12$in thick
Pair glue-on clip earring findings
Glue-on brooch finding with felt pad
Quick-setting glue; fabric glue

Finished size: the cummerbund is $23\frac{1}{2}$in long, but can be adjusted to fit desired waist size. The earrings are $1\frac{1}{8}$in square, the pin $3/4$in square.

WORKING THE CUMMERBUND

Cut a rectangle of muslin measuring $10\frac{1}{4}$in by 36in. Transfer to it the pattern of fold lines at the top and bottom of the central panel shown in Diagram 1 overleaf, using the machine method. These lines act as a guide to the free embroidery as well as being used to fold the fabric when the embroidery is complete.

Select the area to be embroidered and mount the muslin on a ring frame about 10in diameter. Set the machine up for free embroidery and, using the size no.80 needle and the black polyester thread, first work the partial grid pattern for the central embroidered panel shown in Diagram 2. This can be exactly as shown or varied slightly. When all the areas have been worked, fill in individual squares and emphasize the line with random free machine embroidery.

The beads are applied next, either following the pattern or varying it as you prefer. Sew them on by hand, using the black polyester thread and the sharps needle. Make lines of overcasting stitches between beads as shown in the photograph.

Turn under the top and bottom edges of the muslin and machine stitch $1/12$in from the edges using black polyester thread. Fold the muslin as follows to make one fold above and below the central panel alternately. Take fold line A to points B; take fold line B to points C; take fold line C to points D, and fold line D to points E.

MAKING THE CUMMERBUND

Overcast the eight folded edges of muslin using the black pearl cotton. Cut out the rayon piece according to Diagram 3; cut out the interfacing $3/8$in smaller all around. Baste the interfacing to the wrong side of one of the rayon pieces inside the $3/8$in seam allowance. Place rayon pieces right sides together and join $3/8$in

from the edges, leaving the ends open for adjustment. Turn right side out.

Place the embroidered panel in the center of the rayon. Turn the raw edges under and press. Stitch the edges of the panel to the rayon, using small hemming stitches and black thread. Press the cummerbund under a cloth. Top stitch top and bottom edges of rayon to correspond with the hemmed edge of the muslin panel, then apply small black bugle beads along the top and bottom edges as shown. Cover the buttons as instructed by the manufacturer and stitch in place as shown on the Cutting Pattern diagram. Make loops to correspond with the buttons. Remove basting.

WORKING THE JEWELRY

Cut three pieces of cardboard, two $1\frac{1}{8}$in square and one $3/4$in square. Mount a scrap of rayon in the small ring frame and draw around the cardboard pieces, spacing them as far apart as the frame will allow. Using white embroidery thread, and with the machine set for free embroidery,

follow the pattern given in Diagram 4 below. Apply beads using black thread.

Cut three squares of rayon about $3/8$in larger all around than the cardboard pieces. Spread one side of each thinly with fabric glue; stick on rayon squares and leave to dry. Fold edges of rayon over and baste the corners as shown below. Cut pieces of styrofoam sheet to the same size and cut out embroidered squares, leaving a $1/4$in allowance all around to be turned under. Place foam on basted side of square with the embroidered square on top, fold the edges under and sew around them. Glue earring clips and brooch finding to backs.

Designed by Vanessa Richards

DIAGRAM 1: FOLD LINES

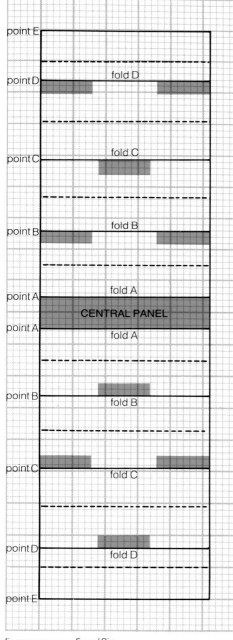

KEY

- ○ clear bead
- ⬓ silver bugle
- ▪ seed bead
- ▬ small black bugle
- ▬ large black bugle
- ▬ free embroidery
- — free embroidery
- ▨ free embroidered areas

DIAGRAM 2: CENTRAL EMBROIDERED PANEL

one square = 1 cm / $3/8$in

DIAGRAM 3: CUTTING PATTERN

one square = 2.5cm / 1in

DIAGRAM 4

EARRINGS PIN

cardboard

five squares = 5cm / 2in

CHOOSING THE DESIGN

The design is a simple geometric one which is marked on the fabric with tailor's chalk before working. The colors chosen here produce a quietly harmonious effect, and the white silk thread shows up as a silvery band on the matte white background. This is a particularly good project for anyone new to machine embroidery, since the only stitches used are straight stitch and satin zigzag.

MATERIALS

Piece of white linen sheeting fabric, sufficient for single or double sheet as desired, plus a piece $1\frac{1}{8}$yds by $\frac{1}{2}$yd for each pillowcase
2 spools each of machine embroidery threads (silk twist or pearl cotton) in white, cream and fawn
Yardstick, T-square, tailor's chalk, pattern-cutting paper

Finished size: The measurement of a sheet depends on the size of the bed. It must be at least 28in wider than the mattress and 38in longer to allow for top and bottom hems and an adequate amount to tuck in.

METHOD OF WORKING

Pillowcases
For each pillowcase, cut two rectangles of fabric each measuring 40in by $25\frac{1}{2}$in, placing the top edges on the selvage if possible. If you cannot use the selvage, allow an extra $\frac{5}{8}$in for hems. If the top edge *is* the selvage, turn fabric from the wrong to the right side $4\frac{1}{2}$in from the top and baste along $\frac{5}{8}$in from the bottom of the flap. If not using the selvage, first turn over $\frac{5}{8}$in from the wrong to the right side as shown, and stitch. Stitch down the sides of the flap, $\frac{5}{8}$in from the edges, trim the corners and clip into the stitching as shown, then remove the basting, turn right side out and press, making sure the corners are well pushed out. This forms the front of the pillowcase.

On the right side, measure 4in in from the top and sides and mark with pins, then draw lines using a yardstick and tailor's chalk. Put two sheets of pattern cutting paper under the fabric. Set the machine to the widest satin stitch (4) and, using white thread, stitch from A to B as shown in the diagram below. (It is advisable to practice the satin stitch on a spare piece of fabric first, since you may have to tighten the bobbin tension and adjust the top a little.) When the stitching is complete, pull the ends through to the wrong side, tie them and cut off.

Turn over $\frac{5}{8}$in on the top edge of the other piece of fabric as before (if not using the selvage) and stitch. Place the two pieces right sides together. Pin and baste the bottom and side edges, then turn over the top of the back piece to match exactly the line of satin stitching worked on the front piece. This forms the flap for the pillow to tuck under. Press the flap, then stitch a seam around the bottom and sides, $\frac{5}{8}$in from the edges. Remove the basting, turn right side out and press again.

Working on the right side of the top piece, mark with tailor's chalk, yardstick and T-square 4in from the joined edges, matching up with the satin stitch already worked. Satin stitch along the marked lines as before, with paper under the fabric. Mark out the designs in each corner, following the Stitching Design diagram below, and satin stitch with the white, cream and fawn threads, varying the width of the stitch to $3\frac{1}{2}$ for the cream and 3 for the fawn. Finally, using the edge of the pillowcase as a guide, stitch all around the edges, first with white, then cream and fawn. Tear the paper away.

Sheet
Hem the fabric at top and bottom; the selvages should be at the sides. At the top, make a hem $4\frac{1}{2}$in from the edge, as for the pillowcase. Make a shallower hem at the bottom edge. Mark the design on the fabric, following the Stitching Design diagram, and stitch as for the pillowcase.

OPTIONS
This design could be used effectively for any article of household linen, such as a tablecloth and set of matching napkins. A tablecloth could be worked with a central as well as a border design. The color range can be varied too.

Designed by Diana Thornton

PILLOWCASE FRONT

PILLOWCASE BACK

STITCHING DESIGN

CHOOSING THE DESIGN

Machine quilting can appear elegant, dramatic and unusual when combined with ready-made decorations such as beads and sequins. It is an ideal technique for articles of clothing such as this jacket in which each piece of the garment is relatively small. The designer has chosen a simple basic shape and a dark fabric, all of which combine to provide an excellent background for the decorative work.

MATERIALS

Fabric
$1\frac{3}{4}$yds black polyester satin, 45in wide
$1\frac{1}{2}$yds black lining fabric, 45in wide
$1\frac{3}{4}$yds lightweight batting, 45in wide
Pair of shoulder pads
Threads
1 spool black polyester sewing thread
Basting thread in two colors
1 spool metallic embroidery thread

$1\frac{1}{2}$yds black satin ribbon, $\frac{1}{8}$in wide
1 self-covered button, $\frac{5}{8}$in diameter
Beading needles
Beads: small black beads, black metallic bugle beads, black metallic sequins (for suppliers, see end of book)
Thin tracing paper for design and pattern

Finished size: the jacket is designed to fit size 34in bust

METHOD OF WORKING

The quilting is worked on the back and front first. The sleeves are quilted individually before being assembled.

Make a jacket pattern on tracing paper by enlarging the pieces shown in the cutting patterns. Trace the basic lines for the quilting design indicated in blue on the pattern for each piece, then pin them to the satin; baste through on the design lines.

Cut out one back piece, two front pieces and two sleeves from satin, lining and batting, allowing a $\frac{1}{2}$in seam allowance all around. Baste the satin and batting for each piece together carefully, starting in the middle (see book, p. 91), then baste around the edges. Use a different color to that used for the design, and make the basting stitches smaller on top of the fabric than underneath, since the machine foot can easily become caught in long stitches.

Baste the front and back pieces together at shoulders and sides, with right sides together. Stitch, using black thread. Trim the batting as close to the seam as possible (this must be done slowly and carefully), then press the seams open, using a dry cloth over the batting.

Tear away the paper and work the quilting, using the metallic thread on top of the machine and the black thread in the bobbin. The stitches should be quite large —about eight per inch. It is advisable to test the stitches on a spare piece of satin and batting first, since you may have

to loosen the top tension slightly. When the quilting is complete, pull all the ends of thread through to the back and fasten them off securely. Sew on the beads and sequins, either following the diagrams or your own design.

Cone tassels
For each tassel cut two pieces of satin $2\frac{3}{4}$in square. Pin them with right sides together, then stitch $\frac{1}{4}$in in from the edges, leaving a $\frac{3}{8}$in gap on one corner for turning. Turn right side out, pushing the corners

out carefully; baste around the edges and press.

Using the metallic thread on top of the machine and in the bobbin, and a fairly long stitch, stitch around the square as close to the edges as possible. Then stitch three or four rows inside this, swivelling the fabric to ease around the corners without removing the needle. Attach a length of ribbon 8in long as shown; thread a double length of bugle beads to reach from the center to one corner and attach it at the center only, so that the beads hang loose as shown. Fold the sides in so that point C overlaps point B, then slipstitch from A to C. Make 10 cone tassels in this way.

Sew the cone tassels to the jacket front. Attach each cone at the top and bottom, and open up the shoulder seams for $3/8$in to tuck the ribbons in. Re-sew the seams neatly by hand and press. Position the cones and ribbons on the sleeves, taking the ribbons down to the edges of the sleeves; baste them in place and attach as before. Press seam, and insert the sleeves, gathering them slightly at the tops to ease.

Cut a square of black satin to fit the button and decorate it with thread and beads as shown in the pattern, then cover the button according to the manufacturer's instructions.

FINISHING

Insert shoulder pads in jacket, sewing them to the shoulder seam allowance, and tacking the ends to the armhole.

With right sides together, seam front and back lining pieces at shoulders and sides. Pin the lining inside the jacket, matching raw edges, and baste all around. Machine stitch $3/4$in from front opening, neck and lower edges, then trim seam allowances. Baste jacket and lining together at shoulders.

Stitch sleeve slams at underarm, right sides together, then make a double row of running stitches at the top to ease. Turn in seam allowance at upper edge, clipping where necessary, and baste. Slip lining over sleeves, matching underarm seams, then slipstitch the basted edges over the armholes. Fold under 1in at the lower

edges of each jacket sleeve, then fold under 2in at the lower edge of each sleeve lining and slipstitch in place.

Top-stitch around the bottom, neck and front openings as close to the edge as possible. Make a buttonhole in the right front and sew the button to the left front to match.

Designed by Barbara Furse

MAKING UP TASSELS

BUTTON PATTERN

CUTTING PATTERNS BACK cut 1

one square = 2.5cm/1in

KEY

- • • • • small beads
- + + + + sequins
- – – – – bugle beads
- quilting design
- tassels

SLEEVE cut 2

LEFT FRONT cut 1

RIGHT FRONT cut 1

CHOOSING THE DESIGN

The original idea for this free machine embroidery came from a collection of photographs, postcards and sketches the designer had built up over several holidays. The final design was achieved by trying out various simple images, then placing these within borders to emphasize the picture-postcard theme.

MATERIALS

24in unbleached calico, 24in wide
Threads
Machine embroidery threads in 50yd spools: 2 mid-green; 1 each of pale blue, mid-blue, dark blue, dark green, yellow, white, pale pink, red, burgundy, dark brown, light brown

Tracing paper and transfer pencil
Piece of mounting board $8\frac{1}{2}$in by 10in

Finished size: the picture measures $8\frac{1}{2}$in by 10in, unframed

METHOD OF WORKING

Transfer the design to the calico, so that it is placed centrally (see book, p. 64). Stretch the calico in a bound ring frame (see book, p. 116).

The technique used is free machine embroidery worked in close lines to form solid blocks of stitches. Set the machine for free embroidery (see book, p. 116) and start working from the center, filling in each area in the color shown in the photograph. Let the outline of each area dictate the direction of the stitch, as though you were drawing with wax crayons. The tree trunks, for example, are worked vertically, while the stitches for the leaves echo the shapes of the leaves themselves. (If you have not done this form of embroidery before, it is advisable to practice on some spare stretched calico before embarking on the design.)

Keep the work drum-taut or the thread will gather and break, and operate the machine at a steady, even speed, moving the frame fairly slowly and smoothly. Work the design outward to the borders. Work a border in green, measuring about $1\frac{1}{4}$in wide at the sides and 1in wide at top and bottom.

FINISHING

Stretch the work by lacing it over the piece of mounting board (see book, p. 138). It can be mounted and framed if desired. The frame in the photograph has been bound with stranded floss, using double-sided tape (see book, p. 52). The bright colors chosen match those used in the embroidery.

Designed by Kay Lynch

CENTRAL DESIGN

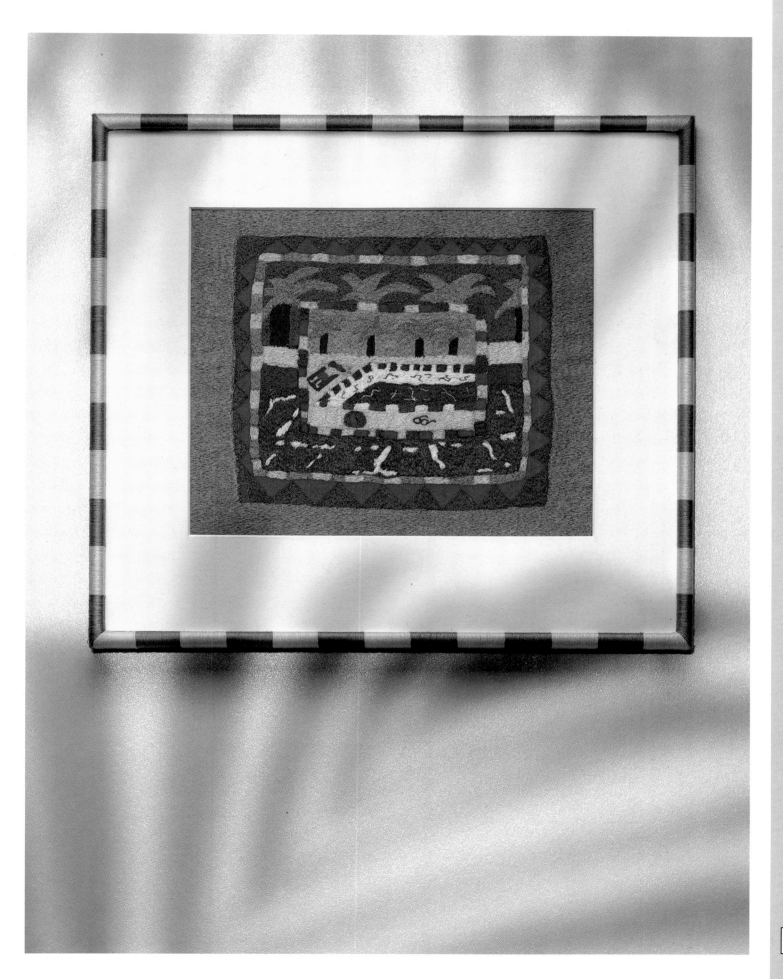

CHOOSING THE DESIGN

This needlepoint design, in which brightly colored geometric shapes are arranged on a dark background, has a simplicity and vividness well suited to a small object. The effectiveness of the design relies on both color and texture. The background is worked in diagonal satin stitch, the rows alternating in direction, with the horizontal bars in mosaic stitch. Stranded floss is used throughout, its slight sheen emphasizing the light and shade effect created by the different directions of the stitches.

MATERIALS

$32\frac{1}{2}$in mono canvas, 13in wide (18 holes to the inch)
$\frac{1}{2}$yd navy blue lining fabric, 36in wide
Stranded floss: 7 skeins navy blue; 1 skein kingfisher blue, yellow, orange, green
1 spool navy blue sewing thread
Tapestry needle, size no. 24
Sewing needle
Thin cardboard, cellophane tape, fabric glue

Finished size: the top of the box measures $3\frac{1}{4}$in square; the height is about $2\frac{1}{4}$in

METHOD OF WORKING

Cut the canvas into two pieces; the box top measures 11in by 11in, the side strip $6\frac{1}{4}$in by $17\frac{3}{4}$in, but allow 2in extra all around if the canvas is to be mounted in a frame.

Stretch the canvas on the stretcher frame, if used, using staples or thumb tacks. Take care to keep the canvas grain straight. If you are not using a frame, bind the edges of the canvas with masking tape or bias binding to prevent fraying.

Using sewing thread, baste the outside lines of the box design on the canvas.

Work the embroidery from the charts below, starting from one corner and using six strands of thread. Work the background areas first in diagonal satin stitch (see book, p. 125) over two horizontal and two vertical canvas threads. Work in vertical rows with the direction of the stitches alternating for each row. When the background is complete, work the colored shapes, using mosaic stitch (see book, p. 133) for the vertical bars and diagonal satin stitch for the zigzags, squares and horizontal bars. The squares are made up of four small blocks of diagonal satin stitch, worked in opposite directions.

Block the finished embroidery (see book, p. 136) to even out any distortions (this is particularly important if you have not used a frame) and allow to dry thoroughly.

FINISHING

Trim the surplus canvas all around to within $\frac{1}{2}$in of the edges of the embroidery. Turn the raw edges under, miter the corners, and secure the hems with herringbone stitch, using two strands of navy blue embroidery thread.

Cut out one piece of lining fabric $\frac{3}{4}$in larger all around than the long strip of embroidery, and three pieces each $\frac{3}{4}$in larger than the square. Join the short edges of the long strip of embroidery by overcasting. Cut a strip of cardboard just smaller than the embroidered strip, score it where each corner is to be, then fold it to make the four sides of the box. Check it for fit (see diagram). When you are sure that the cardboard fits correctly inside the embroidery, cut on the scored lines and re-join with tape to give a neat, square corner. Cover the inside of the cardboard strip with lining fabric, taking the surplus over to the other side and securing it with tape or fabric glue.

Cut two further squares of cardboard,

one the same size as the embroidery for the top of the box, the other just slightly smaller for the bottom. Cover one side of the top piece with lining fabric in the same way as for the sides, and cover both sides of the bottom piece, turning under the edges of the second piece and slipstitching in place around the edges.

Sew the bottom of the box in place by overcasting with a double thickness of navy sewing thread, then slide the lined cardboard into the embroidery and secure it by slipstitching around the upper edge. Join the lined top piece of cardboard to the embroidered square by slipstitching neatly around the edges.

Make tiny hinges for the box by working bar tacks at intervals around the back of the lid as follows. Using three strands of navy blue embroidery thread, take two or three long stitches from the lid to the box, then work buttonhole stitch over them. The bar tack must be long enough to allow the lid to sit neatly on the box and lie flat.

Designed by Jan Eaton

BOX TOP

SIDE work 4 times

KEY

☒ green

◎ yellow

▨ orange

▨ light blue

CHECKING FIT

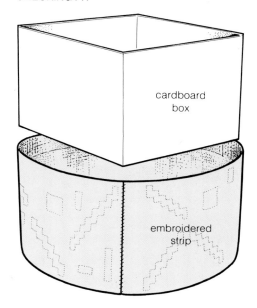

cardboard box

embroidered strip

CHOOSING THE DESIGN

This bright, bold needlepoint frieze of clowns, each performing a separate act, was designed specifically for children. The idea originated from a Christmas decoration. To execute it, the designer first made detailed drawings on tracing paper and then plotted them on graph paper. The idea of jack-in-the-box clowns is carried through by placing each one in a separate box.

MATERIALS

Penelope canvas, 11in by 28in (10 holes to the inch)

Threads

Embroidery yarn: 3 skeins deep yellow; 2 skeins royal blue; 1 skein each cornflower blue, gray-blue, dark green, mid-green, light blue-green, dark red, cherry red, pink-red, pink, bright yellow, light yellow, ginger-brown, black and white
Tapestry needle, size no.20

Finished size: the finished frieze measures 8½in by 26in, unframed

METHOD OF WORKING

Mount the canvas on a stretcher frame (see book, p. 67). The embroidery is worked mainly in tent stitch, with the hats in cross stitch and the flowers for the right-hand clown in French knots. Borders, corners and some other pattern elements, such as the balls for the juggling clown, are worked in long straight stitches.

Work from the chart, following the stitch and color keys, and working all the background stitches first. Note that the straight stitches are worked between the double threads as well as between each pair of threads, as shown in the Pattern Design. Start each new stitch at the end of the previous one, since this is more economical. Work the corners as shown. When all the background has been covered, work the flowers in French knots, and work small straight stitches over the background stitches for the pitcher handle, the straws and the third clown's mouth.

FINISHING

Remove the work from the frame and press it (see book, p. 136). It is recommended that the embroidery be framed professionally. A little of the border may be lost in framing, but this can be minimized by working a few extra rows of tent stitch around the edges.

OPTIONS

The clowns can be worked individually, as a set of pillows, for example, or four separate pictures. Vary the colors to suit personal preferences.

Designed by Louise Lovell

DOUBLE THREAD STITCHING

CORNERING

PATTERN DESIGN

one square = 1.25cm/½in

CHOOSING THE DESIGN

This designer draws out her designs freehand before proceeding to execute them in needlepoint. Her style of drawing, with its somewhat stylized motifs, lends itself well to the technique of needlepoint (petit point here), which imposes an angularity on any design.

The individual motifs are linked by the harmonious colors used in the embroidery, all of them highlighted against the midnight blue of the background "sky".

The gold thread used throughout adds a luster to the work, and a degree of sophistication to the finished article. The richness of the velvet surround, chosen to match the color of the needlepoint background, also gives the bag its evening glamour.

MATERIALS

Fabric
Mono canvas, $6\frac{1}{4}$in by $19\frac{3}{4}$in (18 holes to the inch)
$\frac{1}{2}$yd blue cotton velvet, 36in wide
$\frac{1}{2}$yd blue polyester satin, 36in wide
Threads
1 spool sewing thread to match velvet
Stranded embroidery floss:
12 skeins dark blue; 2 skeins pale gray; 1 skein each pale yellow, cream, gold, pale pink, dark pink, dark gray, sky blue and pale blue
1 spool metallic gold thread

2yds braid for drawstring
Tapestry needle, size no.20
Stiff cardboard for base

Finished size: the bag is 12in high and 18in around at the widest point

METHOD OF WORKING

Mount the canvas on a small stretcher frame (see book, pp.66–67) and work the embroidery from the color chart overleaf using tent stitch throughout (see book, p.125). Use all six strands to cover the canvas entirely. When complete, cut the canvas off the frame, leaving $\frac{1}{2}$in all around the edges of the worked area as a seam allowance.

FINISHING

Cut two pieces of velvet measuring 4in by 19in and $8\frac{3}{4}$in by 19in, the larger piece to be joined to the top of the embroidery and the smaller one to the bottom. Place the velvet and canvas right sides together and stitch a $\frac{1}{2}$in seam by machine, being careful to stitch close to the edges of the embroidery so that no unworked canvas will show on the right side. Trim the canvas close to the seam and press the seam flat toward the canvas. With right sides together, stitch down the long sides to form a tube, making sure the embroidery meets at the edges. Trim seam as before and press.

For the base, cut out a cardboard circle $5\frac{3}{4}$in in diameter, then cut out a piece of velvet $\frac{3}{4}$in larger all around. Place the cardboard in the center of the wrong side of the velvet. Bring the edges up and stitch across the velvet from side to side, as shown, until it is firmly stretched and all the edges are secured. Press well to flatten. Cut a piece of lining fabric the same size as the cardboard, turn the raw edges under and neatly hand stitch to the velvet as close to the edge as possible.

With the main bag piece still inside out, hand stitch the base in place around the bottom, turning the edge of the velvet over by $\frac{1}{2}$in. Cut out a piece of lining fabric 11in by 19in. With right sides together, stitch down the long edge. Press, then turn under $\frac{1}{2}$in at the bottom and $\frac{5}{8}$in at the top. Press again, then turn right side out. Slip the lining over the bag and hemstitch lightly around the base. Turn the whole bag to the right side, fold 3in of velvet at the top to the inside. Turn the top of the lining under to just above the raw edge of the velvet and slip stitch the lining to the velvet.

To make the casings for the drawstrings, cut two pieces of velvet each $2\frac{1}{4}$in by $8\frac{1}{4}$in. Turn under $\frac{1}{2}$in on the short edge and just less than $\frac{3}{8}$in on the long edges. Stitch the short edges and pin the hems on the long ones, then pin the casing to the bag $1\frac{1}{2}$in from the top, placing one so that it covers the seam and the other directly opposite. Machine stitch along top and bottom edges. Cut the braid into two lengths, and thread through the casings in opposite directions so that they pull up easily. Knot the ends of the braid.

OPTIONS
The panel could be larger or smaller in relation to the bag, or the bag could be made in another type of fabric. The needlepoint design could be used as the basis for a panel or incorporated into a pillow.

Designed by Julie Arkell

BASE

MAKING UP

top

canvas

bottom

seam allowance

CHART

middle point

middle point

each square = one stitch

CHOOSING THE DESIGN

The design for this needlepoint picture was based on a garden in rural England. The designer took several photographs and later made drawings from them, concentrating on the idea of a picture within a picture. The selected drawing was then transferred to graph paper to establish the scale and to make any necessary simplifications and modifications.

This designer is particularly interested in the contrasts between textures and areas of flat pattern. Both are combined in this embroidery.

MATERIALS

Mono canvas, 10in by 10in (18 holes to the inch)
Crewel needle
Threads
Stranded embroidery floss: 2 skeins black; 2 skeins dark gray; 2 skeins mid-gray; 2 skeins each in three shades of pale gray; 1 skein each of white, olive green, leaf green, bright green, mid-green, light yellow-green, pale green-white, light blue-green, off-white, pale blue, sky blue, deep blue; 4 shades of red from bright to dark.
1 skein white coton à broder

Finished size: the picture measures 7in by 7in, unframed

METHOD OF WORKING

Enlarge the design from the chart opposite. Transfer the outlines to the canvas, then stretch the canvas over a stretcher frame.

Work the embroidery from the line chart, following the key that clarifies the stitches. The chart indicates which colors to use, but you might also refer to the photograph. Use three strands of floss throughout, except for the inner border, which is worked in a single strand of coton à broder, and the sky, in which one strand of each of the three pale grays are used in the needle. Work the black, white and gray areas first, followed by the white border, the colored inner picture and finally the outer border.

Block the finished work (see book, p. 136) and mount it by stretching it over a piece of board. (Or have it stretched and framed professionally.)

OPTIONS
The central picture could be worked in black and white and the outer area in color. The design could also be enlarged considerably and worked on a coarser canvas with wool threads.

Designed by Liz Mundle

STITCH CHART

MAKING UP

STITCH KEY
A = French knots
B = tent stitch
C = mosaic stitch
D = jacquard stitch
E = cross stitch
F = diagonal satin stitch
G = small chequer stitch (combination of mosaic and tent stitch)
H = tent stitch, reverse direction
I = long and short satin stitch
J = oblong cross stitch with back stitch at edges
INNER BORDER = diagonal satin stitch

CHOOSING THE DESIGN

The design consists of a trellis pattern enclosing diamond shapes. The trellis, in four harmonizing shades of gray, is worked in diagonal satin stitch, giving a smooth background against which the orange diamonds, each filled by a double leviathan stitch, stand out as areas of texture.

The pattern repeat is quite small, so the design can be used for any size of chair seat. Tapestry yarn has been chosen for the embroidery, since it is hardwearing, mothproof and fade-resistant.

MATERIALS

Mono canvas, 30in by 30in (16 holes to the inch), or sufficient for the frame being used
Tapestry yarn: 16 skeins orange; 11 skeins each of dark gray, mid-gray, and two shades of light gray
Tapestry needle, size no. 22
Sharps needle
1 spool sewing thread

Finished size: the embroidery for the chair shown measures 21in along the front, 17in along the back and 21in along each side, to fit the chair seat measuring $16\frac{1}{2}$in by 12in by $16\frac{1}{2}$in and approximately 2in deep. The size will vary according to the chair

seat being covered, but always allow an extra 4in of unworked canvas around the design.

METHOD OF WORKING

Before starting the embroidery, remove the old chair seat covering and use it to work out exactly what area of the canvas needs to be stitched; to avoid excess bulk at the corners, leave unworked those parts that will be overlapped and work only the area that will show when the seat is in position. Any final adjustments may well have to be done after finishing.

Mount the canvas in the frame or pin or staple it to the stretcher, taking care to keep the grain straight and the canvas square. Using sewing thread, baste the horizontal and vertical outside lines of the design on the canvas. Then baste between these two lines to mark the slanting side edges. Mark the center of the design in the same way.

Work the trellis pattern from the chart below, starting at the center of the canvas and using one shade of gray over the whole area at a time. Work the satin stitch (see book, p. 126) over three vertical and one horizontal canvas intersections, all in the same direction. When the trellis background is complete, work a double leviathan stitch (see book, p. 131) in each diamond.

FINISHING

Block the embroidery (see book, p. 136) to even out any distortions; let the work dry.

Trim the surplus canvas around the embroidery to 2in, and lay the work right side down on a clean, flat surface. Position the seat centrally over the canvas and fold the edges of the canvas over the seat.

Insert one staple or tack at the center of each side and check that the embroidery is in the correct position. Staple or tack the canvas to the chair seat around the edges, folding the corners in as neatly as possible. Trim away the canvas to within $\frac{3}{8}$in of the staples or tacks. Drop the covered seat into place on the chair.

OPTIONS

The trellis could be worked in dark colors, with the diamonds in bright primaries, or pastel shades used throughout for a more traditional look.

Since this design has such a small repeat, it can be used for many other items such as pillow covers, bags, glasses cases and pincushions, worked in either tapestry yarn or stranded floss.

Designed by Jan Eaton

STITCH CHART

CHOOSING THE DESIGN

The bowl of flowers is a traditional embroidery theme, but here an unusually subtle and interesting effect has been achieved by an ingenious choice of stitch and color combinations. For the tent stitch background the designer has used a series of gently gradated colors echoed in the outer border, where the colors are arranged to give the effect of a bargello pattern. The stylized Clarkia flowers are worked in straight stitches of varying lengths with four strands of yarn so that they stand out in semi-relief.

MATERIALS

Mono canvas, 18in by 18in (13 threads to the inch)
Tapestry needle, size no. 20
Crewel yarn: 11 skeins off-white; 5 skeins white; 4 skeins palest yellow; 3 skeins shell pink; 2 skeins each sky blue, bright rose pink, orange-red, pale lilac; 1 skein each mid-green, 2 shades leaf green, 2 shades royal blue, 3 shades rose pink, pale ochre, scarlet, flesh pink, palest gray.

Finished size: the picture measures 13in by 13in, unframed

METHOD OF WORKING

Mount the canvas on a stretcher frame (see book, p.66) or bind the edges with masking tape.

Draw the outlines of the main border and mark the center of each side with a fine, indelible marking pen (see book, p.123). The central square is worked over 104 threads, and the border over 34 threads. Make a note of the lengths of the outer sides for reference when stretching the finished work.

Work the straight stitch from the chart for the central square first, referring to the line chart for the lengths of stitches and the colors used, and using four strands of yarn throughout. Then, using three strands of yarn, work the tent stitch background from the same chart. Finally, work the outer border in eight sections, referring to the border line chart for the colors and stitch lengths.

The colors used in the charts have been exaggerated to clarify the "bargello" pattern of the border and the color changes in the background. Refer to the color photograph to note the subtle shades used in the actual picture, or work out your own combinations from the yarns you have.

FINISHING

Remove the work from the frame, if used, and block it (see book, p. 136). Lace the embroidery over a piece of board or have it professionally framed.

Designed by S. Martin and S. Windrum

BORDER

CENTRAL SQUARE

CHOOSING THE DESIGN

The inspiration for this lily pillow came from a series of drawings entitled "A beautiful bunch of lilies," which the designer completed for a series of greetings cards and wrapping paper. The design was drawn straight on the canvas with colored pencils, the aim being to achieve a fresh, spontaneous approach. The illustrative style of the design, and the bright colors used, bring a fresh, modern quality to the traditional technique of needlepoint.

MATERIALS

Fabric
½yd mono canvas, 24in wide (10 holes to the inch)
½yd pink upholstery fabric (cotton/linen), 36in wide
1yd fabric for cording, 36in wide

Tapestry yarn
15 skeins pink I (background pink)
5 skeins white
2 skeins green I
2 skeins green II
2 skeins lilac
2 skeins turquoise
1 skein yellow
1 skein pink II
1 skein pink III

Tapestry needle, size no.20
2yds piping cord, ¼in wide
1 spool pink sewing thread
1 pillow form, 15in by 15in

Finished size: the pillow measures 15in by 15in

METHOD OF WORKING

Mount the canvas in a frame (see book, p. 66) if desired, and work in tent stitch (see book, p.125), following the color-coded design chart.

FINISHING

Block the canvas (see book, p.136) before making it into a pillow. Cut the cording fabric into bias strips and join them together, then encase the piping cord as shown in the book on page 139. Alternatively, use 2 yards of ready made cording in a matching or co-ordinated color. Attach the piping to the canvas front, then join the back of the pillow to the front, following the instructions for Finishing given on page 140 in the book.

Designed by Julie Arkell

KEY

- white
- pink I
- pink II
- pink III
- turquoise
- yellow
- lilac
- green I
- green II

ten squares = 2.5cm/1in

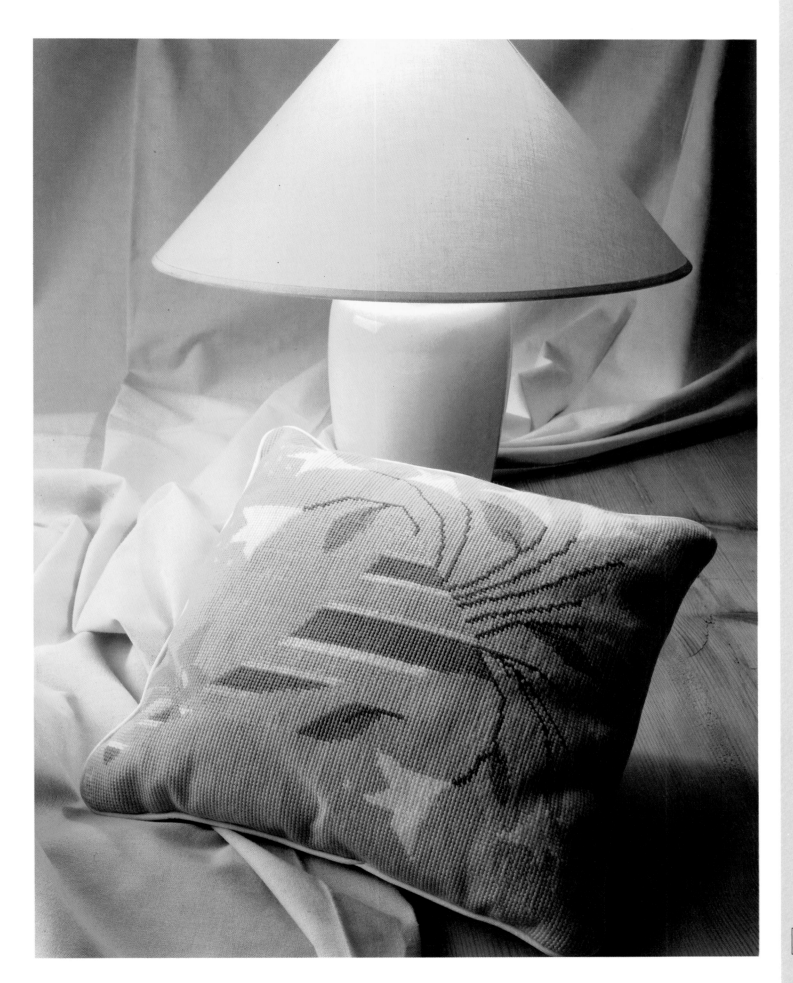

CHOOSING THE DESIGN

Childhood memories of happy days at the beach were the original idea behind this design. The designer then referred to pictures and photographs, and the basic outline came from a photograph of a beach that she knew well. From a list of personal seashore associations, the most suitable elements were chosen to be included in the border. A number of rough sketches were made before arriving at the final design and layout. The design was then plotted out in pencil on graph paper, and the smaller details worked out at this stage.

The colors were chosen to give the impression of a hot sunny day in midsummer. They are stronger than they would be in reality, since the intention was to convey a mood rather than a strict representation of a scene.

MATERIALS

1yd Penelope canvas, 24in wide (10 holes to the inch)
1 skein tapestry yarn in each of the colors shown on the key below, plus 1 extra skein of crimson
Tapestry needle, size no.18

Finished size: the picture measures $10\frac{1}{2}$in by 14in

METHOD OF WORKING

Cut the canvas to size; it should be at least 14in by 18in, but may need to be cut larger to fit on a frame. Mount the canvas on the frame (see book, pp.66–67). Work the design in tent stitch (see book, p.125), following the colors shown on the chart.

Accentuate the outlines around the fishes' mouths, the sunglasses, the crosses on the flags, the bucket handles and the poles of the windbreaks by working back stitch over the tent stitch. Refer to the color photograph as necessary.

Work the people on the beach in only two strands of yarn, using vertical stitches, positioning them as indicated on the chart.

FINISHING

Press the work on the wrong side, using a cool iron. Hold it up to the light to make sure there are no missing stitches: if there are, fill them in.

If you wish to mount the picture yourself, stretch it over a piece of masonite, lacing it at the back as described in the book on page 138. Some of the plain outer edge of the border will be lost in framing. If you are having the picture framed professionally, this will usually include stretching the canvas.

OPTIONS
The various elements of the design could be used in a number of other ways. The central scene could make an effective picture on its own, and would be much simpler to execute. Alternatively, you could use one of the borders as a repeating frieze for a child's room.

Designed by Louise Lovell

CHOOSING THE DESIGN

The design of the rug—which could also be used as a wallhanging—emerged from an exercise the designer set for herself. Using paints and colored pens freely, she set out to create a simple combination of shapes which had an immediate impact.

MATERIALS

Mono canvas, 1yd by $1\frac{5}{8}$yds (5 holes to the inch)
$1\frac{5}{8}$yds burlap for backing, 36in wide
6-ply Turkey rug yarn: 5lb red, $3\frac{1}{2}$lb black, $8\frac{3}{4}$lb white
Large-eyed tapestry needle
Button thread and curved needle

Note The materials suggested are for a quickly worked rug, but a finer rug yarn and smaller gauge canvas can be used if preferred. Penelope canvas can also be used, in which case the rug should be worked in velvet stitch (see book, p. 135).

Finished size: the rug measures approximately 30in by 48in

METHOD OF WORKING

Enlarge the main design elements from the Pattern Design chart (right) and make patterns for each one, from either thin cardboard or newspaper. Arrange them on the canvas and draw around them with an indelible fabric-marking pen. Draw in the smaller shapes freehand.

The rug is worked in knotted stitch (shown right): insert the needle at arrow, holding down a short length of thread with your thumb. Bring through at A, re-insert at B, bring through at C and pull the left-hand thread downward to make a tight knot. Continue as shown, forming loops between each stitch.

In the finished rug the piles are trimmed to different heights, with the white areas trimmed most closely so that they do not pick up too much dirt. When working, regulate the lengths of the loops by working them over a thin knitting needle for the close pile and a larger object, such as a ruler, for the deeper pile. Work the white areas first, leaving the loops uncut until each area is complete.

FINISHING

Trim the canvas to 1in outside the design and turn the edges under. Cut the burlap to the same size plus 1in extra all around and turn the extra allowance under also. Using the curved needle and button thread, sew the burlap to the edges of the canvas.

If the rug is to be used as a wallhanging, make a simple frame slightly smaller than the rug (or use a canvas stretcher) and sew the burlap backing to it.

Designed by Caroline Slinger

SINGLE KNOTTED STITCH

PATTERN DESIGN

one square = 2.5cm/1in

CHOOSING THE DESIGN

The design of this unusual needlepoint resulted from a long series of experiments with color. The effects are created by the technique of optical color mixing, in which pure colors are laid side by side so that they appear to blend. In this piece, six colors of thread—two reds, two yellows and two blues—are laid on canvas over different sizes of squares. The order of working the colors produces a wide variety of both color "mixes" and shapes—squares, diamonds and triangles.

MATERIALS

Mono canvas, 9in by 9in (12 holes to the inch)
Perlé size no.5: 1 skein each bright red, dark red, bright blue, dark blue, bright yellow and yellow-orange
Basting thread
Tapestry needle, size no.22

Finished size: the finished embroidery measures 5¾in by 5¾in, unframed

METHOD OF WORKING

Mount the canvas on a small scroll or stretcher frame. The design is based on nine squares of 21 by 21 holes each, the three squares on the left then being subdivided into smaller squares. Mark the nine squares with basting thread: first count 10 threads to left and right of the central hole to give the vertical lines, then repeat the process for the horizontal ones.

Working the large squares
Lay a grid of 10 dark blue threads vertically on the central square, leaving two threads between each stitch, as shown. Fasten off, then work 10 diagonal stitches in bright red, leaving two threads between each one as before. Work another 10 diagonal stitches in bright yellow. Work 10 bright blue stitches horizontally, then work diagonally halfway across from the top lefthand corner with the yellow-orange. This completes the central square.

Work five other squares above, below and to the right of the central square in the same way, butting them by starting each one in the hole in which the previous square finished. Use a different color each time for the foundation stitches, as shown in the Pattern Design, and vary the succeeding layers of colors so that there are never two adjacent blocks of the same color.

Working the small squares
Each of the squares on the left is divided into four. The total is worked as 12 small squares over 10 threads each. Work the foundation stitches of each group of four squares in dark red, dark red, bright blue and yellow-orange, as shown, then complete as for the large squares, taking care to arrange the colors to contrast with those adjacent to them.

Working the edging
Using two strands of the dark and bright red and the dark and bright blue, lay long threads from corner to corner as shown in the edging diagram, leaving two threads between the outer and inner laid threads. Using single strands of each of the colors in turn, work across the laid threads with vertical stitches.

FINISHING

Remove the work from the frame. It should not need blocking if it has been framed correctly. Lace it over a piece of mounting board and mount and frame as desired (see book, p. 138), or have this done professionally.

Designed by Jeannie Parry

WORKING THE LARGE SQUARES

WORKING THE FOUNDATIONS

WORKING THE EDGING

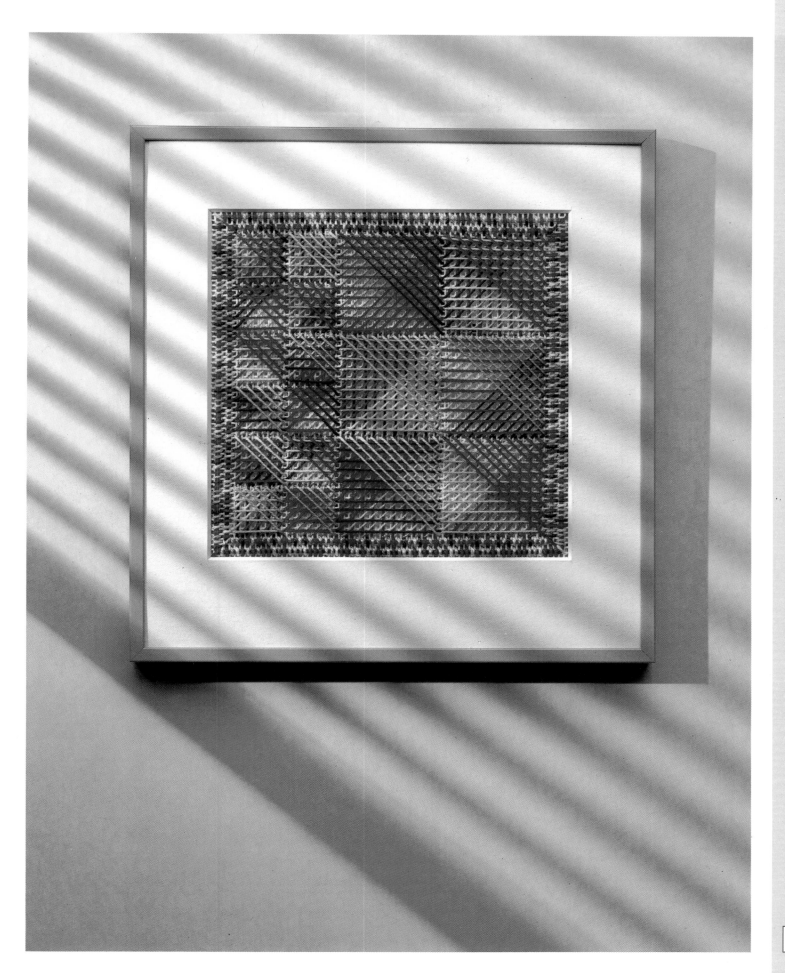

CHOOSING THE DESIGN

The idea for the central part of this design came originally from a patterned piece of ribbon seen twisted on the floor. The embroiderer sketched this as a symmetrical motif on graph paper and then charted the whole design, working outward to echo the shape in the center. The stitch used is bargello, worked over four and six threads, and is quite simple and quick to work (see book, pp. 128–129).

MATERIALS

Mono canvas, 16in by 22in (14 holes to the inch)
Tapestry yarn: 4 skeins dark brown, 4 skeins mid-brown, 2 skeins light brown, 9 skeins dark cream, 5 skeins light cream
Tapestry needle, size no. 22
Piece of carpet felt or similar for backing
Spray glue (optional)

Finished size: the mat measures 13in by 19in

METHOD OF WORKING

Find the center of the canvas by folding it across the length and the width and mark the point. Mount the canvas on a stretcher frame or bind the edges with tape.

Work from the Pattern Design chart, starting in the center with the light cream thread. Note that this area is worked over four threads throughout. Continue working outward from the center, following the colors indicated, over four or six threads as shown.

The background area also alternates the length of the stitches, with the row outside the light brown zigzag line being worked over six threads, the next row over four, the next six again, and so on.

The border is worked in interlocking long and short stitches worked over six, four and two threads as shown.

FINISHING

Block the work if necessary (see book, p. 136). Trim the canvas to about $\frac{1}{2}$in outside the stitching and turn under the edges. Cut the carpet felt to the same size and either glue it to the back of the embroidery with spray glue, or stitch all around the edges with button thread or a double thickness of sewing thread.

OPTIONS

The design could be adapted to a full-scale rug, using rug yarn and a heavy gauge rug canvas. It could equally well be reduced, for a much smaller item worked in embroidery threads. The colors could be varied as you please, and a wider range could be used: for instance eight or ten harmonizing shades would give a more traditional bargello look as well as making the pattern appear more intricate.

Designed by Gisela Banbury

MAKING UP

BORDER

PATTERN DESIGN

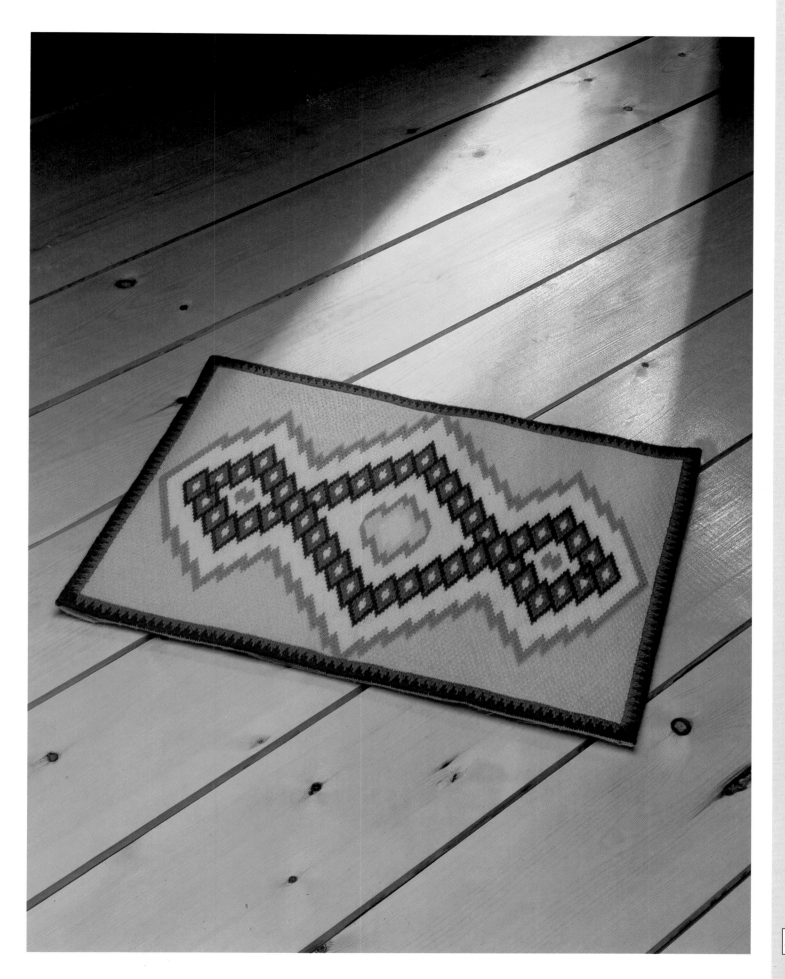

INDEX

ACKNOWLEDGMENTS

We would like to thank all the following people who helped put this book together:

SUPPLIERS' CREDITS
The publishers are particularly indebted to Dunlicraft Ltd of Leicester, the sole distributors in the UK for DMC threads, who provided the threads for many of the patterns in the Embroidery Design Collection as well as for the embroidered samples illustrated elsewhere in the book.

10/11 C.J. Graphic Supplies Ltd.
   13 Threads: DMC/Dunlicraft Ltd, Leicester;
          Royal School of
          Needlework, London
       Beads: Ells & Farrier
14/15 Sewing equipment and canvas samples:
       Royal School of Needlework, London
   63 Embroidery frame:
       Royal School of Needlework, London

PHOTOGRAPHIC CREDITS
½ title Roger Phillips; title Roger Phillips; contents Peter Rauter; 8–9 embroidery: Peter Rauter, surrounding objects: John Barlow; 10–11 Roger Phillips; 12 John Barlow; 13–14 Roger Phillips; 15 John Barlow; 23 Roland Lewis; 25–29 John Barlow; 31–33 Roger Phillips; 34–35 Peter Rauter; 36–37 John Barlow; 38–39 Roger Phillips; 39 John Barlow; 40–41 John Barlow; 42–43 Roger Phillips; 44–45 John Barlow; 46 Roger Phillips; 47–49 John Barlow; 50–52 Roger Phillips; 53 John Barlow; 54–55 Roger Phillips; 56–57 John Barlow; 60–63 John Barlow; 69–135 Grade One Photographic

ARTWORK CREDITS
Key: t top; b bottom; l left; r right; c center

16–17, 18–19 Richard Phipps; 19 (color butterfly) Alan Male/Linden Artists; 21, 22 Richard Phipps; 23 tr Hayward & Martin; bl Terry Evans; 24 Richard Phipps; 25, 27 (collage) John Bigg; 29 tr, cr John Bigg; b Hayward & Martin; 30, 31 (line drawings) Richard Phipps; 40 (color swatches) John Hutchinson; 44 (rubbing) Jenny Chippendale; 52 Richard Phipps; 58–59 *Favorite Charted Designs* by Anne Orr/Dover Publications Inc.

64–141 Special thanks to Coral Mula for all the step-by-step illustrations

EMBROIDERERS' CREDITS
Key: t top; b bottom; l left; r right

½ title Margaret Horton; title Irene Ord; contents Jennie Parry; 8–9 Louise Lovell; 31–33 Irene Ord; 34 Jennie Parry; 35 Chris Crilly; 36 Sheila Miller; 37 Patricia Few; 39 Jenny Chippendale; 42–43 Irene Ord; 44 Jenny Chippendale; 45 t Isabel Dibden; 45 b Robin Giddings; 46–47 Jenny Chippendale; 48 t Irene Ord; 48 b Avril Farley; 49 t Diana Thornton; 49 b Judith Groves; 50–51 Margaret Horton; 52 Irene Ord; 53 Liz Cooksey; 54–55 Jenny Chippendale; 55 Barbara Siedlecka; 56 Jenny Chippendale; 57 Liz Mundell; 60 tl Jan Eaton; 60 tr Jenny Chippendale; 60 bl Margaret Horton; 60 br Jenny Chippendale; 61 tl Irene Ord; 61 tr Gisela Banbury; 61 bl Angela Dewar; 61 br Diana Thornton; 63 Helen Conrad; 69–87 Irene Ord; 88–95 Angela Dewar; 97–99 Caroline Davis; 100–101 Angela Dewar; 103–105 Caroline Davis; 107–108 Helen Conrad; 109–111 Margaret Darby; 113 Gisela Banbury; 115 l Pauline Brown; 115 r Gisela Banbury; 116–121 Diana Thornton; 124 Eleanor Van Zandt; 125–135 Gisela Banbury.

We would like to thank the following people who assisted in the preparation of the Embroidery Design Collection patterns:

PHOTOGRAPHIC CREDITS
Peter Rauter 1, 4–5, 13, 15, 19, 22, 35, 37, 39–41, 43–46
Christine Hanscomb 2–3, 6, 8–12, 14, 16–18, 20, 21, 26–28, 30, 31, 33, 36, 38, 42 John Barlow 7, 23 Heinz Lautenbacher 24, 25, 29, 32, 34

ARTWORK CREDIT
All diagrams and charts drawn by John Hutchinson

SUPPLIERS' CREDITS
1 Frame: The Court Gallery

3 Fountain pen: Philip Poole
  Pen & inkwell: Mansfield

6 Table: Country Pine

8 Towels: The Reject Shop

9 Shirt: Simpson Scarf: Aquascutum

11 Sweater: Benetton 012

14 White tablecloth:
   Antiquarius/Sue Madden X9–10
   Plate, cup, saucer:
   Josie Firmin at Strangeways

16 Pants: Benetton 012

17 Sheets and pillowcase made by Avril Farley

26 Cutlery: David Mellor

27 Box: Antiquarius/Gerald Mathias R3
   Hat pin: Antiquarius/Persiflage Y8
   Threads: Royal School of Needlework

29 Dress made by Avril Farley

32 Tuxedo: Dickins & Jones
   Shirt: Jaeger
   Scarf: Aquascutum

33 Lampshade: The Reject Shop
   Bedside chest: Scallywag Pine Furniture

34 Pants: Dickins & Jones
   Scarf belt: Aquascutum
   Bracelet: Merola
   Necklace and earrings: Michaela Frey

35 Handbound frame by Zilda Tandy

36 Buttons: The Button Box

38 Opera eyeglasses: Antiquarius/Sedler F3–5

39 Frame: The Court Gallery

40 Chair kindly loaned by Suzanne Tandy

41 Frame: The Court Gallery

42 Lampshade: The Reject Shop

43 Frame: The Court Gallery

45 Frame: The Court Gallery

USEFUL ADDRESSES

Most of the suppliers listed below make a nominal charge (usually 1–3 dollars) for their catalog, which is usually offset against the customer's first order. Almost all stockists sell embroidery kits as well as supplies.

DESIGN EQUIPMENT, FABRIC DYES AND PAINTS

Aiko's Art Materials Import Inc.
714 N. Wabash Avenue
Chicago, ILL 60611

Cerulean Blue Ltd.
PO Box 21168
Seattle, WA 9811

W. Cushing & Co.
North Street
Kennebunkport, MA 04046

Decart Inc.
Lamoille Industrial Park
Box 208
Morrisville, VE 05661

Dharma Trading Co.
PO Box 916
San Rafael, CA 94902

Farquhar International Ltd.
56 Harvester Avenue
Batavia, NY 14020

Pentalic Corporation Inc.
122 West 22nd Street
NY, NY

Savoir-Faire
3020 Bridgeway
Suite 305
Sausalito, CA 94965

Winsor & Newton Inc.
122 555 Winsor Drive
Secausus, NJ 07094

SPECIALIST SUPPLIES

FRAMES
Frames
711 Gumrock
Newport News, VA 23606

QUILTING
Quilt Patch
1015 Boston Post Road
Marlboro, MA 01752

SMOCKING
Carolina Classics
2402 Jamestown
Somerville, NJ 08876

THREADS
DMC Corporation
107 Trumbull Street
Elizabeth, NJ 07206

Susan Bates Inc
PO Box E
Route 9A
212 Middlesex Avenue
Chester, CO 06412

Appleton Bros. of London
West Main Road
Little Compton, RI 02837

Paternayan Bros. Inc
312 East 95th Street
NY, NY 10028

TRIMS
Creative Trims
18 Woodland Drive
Lincroft, NJ 07738

Novtex
510 State Road
North Adams, MA 01247

The Greatest Sew on Earth
PO Box 214
Fort Tilden, NY 11695

CROSS STITCH

American Cross Stitch Inc
Box 4039
Parkersburg, WV 26104

Amy's Place
PO Box CC
South Lyon, MI 48178

Crosscreek
717 Jones Street
Berkely, CA 94710

Crosspatch
Rt 9
Garrison, NY 10524

Diane's Crafts
PO Box 250
Talbott, TN 37877

Heartdrops
PO Box 181
Oneonta, NY 13820

Mary Jane's Cross 'n' Stitch
2807 Cooper Court
Woodridge, IL 60517-1999

The Cross Stitcher
PO Box 10779
Jackson, MS 39209

GENERAL SUPPLIES

Boycan's
Box 897
Sharon, PA 16146

Carol's Crafts Inc.
PO Box 230
Winchester, MA 01890

Celebrations
PO Box 578–A
Mt. Laurel, NJ 08054

Circle Craft Supply
PO Box 3000
Dover, FL 33527

Craft King
Mail Order Dept.
741 No. Wabash Avenue
Lakeland, FL 33801

Create Your Own
PO Box 354
Salem, MI 48175

Elite Design
PO Box 894
Dalton, GA 30720

Heather Hill Ltd.
141 West 87th Street
NY, NY 10024

Homespun Crafts
PO Box 530
Lawrence, MA 01842

House of Crafts & Stuff
409 No. Gall Blvd
Zephyrhills, FL 34248

Island Crafts
PO Box 281
Kentfield, CA 94914

Kelpar Needlecraft
PO Box 5177
Scottsdale, AZ 85261

Kirchen Brothers
Box C–1016
Skokie, IL 60076

Priced Rite
PO Box 2764
Dublin, CA 94568

Ron's Craft Supply House
177 Main Street
Greenville, PA 16125

Scrock's Crafts
Box 1136
Massillon, OH 44648

Stitch 'n' Stuff
24401 Carla Lane
North Olmsted, OH 44070

The American Needlewoman
Box 6472
Fort Worth, TX 76115

The Craft House
College Estates Station
Box 1043–B
Frederick, MD 21701

The Crewel Elephant
124 E. 13th Street
Silverton, CO 81433

The Needlecraft Shop
PO Box 1406
Canoga Park, CA 91304–0406

The World in Stitches
82 South Street
Milford, NH 03055

Thumbelina
PO Box 1065
Solvang, CA 93463

WE Design
401 Phillips Hill Road
New City, NY 10956

FOR REFERENCE

Do Not Take From This Room

Date: 4/25/22

**REF 670.25759 HAR 2021
Harris Florida manufacturers
directory.**